Legal Battles That Shaped
the Computer Industry

Legal Battles That Shaped the Computer Industry

Lawrence D. Graham

Q

QUORUM BOOKS
Westport, Connecticut • London

Library of Congress Cataloging-in-Publication Data

Graham, Lawrence D., 1964–
   Legal battles that shaped the computer industry / Lawrence D.
Graham.
      p.   cm.
   Includes bibliographical references and index.
   ISBN 1-56720-178-4 (alk. paper)
   1. Computers—Law and legislation—United States.   2. Copyright—
Computer programs—United States.   I. Title.
KF390.5.C6G73   1999
346.7304′82—dc21   99-13620

British Library Cataloguing in Publication Data is available.

Library of Congress Catalog Card Number: 99-13620
ISBN: 1-56720-178-4

First published in 1999

Quorum Books, 88 Post Road West, Westport, CT 06881
An imprint of Greenwood Publishing Group, Inc.
www.quorumbooks.com

Printed in the United States of America

The paper used in this book complies with the
Permanent Paper Standard issued by the National
Information Standards Organization (Z39.48–1984).

10 9 8 7 6 5 4 3 2 1

For Sharon and Jordan,
who endured too many evenings and weekends alone.

Contents

Figures and Tables

Preface

From the day the first crude computer turned a logical 0 (zero) into a logical 1 (one), the computer industry has mushroomed. Most Americans today either have a computer at home or use one at work, or both. With more than two million professional programmers and several million additional employees, the computer industry is well on its way to becoming a $1 trillion industry.

The growth of litigation in the computer industry has substantially paralleled the growth of the computer industry itself. Considering the enormous increase in computer-related litigation, it is not surprising that intellectual property is the hottest specialty in the legal profession.

Although computer law has been an active field, it has also been an unpredictable one. The law governing computers was particularly sketchy during the industry's nascent period. Prior to 1976, it was unclear whether programmers had any legal rights in the software they developed. In 1976, Congress modified the copyright statutes to specify that software was eligible for copyright protection. Unfortunately, Congress offered little guidance to the courts about how to apply the copyright laws to software. With each lawsuit, the courts added to the sketchy foundation of the copyright laws, developing "the law" (the combination of statutes and court opinions) as they went along. Because the courts have so often *made* the law at the same time that they *applied* it, many computer-related lawsuits have greatly affected the industry.

My primary purpose in writing this book is to outline some of the significant legal battles that helped lay the foundation for the development of both the computer industry and computer law. In many instances, these legal battles have changed the course of the computer industry. By studying the history of the development of computer law and its effect on the computer industry, this book also serves as a resource for the state of computer law today. To facilitate its use as a legal handbook, each chapter concludes with a very brief summary of the law related to the applicable hardware or software element. Despite this inclusion of general legal summaries, this book is not intended to be a comprehensive legal resource for attorneys. Rather, my intention has been to hit the legal high points without getting bogged down in the complex minutiae of legal *wherefores* and *parties-of-the-second-parts*. In doing so, I hope to have created a book that serves as an easy-reading, accessible legal resource while outlining major litigation and the way that litigation has shaped the industry.

This book was written with two primary groups of readers in mind. The first group is comprised of those who work in the computer industry—for example, managers, programmers, or engineers. This group can benefit by learning more about the development of the computer industry and the way their professions have been influenced by the law. The secondary audience more broadly includes those who either have a computer at home or are otherwise interested in computers but work outside the industry. Anyone who is curious about litigation and the way the courts can alter the development of an industry should find many of the legal battles in this book to make interesting reading.

No book addressing the law and written by a lawyer would be complete without a disclaimer, and this book is no exception. Any tips or suggestions offered in this book are intended for general informational purposes only, and not to be construed as legal advice. Critically, the law may vary significantly from state to state and from time to time. Equally important, although the law may be discussed in the abstract, it is always applied to a particular set of facts that varies widely from case to case. Accordingly, the chapter ending summaries and the chapters themselves cannot be relied upon as conclusive legal authority, nor can they be taken as legal advice. Rather, they should be used as a starting point, offering a general summary of the prevailing condition of the law at the time of publication. You should conduct additional research, or consult an attorney, to evaluate the application of the law to the facts of any particular case.

Likewise, none of the opinions expressed in this book should be attributed to my firm or to any of the clients it represents. I have attempted to report on legal disputes and outcomes without taking sides along the way. To the extent this book offers any opinions, they are mine alone.

Introduction

The enemy was a moving target, separated from the sentry by a dense, swirling fog. Beads of sweat formed on the sentry's forehead as he contemplated his very survival. His superiors at the Ditto Computer Company had taken tremendous risks to build the empire he now sought to protect. If the enemy got the upper hand this time, Ditto's fortunes surely would be lost forever. The tension was severe as the enemy drew nearer, preparing to launch its final attack.

The sentry never really had a chance. Despite excellent training and vast resources, the Ditto Computer Company had been caught stealing secrets from the enemy—violating a major rule of engagement. Justice was swift and severe. With a loud "Crack!" the judge's gavel pounded the polished walnut, bringing the case, and the Ditto Computer Company's hopes, to an end.

Although the combatants and their treasures differ from one battle to the next, scenes like this one have been replayed countless times. During the past two decades, personal computer hardware and software companies have engaged in an endless string of battles to control personal computers.

THE BREADTH OF THE COMPUTER BATTLEFIELD

To a significant extent, these battles have shaped the computer hardware and software we now use. Have you ever wondered why there are so many "PC-compatible" or "clone" computers but (until recently) no Apple Macintosh compatible machines? Or why competing spreadsheet programs look so similar to one another? Do you know who owns programming languages like Basic or C++? Or why there are so many similar fonts with different names? Do you know why software comes with a "shrink-wrap" license? And does it matter that you have never read one?

The answers to these and a surprising number of other questions about computers are found in the legal battles waged by competitors in the computer industry. Legal battles have touched virtually every aspect of personal computers. Figure 1 shows a typical personal computer, equipped with commonly found software and hardware. Each of

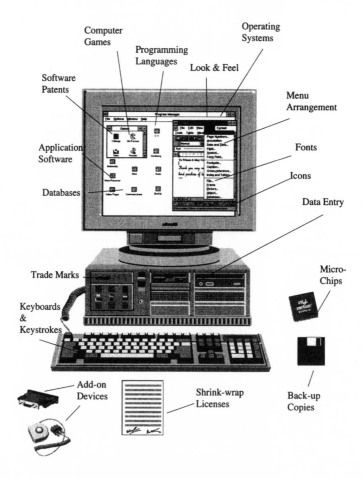

Figure 1. The reach of the law. Virtually every aspect of the typical personal computer has been touched by the law.

the labels in Figure 1 identifies a part of the computer that has been affected by the law. In most cases, a major lawsuit between computer hardware or software companies has led to a legal ruling that significantly changed the computer industry.

In this book, we take a tour of the typical personal computer, examining the software, hardware, and other elements commonly encountered by the average computer user. Along the way, we note how each of these particular elements has been shaped by the court battles between major players in the computer industry.

THE ATTRACTION AND INFLUENCE OF THE LEGAL BATTLEFIELD

Why has the law affected computers so deeply? There are many possible answers, not the least of which is money. One of the first lessons in law school is that it is seldom worthwhile to sue those who have no money. Although the law affects everything, the depth of its reach is directly related to the depth of the pockets it reaches into. As an old lawyer joke goes, "How cold was it? It was so cold outside that I saw a lawyer with his hands in *his own* pockets!"

The computer industry's deep pockets attract litigation. Total international revenues in the computer industry now exceed $1 trillion annually, and domestic revenues are in excess of $400 billion, divided nearly equally between hardware and software.[1] Considering the enormous size of the computer industry, it isn't surprising that those with millions of dollars at stake are willing to take their cases to the courts.

The uncertain nature of the law also has contributed to the degree of influence that court battles have had on computers. What lawyers call "the law" typically includes a number of statutes, passed by Congress, that define what is legal or illegal. When adjudicating a lawsuit between two parties, a judge interprets and applies the statutory law to the particular facts of the case. If the statute is unclear or does not address the precise issue the judge is facing, the judge must first decide what the law is, filling in the "gaps" in the statute. "The law" is therefore a combination of statutes and court decisions that fill in statutory gaps and interpret statutory language. If the statutes contain numerous gaps, judicial decisions filling in those gaps take on a greater importance.

Judges in computer cases have been required to perform an inordinate amount of gap-filling and interpretation. The computer industry's rapid growth came before there were laws specifically designed to handle computer software and hardware disputes. The lack of specific computer laws forced judges to apply laws that were developed for other purposes to computer disputes in make-shift fashion, leading to awkward, uneven applications of the law. The net effect is like handing an older brother's hand-me-down clothes to a younger sister—they don't fit all that well, and the younger sister isn't all that happy to wear them.

The complex nature of computers has also contributed to the significance of the law. Software and hardware disputes are often somewhat technical, taxing the understanding of judges and lawyers. Misunderstandings by lawyers and judges have introduced elements of randomness into the law.

Finally, intellectual property laws provide valuable protection to the U.S. economy. The software industry provides a telling example. American companies account for as much as 75 percent of the global market for software. Without strong laws to protect intellectual property rights in software, foreign companies could easily copy American works and rapidly cut into the dominant market share.

THE IMPORTANCE OF UNDERSTANDING LEGAL BATTLES

Okay, so the law has played a significant role in defining the computer industry, but you wonder, "What's in it for me?" Aside from attaining a clearer understanding of the computers and software most of us use everyday, there are several reasons to learn more about the relationship between computers and the law.

Even though the law has thus far played a major role in defining the computer industry, the development of both the industry and the law is far from complete. The following chapters, examining where we are today and how we got here, provide valuable insight into where we are headed.

In addition, because computers are such an integral part of our lives, they are a ready source of opportunity and risk. Though computers may make our lives easier and more rewarding, the tangle of associated intellectual property laws can trip the unwary.

For those who are in the computer industry, knowledge of computer law is vital. The history of the computer industry is littered with companies that have gambled—and lost—their entire fortunes on products that ultimately infringed another's intellectual property rights. An understanding of intellectual property law can help you avoid a similar fate.

Note

1. Statistics regarding the size of the electronics and software industries are contained in Kathleen Morris, "The Soft War," *Financial World* March 15, 1994: 34.

Hardware, Software, and the Law

I

2

Legal Protection for Hardware and Software: A Primer

Computer hardware and software may be legally protected in a variety of ways. For example, patents may protect functional aspects of computer hardware and software, and copyright law may prevent expressive aspects of software from being copied. This chapter presents an overview of patents, copyrights, and several other means for protecting intellectual property in general, and computer hardware and software in particular.[1]

WHAT IS THE LAW?

An initial question worth considering before examining the various intellectual property laws is, "What is the Law?" Considering the labyrinth of statutes and court rulings, the question itself virtually defies answer. An old joke illustrates the answer many lawyers are likely to give to the question, "What is the Law?" An engineer, a physicist, and a lawyer are each asked, "How much is two plus two?" The engineer, trusting his pocket calculator, enters two plus two, reads the answer and says, "Four." The physicist goes to the library to find out what others have found for the same question, designs and conducts a set of experiments, and responds, "In most cases, the answer is likely to be four." The lawyer draws the curtains, dims the lights, and says, "How much do you want it to be?" Similarly, the answer to "What is the law?" is often "What do you want it to be?"

In many cases, "the law" begins with one or more statutes, passed by Congress, that define what is legal or illegal. Unfortunately, deciphering the law is far more complex than simply looking up the statute and reading it. When adjudicating a lawsuit between two parties, a judge interprets and applies the statutory law to the particular facts of the case. If the statute is unclear or does not address the precise issue the judge is facing, the judge must first decide what the law is, filling in the "gaps" in the statute. Alternatively, when the statutory language is seemingly clear, the judge may interpret the statute in a manner that alters the apparent meaning of its terms. "The law" is therefore a combination of statutes and court decisions that fill in statutory gaps and interpret statutory language. If the statutes contain numerous gaps, judicial decisions filling in those gaps take on a greater importance.

In other cases, there are no statutes to form the foundation for the law. While court decisions always play an important role in defining the law, in the absence of an applicable statute the law is formed entirely of court decisions that build the law one case at a time. Accordingly, the law must always be viewed as a "work in progress."

The organization of the federal court system adds additional complexity and uncertainty to the law. Each state is divided into one or more judicial districts that are comprised of federal trial courts, or "district courts." Decisions from the district courts may be appealed to the appropriate one of the thirteen regional federal courts of appeal, called "circuit courts." Finally, parties may petition the Supreme Court to review decisions of the circuit courts.

Each court must follow the rulings of its superior courts. Thus, the district courts are bound by the decisions of their assigned circuit courts, and all courts must follow the decisions of the Supreme Court. District courts, however, are not bound by the rulings and statutory interpretations made by other district courts or by circuit courts in other geographic regions. Consequently, statutes are often interpreted differently in different circuits, and the law—even federal statutory law—differs from one state to the next.

In sum, "the law" is a dynamic, amorphous set of rules, varying from state to state and from one court ruling to the next. To truly know the law, one must consult any applicable statutory authority, as well as relevant judicial opinions interpreting those statutes.

PATENT LAW BASICS

Perhaps the strongest form of protection for intellectual property is provided under the patent laws. Patent and copyright laws enjoy a rich tradition in the United States. Each has its foundation in the Constitution, which provides that Congress shall have the power "to promote the Progress of Science and the useful Arts, by securing for limited

Times to Authors and Inventors the exclusive right to their Writings and Discoveries." Congress exercised this power in the second session of the first congress by passing the patent and copyright statutes.

The Constitutional authority for patent law is therefore aimed at advancing the "useful Arts" by providing limited exclusive rights to Inventors for their Discoveries. There are several different types of patents available to accomplish this purpose, including "utility" patents for functional devices and methods of operation, "design" patents for the aesthetic qualities of functional devices, and plant patents for newly discovered plants. Of these three, the most common is the utility patent.

To obtain a utility patent, an inventor must have an invention that meets four stringent requirements. First, the invention must be useful, or have "utility." This first requirement is seldom invoked but prevents inventors from obtaining patents for devices that do not work, such as perpetual motion machines. Second, the invention must be new, or "novel." Third, it must not be an "obvious" extension of previously existing devices or methods, as judged by a person of ordinary skill in the relevant art. Finally, the type of invention must be a process, machine, manufacture, or composition of matter.

If each of these requirements is met, an inventor (or the inventor's attorney) may prepare and file a patent application that fully discloses the invention. After it is filed, an examiner from the U.S. Patent and Trademark Office reviews the application to determine whether it meets the stated requirements, in addition to numerous others that may apply. Typically, the examiner will reject the application and give the inventor an opportunity to provide an argument or amendment to the application in response. After a number of such exchanges between the examiner and the inventor over an average period of about eighteen months, the application will either be finally rejected or allowed to issue as a patent.

Once all the requirements are met and a patent issues, the inventor, or "patentee," is given the right to exclude others from making, using, offering for sale, or selling the invention in the United States. Presently, these patent rights last for a period of twenty years from the date of filing the patent application. Unauthorized making, using, offering for sale, or selling of the patented invention during the patent term is an infringement of the patentee's rights.

From the very beginning of the computer industry, patents have been an available source of protection for computer hardware. But software has not always qualified for patent protection. Until the mid-1990s, the Patent and Trademark Office routinely rejected software patent applications, arguing that computer programs amounted to mathematical algorithms, which are not patentable in themselves because they are not processes, machines, manufactures, or compositions of matter. Consequently, only a handful of patents were granted for pure software inventions. But a 1994 decision by the Federal Circuit Court of Appeals ruled that software is patentable because it transforms a general purpose computer into a special purpose machine, and as a process or machine, it is patentable. Presently, patents are available for both hardware and software inventions.

COPYRIGHT LAW BASICS

In the language of the Constitution, copyright law promotes the progress of Science by extending exclusive rights to Authors for their Writings. Thus, as patents provide protection to inventors for their inventions, copyrights provide protection to authors for their writings. Eight specific categories of "writings," or "works of authorship," are given protection in the Copyright Act, including literary, musical, dramatic, choreographic, pictorial, graphic, and sculptural; architectural works; motion pictures and audiovisual works; and sound recordings. This list is intentionally made nonexclusive so that copyright protection may be extended to new forms of expression like computer software.

Unlike a patent, a copyright is relatively easy to obtain. Whereas an invention must be new, useful, and unobvious to qualify for patent protection, an author's work must only be "original" and fixed in a tangible medium of expression to receive copyright protection. The originality requirement of copyright law is much less stringent than the combination of novelty and unobviousness under patent law. Quite simply, to be "original," a work need only be created by the author and contain a "modicum" of creativity. Although there are distinct advantages to obtaining a copyright registration, no registration is required to receive copyright protection; rather, an author's work is protected under copyright law as soon as it is fixed in a tangible medium of expression, for example by printing it on paper or recording it on videotape.

Copyright law gives authors several separate exclusive rights, depending on the type of work. First, authors receive reproduction and distribution rights. Because these are separate and distinct rights, the unauthorized acts of copying (or reproduction) and selling (or distribution) constitute separate infringements of the author's rights. Second, the author obtains the exclusive right to prepare derivative works based upon the copyrighted work. Third, the author receives the exclusive rights to perform and display the work publicly.

The length of the copyright term varies according to the date of its origin. For works created after January 1, 1978, the copyright endures from the creation of the work until 70 years after the author's death. In the case of anonymous works owned by a corporation or other employer, the copyright term runs for 95 years from the year of the work's first publication, or 100 years from the work's creation, whichever occurs first.

Any unauthorized exercise of the author's exclusive rights constitutes an infringement. Obviously, a protected work cannot be copied without first obtaining the original work. Thus, in contrast to patent law, one must have access to a copyrighted work in order to infringe it. An independently created work, no matter how similar, is not an infringement of a copyrighted work. Nevertheless, copying need not be intentional in order to constitute an act of infringement. As long as there has been access, even a subconscious copying or derivation constitutes infringement.

TRADEMARK LAW BASICS

A trademark is a symbol or word that identifies a particular person or organization as the source of the goods or services bearing the mark. Unlike patents and copyrights, trademarks do not give trademark owners exclusive rights in any goods themselves; rather, trademark owners hold exclusive rights to use the particular trademarks in association with such goods.

As with copyrights, no registration is necessary to obtain trademark rights; trademark rights attach with the first use of the trademark. But there are numerous advantages that make obtaining a federal trademark registration worthwhile. Among others, these advantages include the presumption that the trademark registrant holds exclusive rights in the mark throughout the United States. Five years after the registration issues, this presumption becomes incontestable.

Trademark owners hold the right to prevent others from using the same mark or similar marks in a manner that is likely to confuse the public as to the source of the competing goods. There are two general parameters that define the strength of a trademark. The first is the extent to which a competing mark can be similar while avoiding infringement. If a trademark is not well known, or if it is highly suggestive of a class of goods, a competing mark may have to be quite similar in order to infringe. On the other hand, if a trademark is famous, customers may be confused by the use of competing trademarks that are less similar. The second parameter is the extent to which competitors may use the identical mark on dissimilar goods. Again, protection will vary with the fame of the mark. If the mark is not particularly well known, others may use the identical mark on dissimilar goods. But the owner of a famous mark may be able to prevent others from using the mark on all goods, no matter how dissimilar.

TRADE SECRET LAW BASICS

Computer hardware and software may also be protected under trade secret laws. Unlike patent, trademark, and copyright laws, presently no federal trade secret statutes exist that have civil penalties, although there are federal criminal laws prohibiting trade secret theft. Nevertheless, every state has a civil statute to protect trade secrets, and most state trade secret laws are either identical or substantially similar to one another.

A trade secret is competitively sensitive information that derives its value, at least in part, by not being generally known by others. In general, any type of information may be trade secret information, including scientific, technical, or business information. To qualify as a trade secret, however, the information must be secret and subject to reasonable efforts to maintain its secrecy.

One who improperly obtains or uses trade secret information or improperly provides trade secret information to others may be liable for trade secret misappropriation. Reverse engineering is generally allowed under trade secret law. Consequently, one who properly obtains computer hardware or software may reverse engineer them without running afoul of trade secret laws, though it may violate other laws.

SEMICONDUCTOR CHIP PROTECTION ACT BASICS

In 1984, Congress created a special form of intellectual property protection for the "masks" that are used to produce semiconductor chips. The Semiconductor Chip Protection Act (SCPA) is an original statute that borrows extensively from the copyright laws. Under the SCPA, a "mask work" is defined as a series of related images representing the three-dimensional pattern forming the layers of a semiconductor chip product. Essentially, masks are stencils used to etch an electronic circuit on a semiconductor chip. A mask work is the sum total of the individual masks that are used to fabricate an entire chip.

To receive protection under the SCPA, the owner of the mask work must register the work with the Copyright Office within two years of the first commercial exploitation of the work anywhere in the world. Commercial exploitation is defined as public distribution for commercial purposes of a semiconductor chip product embodying the mask work. A written offer to sell existing semiconductor chip products also constitutes a commercial exploitation. If the mask work is not registered within the two-year grace period, the work becomes unprotected.

Under the SCPA, a mask work owner receives the exclusive right to reproduce the mask work and to import or distribute semiconductor chip products embodying the mask work. Whether an accused product is an infringing reproduction is determined using copyright-like concepts. Thus, an accused mask or product must be substantially similar, but not identical, in order to infringe. Likewise, a functionally equivalent but different design does not infringe, and an independently produced design does not infringe even if it is substantially similar to the protected mask work.

There are several additional important limitations on the rights granted to a mask work owner. It is not an infringement to reproduce a mask work to evaluate the concepts or techniques embodied in the work, or to analyze the circuitry, logic flow, or organization of components used in the mask work. Nor is it an infringement to incorporate the results of the analysis in the creation of another original mask work.

If a mask work owner can prove that its protected work has been infringed, the owner can obtain "injunctive relief" ordering the infringing party to refrain from further infringement. The owner may also receive monetary damages and attorneys' fees.

RULES OF BATTLE

The enforcement of legal rights in court under the laws described here begins with the filing of a "complaint." The complaint is filed by the "plaintiff," the party that has been damaged, against the "defendant," the party that allegedly committed the wrongful acts. The complaint generally sets forth an outline of the improper acts and the laws that make the acts illegal. After the complaint is filed, the defendant must file an "answer" that admits or denies the allegations in the complaint.

After the complaint and answer are filed, the parties engage in an information-gathering process called "discovery." During discovery, each party may submit written questions to the other, request documents and other items, and request that the other party admit that certain things are true. The parties may also conduct "depositions," the formal questioning of witnesses under oath. The courts favor a broad range of discovery, theorizing that discovery will ultimately lead to the truth and that the parties are more likely to settle the dispute out of court if they have access to all the facts.

There are many other events that may occur after a lawsuit is filed but before the actual trial. If the plaintiff believes that it needs immediate relief that cannot wait until trial, the plaintiff may file a "motion" with the court seeking a "preliminary injunction." An "injunction" is a court order that stops, or "enjoins," the other party from taking or continuing a particular action. It is "preliminary" if it is obtained prior to trial, enjoining the other party's actions between the time the order is issued and the date of the trial. To obtain a preliminary injunction, the plaintiff typically must prove that it is likely to succeed if the case goes to trial and that the failure to grant the preliminary injunction would harm the plaintiff more than the preliminary injunction would harm the defendant.

Either party may also file a motion for a "summary judgment." A summary judgment is a ruling by the court on the substance of the case prior to trial. But unlike a preliminary injunction, a summary judgment order may be final, ending the case. A court will grant a motion for a summary judgment if there is no genuine issue of material fact; that is, if the case is so one-sided that all reasonable persons would rule for that side.

Finally, if the case has not settled or been disposed of on summary judgment, it will proceed to trial. In most cases, either party may request that the case be tried by a jury; if neither party requests a jury, it will be decided by the judge instead. After the jury verdict has been entered, either party may file a motion for "judgment as a matter of law," or JMOL. A motion for JMOL asks the judge to overturn some aspect of the jury verdict because, based on the evidence presented, no reasonable jury could reach that result. After the jury verdict and any post-trial motions have been decided, the decision may be appealed to the court of appeals.

Note

1. The information from this chapter comes primarily from the statutes that govern each substantive area of the law: 35 U.S.C. § 101 et seq. (patents); 17 U.S.C. § 101 et seq. (trademarks); 15 U.S.C. § 101 et seq. (copyrights); the Uniform Trade Secrets Act; the Semiconductor Chip Protection Act; and the Federal Rules of Civil Procedure.

3

Can I Go to Jail for This?

A survey conducted in cooperation with the Senate Permanent Subcommittee on Investigations found that hackers broke into the computer systems of nearly six out of every ten major U.S. corporations in 1996. Most of the victims suffered substantial monetary losses: more than two-thirds lost $50,000 or more; almost 20 percent sustained damages of more than $1 million.[1] As more and more companies connect valuable computer systems to the Internet, the rate of infiltration and the magnitude of the damage seem certain to rise.

Meanwhile, software companies have lost enormous sums to piracy. Although the exact amount lost to piracy is unknown, the Software Publishers Association has estimated that software manufacturers lose several billion dollars each year due to the unlawful copying of computer software.[2]

Considering the magnitude of these statistics, it isn't surprising that many companies have lobbied Congress to increase the number of criminal provisions for such acts. The commission of any of the acts discussed in this chapter is subject to civil penalties. In other words, an injured party may recover monetary damages as a legal remedy for the wrongful acts. But in many cases it is simply not worthwhile to file a civil lawsuit to recover what may well be nominal damages. Even if the damages are potentially large, many small companies may not have the resources to pay the legal expenses required to recover them. The lack of criminal provisions and the remoteness of being sued in a civil action have contributed to the growth of software piracy and other acts of infringement. Congress has responded to these concerns with several new criminal statutes aimed at curbing intellectual property theft and destruction.

This chapter surveys several intellectual property crimes, including new laws making it a crime to steal trade secrets or to distribute copyrighted software. Importantly, this chapter is only intended to provide a feel for the types of acts that carry criminal penalties and is not an exhaustive summary of intellectual property crimes. In addition to the federal laws discussed in this chapter, most states have enacted laws aimed at curbing various intellectual property crimes. Even in the absence of such specifically tailored laws, creative prosecutors are often able to apply more general laws to misdeeds involving intellectual property. If there is any doubt about the legality of a particular act, you should seek legal advice or act at your own risk.

COPYING SOFTWARE FOR FUN AND PROFIT

Software is a unique good in that it is typically expensive and time-consuming to develop but easy and cheap to copy and distribute. Unfortunately for software makers, pirates or competitors can copy and distribute software nearly as easily as the original developer. From time to time, software companies have experimented with various schemes that prevent others from copying disks entirely or that require users to enter special codes from the software's documentation before the program may be installed or used. But consumers have complained about the inconveniences caused by such protection devices, and copiers have routinely found ways to defeat them.

Until recently, there were few legal alternatives available to software companies. Prior to December 16, 1997, the federal copyright statutes contained only limited criminal provisions that were aimed at large-scale piracy. The Copyright Act made it a crime to "infringe a copyright willfully and for purposes of commercial advantage or private financial gain." In drafting the law in this manner, Congress wanted to avoid making criminals out of the millions of personal computer owners in the United States. This criminal provision very clearly and intentionally excludes small-business owners and home computer users who occasionally improperly copy a computer program for private use. But when Congress debated the criminal provisions of the Copyright Act in 1992, it did not foresee the new opportunities for copying that would accompany the growth of the Internet. It discovered a major loophole in the existing criminal copyright provisions in the 1994 lawsuit *United States v. LaMacchia*.[3]

On April 7, 1994, a federal grand jury returned an indictment against David LaMacchia, charging him with conspiracy to violate the federal wire fraud statute. At the time, LaMacchia was a twenty-one-year-old student at the Massachusetts Institute of Technology (MIT). Using a pseudonym and an encrypted address, LaMacchia allegedly used MIT's computers to set up an Internet bulletin board and encouraged others to upload software applications such as Microsoft Excel 5.0 and Word-Perfect 6.0, and computer games such as Sim City 2000. These programs were then transferred to a second encrypted address where they could be downloaded by others. Despite efforts to maintain a low profile and avoid notice, the offer of free software generated substantial worldwide traffic and attracted the attention of university officials and federal authorities.

Because LaMacchia did not receive a "commercial advantage or private financial gain," he could not be prosecuted under the Copyright Act's criminal provisions. Nevertheless, prosecutors believed that LaMacchia's acts were wrongful and charged him with conspiring with "persons unknown" to violate the federal wire fraud statute. According to the indictment, LaMacchia devised a scheme to defraud that sought to facilitate "on an international scale" the "illegal copying and distribution of copyrighted software" without payment of licensing fees and royalties to the software manufacturers. The scheme allegedly caused losses of more than $1 million to the copyright holders. Importantly, the indictment did not allege that LaMacchia sought or derived any personal financial benefit.

LaMacchia's supporters and detractors were organized into predictably distinct groups. Software companies applauded the decision to prosecute LaMacchia as a sign that the government was finally taking an active stance against software piracy. Students, hackers, and many in academia decried criminal prosecution of what some categorized as a prank or the perfectly legal distribution of software. Some of LaMacchia's supporters even organized a legal defense fund, collecting nearly $10,000 in pledged donations.

Shortly after the indictment, LaMacchia filed a motion to dismiss the case, arguing that the government could not use the wire fraud statute to punish an act that was not a crime under the Copyright Act. Essentially, LaMacchia argued that Congress had considered the matter when it enacted the Copyright Act and intentionally decided that acts such as his were not criminal in the absence of commercial advantage or financial gain. The district court agreed with LaMacchia and granted the motion to dismiss. As the court explained, the Copyright Act is carefully crafted to provide a well-defined set of protections. Although the mail and wire fraud statutes are admittedly broad, so much so that they have been called the federal prosecutor's "weapon of choice," they cannot be applied to criminalize an act expressly carved out by Congress when it drafted the criminal provisions of the Copyright Act.

Despite dismissing the charge against LaMacchia, the court found nothing redeeming in LaMacchia's alleged acts. As the court explained, "If the indictment is to be believed, one might at best describe his actions as heedlessly irresponsible, and at worst as nihilistic, self-indulgent, and lacking in any fundamental sense of values." In sum, although the court believed that the acts should be criminally punished, it concluded that they were not punishable under the federal wire fraud statute.

On December 16, 1997, President William Clinton signed into law a bill intended to close the loophole discovered in *United States v. LaMacchia* that required proof of commercial gain or financial advantage before criminal penalties would apply. The new law provides criminal penalties for anyone who willfully infringes a copyright "by the reproduction or distribution, including by electronic means, during any 180-day period, of 1 or more copies or phonorecords of 1 or more copyrighted works, which have a total retail value of more than $1,000." Software makers have hailed the new law as an important tool to prevent the piracy of copyrighted works. While closing the electronic distribution loophole, the law retains the limited exception for private, home copying, which typically will not exceed the $1,000-in-180-days limitation.[4]

VIRUSES AND HACKING

In addition to the laws criminalizing the copying of software, there are several laws imposing criminal penalties for certain acts of "hacking," such as unauthorized access, theft, and destruction of computer systems and data. In the early days of computers, the term "hacker" was used to denote energetic programmers developing pioneering software. The positive qualities of the term have slowly eroded to the point that today it is generally used to refer to pranksters who illegally tap into computer systems to commit acts of theft or destruction. Despite the negative connotations, there is little doubt that many hackers are intelligent and innovative. In fact, the Electronic Frontier Foundation was formed, in part, to protect the civil rights of hackers, believing that they are the technological innovators of tomorrow.

Whether they are innovators or not, hackers cause an enormous amount of damage every year. Hackers commit a wide array of destructive acts, including creating and spreading viruses, stealing trade secrets, destroying data, and stealing computer time. To combat these acts, nearly every state has enacted legislation aimed directly at curbing computer-related offenses. Though these statutes vary widely from state to state, they generally make it unlawful to intentionally access a computer to commit fraud, steal money, steal secret information, or damage or destroy data or hardware.

In addition to the many state statutes, there are a few federal statutes directly aimed at computer abuse. One such statute, the Computer Fraud Abuse Act of 1986, 18 U.S.C. § 1030, makes it a crime to access a computer without authorization to obtain classified government information, steal financial information, commit fraud, or to conduct other criminal activity. It also makes it a crime to access a protected computer to cause damage without authorization, and to improperly sell computer passwords to others.

The Computer Fraud Abuse Act of 1986 has been used to prosecute the spread of computer viruses. In October 1988, Cornell University student Robert Morris allegedly began work on a computer virus to demonstrate the inadequacies of the security of computers connected to the Internet.[5] Morris's virus was known as a "worm," which differs from a typical virus in that it travels from one computer to another but does not attach itself to the operating system of the infected computer. Morris apparently intended that the worm would spread widely but not interfere with the normal operation of the computers. Unfortunately, he underestimated the rate at which the virus would replicate itself on a single host computer. Within a few weeks, Morris discovered that the virus was replicating itself and reinfecting machines so quickly that it caused many machines across the country to crash or lock up.

When Morris discovered the damage being caused by the worm, he contacted a friend at Harvard to discuss possible solutions. Eventually, he sent an anonymous message over the Internet that instructed users how to eliminate the worm and prevent reinfection. But by the time his anonymous message was received by many users, the damage had already been done. Morris was caught and charged with violating the Computer Fraud Abuse Act of 1986. Following a jury trial, Morris was found guilty of violating the Act and sentenced to three years of probation, 400 hours of community service, and a fine of $10,050 plus the costs of his supervision.

TRADE SECRET THEFT

At about the same time Congress was drafting the amendments to the Copyright Act in response to the *LaMacchia* case, it passed a new law that criminalizes the theft of trade secrets. Under the Economic Espionage Act of 1996, individuals found guilty of intentional trade secret theft can be fined up to $250,000 and imprisoned for up to ten years.[6] Corporations or other business organizations found guilty of trade secret theft may be subject to fines of up to $5,000,000.

Because the law is so new, it is not yet clear how it will be applied. So far, the law has primarily been used in cases involving foreign agents who have attempted to use bribery to purchase important trade secrets. The considerable discretion held by federal prosecutors in deciding whether to prosecute individual cases makes it likely that cases that do not contain substantial evidence, such as the presence of a bribe, and high-profile appeal, such as the involvement of foreign agents, will not be prosecuted.

With regard to computer hardware or software, several conclusions may be drawn. The law certainly applies to the theft of software-related documents and files containing trade secrets. Presumably, the law applies to the misappropriation of either source code or object code that contains protectable trade secrets. Likewise, the law probably retains long-standing doctrines that allow reverse engineering as long as the original hardware or software was properly obtained. Despite these presumptions about the application of the law, it would be best to let others provide the test cases that will define the reach of the Economic Espionage Act.

PACKAGING, LABELS, AND ADVERTISING

In 1984 Congress substantially bolstered the criminal penalties for trademark counterfeiting by passing the Trademark Counterfeiting Act. The Trademark Counterfeiting Act makes it a crime to intentionally traffic or attempt to traffic counterfeit goods, knowingly using a spurious, counterfeit trademark that is identical or substantially indistinguishable from a federally registered trademark, when such trafficking is likely to cause confusion, mistake, or deception. Individuals convicted under the Act are subject to maximum penalties of $2 million dollars, ten years in prison, or both; corporations are subject to a maximum penalty of $5 million.

The Trademark Counterfeiting Act is primarily aimed at stopping the sale of counterfeit goods such as Rolex watches, Gucci purses, and Polo clothing. In such cases, the counterfeiter is not acting in good faith. Rather, the counterfeiter intends to profit by fooling consumers into believing that the goods are genuine or seeks to take advantage of the public's desire to obtain goods that look like the real thing but are much cheaper.

As applied to computer hardware, the Act would provide criminal penalties for the trafficking of computers, peripheral devices, and any other goods bearing spurious marks that are identical or substantially indistinguishable from registered trademarks for those same goods. For example, selling counterfeit microprocessors intentionally bearing a

Pentium or Intel Inside logo would likely be criminal conduct under the Act. The same standard applies to computer software, so that the sale of counterfeit software bearing a Microsoft Windows trademark would be subject to criminal penalties.

In addition to the federal Trademark Counterfeiting Act, there are several other criminal provisions to combat counterfeit goods. For example, in 1996 Congress increased the criminal penalties available by making trafficking in counterfeit goods a "predicate act" under the Racketeer Influenced and Corrupt Organizations Act (RICO). Many states also have additional laws that criminalize trafficking in counterfeit goods.

Legitimate businesses need not worry about the criminal aspects of trademark infringement. In general, criminal penalties will not apply to anyone who has an honest, good faith belief that the applicable trademark is not counterfeit. If honest, good faith belief is not comforting enough, two additional steps will provide further protection for legitimate businesses. First, notify the trademark owner of the plans to use the mark thirty days before such use; second, include a notice on the goods disclaiming any association with the trademark owner.

NONCRIMINAL ACTS

Not all intellectual property infringements carry criminal penalties. Considering the number of ways that you can land yourself in jail, it may be surprising to learn that it is possible to infringe another's intellectual property rights without committing a crime. Though there are still a few acts that do not carry criminal penalties, it is extremely important to note that intellectual property law, particularly the criminal aspects of intellectual property law, is constantly changing. If you have any doubt about the propriety of any particular act, you should consult an attorney or act at your own risk.

In general, there are no criminal penalties associated with pure acts of patent infringement. The patent statutes have long left it up to individual patent owners to enforce their patents against alleged infringers. Although there is presently no pending legislation to add criminal penalties for patent infringement, the recent amendments to the copyright and trade secret laws provide ample evidence that Congress could be persuaded to add criminal penalties for patent infringement in the future.

There are several other acts that may constitute infringement but are free from criminal penalties. For example, copying a single software product having a value of less than $1,000 for individual use without commercial gain is not punishable by fine or imprisonment. In addition, the Copyright Act expressly allows software users to make backup copies of their software and to modify it as necessary to enable it to run on their hardware. Likewise, reverse engineering is generally understood to be a noncriminal act.

Intellectual property plays an increasingly important role in the U.S. economy. Because of its prominence, Congress and the states have enacted many criminal statutes aimed at protecting intellectual property. Although a few acts of intellectual property infringement still do not carry criminal penalties, the number of such acts is dwindling. The best course of conduct would be to avoid any act that arguably infringes the intellectual property rights of others.

Notes

1. The introductory statistics are contained in a study done by the Senate Permanent Subcommittee on Investigations in 1996.

2. Statistics regarding estimated losses incurred by the software industry to piracy are cited in "U.S. Combats International Software Piracy," *Journal of Proprietary Rights* (July 1993): 31.

3. The LaMacchia case is primarily based on the reported court decision at *United States v. LaMacchia*, 871 F. Supp 535 (D.Mass. 1994).

4. The new copyright criminal provisions are contained in the "No Electronic Theft Act," signed by President Clinton on December 16, 1997, and incorporated into the copyright act at 17 U.S.C. § 506. The law, originating in the House as HR 2265, also contains penalty provisions that modify Section 2319 of Title 18.

5. The Morris case is primarily based on the reported court decision at *United States v. Morris*, 928 F.2d 504 (2d Cir. 1991).

6. Information regarding the Economic Espionage Act comes from the act itself. See also Joseph N. Hosteny, "The Economic Espionage Act: A Very Mixed Blessing," *Intellectual Property Today* (February 1998): 8; Lawrence B. Ebert, "More on the Economic Espionage Act of 1996," *Intellectual Property Today* (February 1998): 13.

II

Control of Screen Displays

4

Video Game Wars

Video games have been tremendously popular from the time they were first introduced. Though the first popular computer game, Pong, was merely a crude version of table tennis, consumers were fascinated by the blinking lights and sound effects. The demand for computer games has continued to grow in parallel with the ability to make increasingly sophisticated games for ever more powerful computers. This combination has created a video game market that now exceeds $1 billion annually.

Most of the popular video games of the 1980s were arcade games, rather than personal computer games. Although many personal computer games were available, personal computers simply were not powerful enough to operate the more sophisticated games, which required dedicated computers and stand-alone arcade machines. Today's personal computers are now powerful enough to operate complex games, including many of the arcade games of the past. Because of the power of personal computers, many of today's popular video game titles are originally created for personal computers rather than arcades. Nevertheless, arcades continue to provide a forum for some of the more advanced and expensive computing tasks, particularly including networked gaming.

PAC-MAN

Predictably, many important legal skirmishes have involved arcade games and the right to make similar, competing games or to make home versions of popular arcade games. Several of these legal battles were fought over Pac-Man, one of the most popular arcade games.[1] Namco Limited created Pac-Man in 1979 for the Japanese market. When Midway Manufacturing introduced it in the United States in 1980 under a license from Namco, Pac-Man became an instant success. Virtually overnight there were thousands of Pac-Man arcade games throughout the United States, ready and waiting to take quarters from anyone willing to play. Pac-Man was soon followed by Ms. Pac-Man, Pac-Man Jr., and a dozen other Pac-Man sequels.[2] After the technology advanced enough to support a home video game version, Atari, Inc. obtained a license to make a Pac-Man game for home use. The Pac-Man arcade game was so popular that Pac-Man appeared in television cartoons and on T-shirts, dishes, trays, radios, and nearly every other form of paraphernalia imaginable.

In Pac-Man, a circular yellow "gobbler" is pursued through a maze by four ghost monsters. (See Figure 2.) The four original Japanese monster names Oikake, Machibuse, Kimagure, and Otoboke were translated to Blinky, Pinky, Inky, and Clyde in the U.S. version. Several hundred dots line the pathways of the maze, with four larger dots, called "power capsules," located in the four corners of the maze. During the play of the game, various fruit symbols appear in the middle of the maze to be eaten by the gobbler.

With the use of a joy stick, the gobbler is guided through the maze, gobbling up dots while trying to avoid contact with the ghost monsters. Each play ends when a monster catches the gobbler, and after three

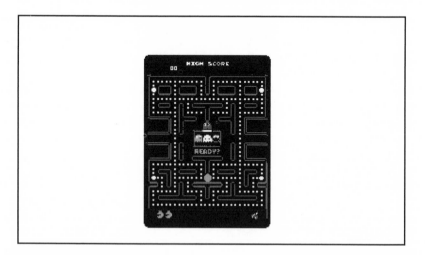

Figure 2. Maze-chase video games. The Pac-Man maze-chase video game was extremely popular—and copied by other game makers.

plays the game is over. If the gobbler consumes a power capsule, the monsters change color and can be consumed by the gobbler. The object of the game is to score as many points as possible by gobbling dots, power capsules, fruit symbols, and monsters.

The Pac-Man maze is drawn in bright blue double lines and contains central openings at the left and right sides of the maze. A player can evade capture by a pursuing monster by exiting through one opening and reentering through the opposite side. The center of the maze contains a "corral" with a small opening on the upper side. The monsters begin the game from within the corral, exiting one at a time after play begins. If a monster is gobbled after the gobbler consumes a power capsule, the monster's body disappears and the monster's eyes race back to the corral, where it regenerates and returns to resume its pursuit of the gobbler.

Pac-Man also uses several sound effects during play. A distinctive gobbling sound is played as the gobbler's V-shaped mouth opens and closes while traveling through the maze and consuming dots. When the gobbler consumes a power capsule, a siren sounds to indicate that the monsters are vulnerable to the gobbler. When fruit or monsters are gobbled, musical sounds are played. If the gobbler comes in contact with one of the monsters, the action freezes and the gobbler folds back on itself, making a sympathetic whining sound and disappearing with a starburst.

THE COMPETITION: K.C. MUNCHKIN

North American Philips Consumer Electronic Corp. ("Philips") recognized the popularity of Pac-Man and decided to develop a modified version for sale as a home video game called K.C. Munchkin. Principals at Philips, including its programmer, played Pac-Man at least once before beginning work on K.C. Munchkin. When Philips finished K.C. Munchkin, it concluded that it was "totally different" from Pac-Man. Nevertheless, Philips changed some of the game characters to reduce the likelihood of confusion.

Like Pac-Man, K.C. Munchkin is a maze-chase game in which a player directs a gobbler to consume dots and power capsules while avoiding contact with ghost monsters. By gobbling a power capsule, the monsters become vulnerable and can be consumed by the gobbler. The goal is to accumulate as many points as possible by gobbling the dots and monsters.

K.C. Munchkin's maze contains two tunnel exits and a centrally located monster corral. Pac-Man's maze is drawn in blue double lines, the K.C. Munchkin maze is drawn in single purple lines. The K.C.

Munchkin maze also contains a dead-end passageway not found in Pac-Man. The corral, stationary in Pac-Man, rotates ninety degrees every two or three seconds in K.C. Munchkin.

The gobbler of K.C. Munchkin is somewhat different from the gobbler of Pac-Man. Though both gobblers move through the maze with a V-shaped gobbling mouth accompanied by a distinctive gobbling noise, the K.C. Munchkin gobbler is blue-green, rather than yellow, and includes horns and eyes. When attacked by a monster, the gobbler's normally impish smile turns to a frown. If it is successful in consuming all the dots, the gobbler turns to the viewer and chuckles. But if it is captured by a monster, the gobbler folds back on itself and disappears in a starburst.

Although K.C. Munchkin has three monsters to Pac-Man's four, the ghost monsters are similar to their Pac-Man counterparts in shape and movement. Though the monsters of K.C. Munchkin have two short antennae not found on the Pac-Man monsters, in both games the monsters have centipede-like legs and eyes that look in the direction the monster is moving. In both cases, the monsters are initially placed within the corral and exit as soon as the game begins.

When the gobbler of K.C. Munchkin consumes a power capsule, the monsters change color and become vulnerable, moving away from the gobbler at a slower speed as in Pac-Man. If caught by the gobbler, the monster vanishes except for its eyes and "feet." Instead of returning directly to the corral as in Pac-Man, the monster wanders harmlessly about the maze. The monster only returns to the corral if the corral happens to be open toward the monster as it travels toward the corral.

Both games also include dots to be gobbled, although K.C. Munchkin has only twelve dots compared to the over two hundred dots in Pac-Man. In addition, the K.C. Munchkin dots are randomly spaced, rectangular, and continuously moving, whereas the Pac-Man dots are evenly spaced, round, and stationary. When the game begins, a power capsule is located in each of the maze's four corners.

As in Pac-Man, K.C. Munchkin uses a set of sounds that accompany each of the various events that occur during game play. Many of the sounds are different from the sounds used in the Pac-Man game.

Despite the differences between Pac-Man and K.C. Munchkin, the public recognized the many similarities. Retailers in Chicago ran newspaper advertisements describing K.C. Munchkin as a "Pac-Man type game" and "as challenging as Pac-Man." Other advertisements directly referred to K.C. Munchkin as "a Pac-Man game." When Atari and Midway sent private investigators into stores to purchase K.C. Munchkin games, retailers told the investigators that the game was just like Pac-Man. Atari and Midway then sued Philips and its retailer Park

Magnavox Home Entertainment Center for copyright infringement and unfair competition.

VIDEO GAME WARS: *ATARI, INC. v. NORTH AMERICAN PHILIPS CONSUMER ELECTRONICS CORP.*

Shortly after initiating the lawsuit, Atari and Midway filed a motion for a preliminary injunction, seeking an order from the court preventing Philips from any further sales of K.C. Munchkin prior to a final determination at trial. As a practical matter, the award or denial of a preliminary injunction often ends the case because one of the required elements to be proven to obtain a preliminary injunction is likelihood of success at trial. Parties are often unwilling to risk trying to prove their case at trial after receiving an order from the court concluding that there is no likelihood of success.

The trial court denied Atari's request for a preliminary injunction, deciding that Atari had not proven a likelihood of success on the merits of the case. As often occurs in copyright infringement cases, there was no evidence of direct copying by Philips. Consequently, Atari was required to prove copying by showing that Philips had access to Pac-Man and that Pac-Man and K.C. Munchkin are substantially similar. Because the issue of access was not contested by Atari, the case hinged on whether K.C. Munchkin was substantially similar to the protectable portion of the Pac-Man game. The trial court focused on the many differences between the two games in finding them not to be substantially similar. The court stressed that the games play differently because of the moving dots, different maze configurations, and other differences found in K.C. Munchkin.

Atari appealed the trial court's denial of its request for a preliminary injunction to the Seventh Circuit Court of Appeals. The Court of Appeals began its analysis by observing that copyright law only protects the particular expression of an idea, rather than the underlying idea itself. Consequently, copyright protection does not extend to games as such. With regard to the Pac-Man game, copyright protection would not be broad enough to allow Atari to prevent others from making and distributing maze-chase video games. Instead, Atari would be limited to preventing others from making and distributing maze-chase video games that are substantially similar in expression to the Pac-Man game.

Because of this limitation on the scope of copyright protection, many aspects of Pac-Man would not be protected by themselves. Thus, the broad concepts of providing a maze, a central character, and opponents that pursue the central character through the maze can be used by anyone. Similarly, the court noted that the elements of tunnel exits, scoring tables, and dots to reward performance are so essential to a maze-chase type video game that they can only be protected against virtually identical copying. K.C. Munchkin's implementation of these elements was sufficiently different to avoid infringement.

But numerous other central elements were not inherently required by a maze-chase game and were substantially similar to the features found in the Pac-Man game. For example, the creation of a maze-chase game does not inherently require a "gobbler" and "ghost monsters." K.C. Munchkin's gobbler and ghost monster characters contained blatantly similar features that would lead most ordinary observers to conclude that Philips copied them from Pac-Man.

Unlike the trial court, the appeals court discounted Philips' laundry list of specific differences between the two games. As the court explained, the test for copyright infringement in the Seventh Circuit is whether the "ordinary observer" would conclude that the second work was copied from the first. According to the court, the *sine qua non* of the "ordinary observer test" for copyright infringement is the overall similarities, rather than the minute differences, between the two works. Exact reproduction or near identity is not required to establish copyright infringement. This is particularly true with respect to video games because a person who is entranced by the play of the game would be disposed to overlook many of the minor differences in detail and regard their aesthetic appeal as the same. In sum, it is enough that substantial parts of the original work were lifted; no plagiarist can excuse the wrong by showing the amount of his work he did not pirate. Based on these conclusions, the court of appeals reversed the trial court's holding and entered a preliminary injunction against continued copying of the Pac-Man game.

PERIPHERAL PAC-MAN DISPUTES

Pac-Man's commercial success attracted other imitations in addition to K.C. Munchkin. For example, in 1981, Midway sued a group of defendants for making and distributing "Mighty Mouth," an arcade game that was virtually identical to Pac-Man.[3] Midway also sued Bandai-America, Inc. for making and selling "Packri-Monster," a handheld video game that the court found to be substantially similar to Pac-Man. In each case, the court entered a preliminary injunction preventing further sale of the copied games.

In late 1980, Artic International, Inc. began selling a printed circuit board that was used to create a "Puckman" video game. The similarity between the names "Puckman" and "Pac-Man" is even closer than it appears—Namco Limited, the Japanese company that originated the Pac-Man game and licensed it to Midway and Atari for sale in the United States, first sold it in Japan under the name "Puckman." Except for a few trivial differences, Artic's Puckman game was identical to Pac-Man; the printed circuit board even included an error found in Midway's Pac-Man game. As with the other cases, the court entered a preliminary injunction preventing Artic from further infringement of Midway's copyrights.

VIDEO GAME WARS AND THE COMPUTER INDUSTRY

Since the early days of Pong and Pac-Man, the video game market has continued to grow at an exponential pace. Many new companies have been drawn to this booming industry, hoping to cash in. The unprecedented success of Pac-Man naturally led many companies to create similar games, some of which were nearly exact copies of previously existing games such as Pac-Man.

When Pac-Man was first introduced in the United States, the scope of copyright protection for software in general, and video games in particular, was unclear. Video game makers had little guidance regarding how close their competing maze-chase games could get to Pac-Man while avoiding the reach of copyright law. Because there was so little legal precedent involving video games, the courts were creating the law as they applied it. The Pac-Man cases helped to establish that copyright law does not protect video games as such, but does protect the particular expressive content of video games.

Later cases continued to define the boundary between the unprotectable video game idea and the protectable expression. For example, in 1988 the Ninth Circuit Court of Appeals held that the video game "World Karate Championship" made by Epyx, Inc. did not infringe the copyright in the Data East USA, Inc. game "Karate Champ."[4] Each was a video karate game that was similar to the other in numerous respects. Each had fourteen possible karate moves, including forward and backward somersaults, about-face moves, a squatting reverse punch, an upper-lunge punch, a back-foot sweep, a jumping side kick, and a low kick. Each game also had a referee, thirty-second countdown rounds, changing background scenes, and similar scoring systems.

Despite these similarities, the World Karate Championship game did not infringe the copyright in the Karate Champ game. Each of the common features resulted from either constraints found in the sport of karate or in the limited ways to transfer the karate game to a computer. Accordingly, a game like karate has very narrow copyright protection, limited to the particularly expressive elements such as the type of background scenery.

The video game cases have defined the scope of copyright protection for video games in a manner that leaves plenty of room for competition. Because copyright law protects only the particular expression found in a game rather than the underlying idea for the game itself, others can make competing games as long as they do not copy the original expression. Thus, a competitor can make a maze-chase game as long as it does not copy the particular expressive elements found in the Pac-Man game. The resulting computer game market includes a wide variety of video game categories and healthy competition within each category.

VIDEO GAMES: A BRIEF SUMMARY OF THE LAW

Copyright law protects the expressive content found in video games but does not protect the basic, underlying idea of a particular game. Because of this dichotomy, game makers can make competing video games of the same general type as an existing game as long as the later game does not copy the expression found in the original game.

Notes

1. This chapter is based on the court ruling in *Atari, Inc. v. North American Philips Consumer Electronics Corp.*, 672 F.2d 607 (7th Cir. 1982).

2. There are many useful Internet sites devoted to the history of Pac-Man and other video games. Some of the information used in this chapter comes from one such site at *www.gamecenter.com*.

3. The citations for the peripheral Pac-Man battles are *Midway Mfg. Co. v. Bandai-America, Inc.*, 546 F. Supp. 125 (D.N.J. 1982) and *Midway Mfg. Co. v. Artic International, Inc.*, 547 F. Supp. 999 (N.D. Ill. 1982).

4. The Karate Champ case is reported at *Data East USA, Inc. v. Epyx, Inc.*, 862 F.2d 204 (9th Cir. 1988).

5

The Icon Explosion

Icons are increasingly common in computer software—so much so that it is difficult to think of a computer program that contains no icons at all. Nearly all software on the market today uses icons that, when clicked with a mouse, direct the software to perform particular functions. For example, word processors commonly use icons to perform editing functions such as "cut," "copy," and "paste." Icons for such typical functions tend to take on similar looks, even in programs sold by competing software companies. At least for the more basic computing tasks, consumers have learned to associate certain images with particular operations.

Considering that icons are so widespread and often appear quite similar to each other, you might have assumed that the law has not allowed any single company to corner the market on icons. Does that mean that you can copy another's icon designs with impunity? And does it mean that there is no way to protect your own icon designs from being copied by others? The answer to both these questions is a resounding "no."

THE HISTORY OF COMPUTER ICONS

The history behind the use of computer icons to operate computers begins with Xerox Corporation.[1] Although many people assume that icons originated with Apple Computer, Xerox was actually the first to develop graphical user interfaces using icons to control a computer. As early as the mid-1970s, Xerox employee David Canfield Smith adopted the term *icon* to refer to graphical images that represent computer tasks or functions. Xerox made extensive use of icons in its Smalltalk software in 1979 and its 8010 Star Information System workstation in 1981.

Although Apple was not the first to introduce icons to the computing community, it did introduce them to the world of personal computers. The Apple Lisa, introduced in 1983, and the Apple Macintosh, introduced in 1984, both used an icon-driven graphical user interface.

Almost certainly, Apple's idea to use icons in its user interfaces came from Xerox. In December 1979, Apple founder Steven Jobs and other Apple personnel visited Xerox's Palo Alto Research Center ("PARC") to view Xerox demonstrations of its Smalltalk software. Apple apparently liked what it saw. A few months after the December demonstration, Xerox's Larry Tesler (who demonstrated the Smalltalk software to Apple) left Xerox to work for Apple. Subsequently, several other Xerox employees joined Tesler. As Henry David Thoreau once said, "Some circumstantial evidence is very strong, as when you find a trout in the milk." Like a trout in the milk, Apple's visit to Xerox and its hiring of Xerox employees are strong circumstantial evidence that Apple's icon ideas came from Xerox.

While Apple was developing the Lisa and the Macintosh, IBM was launching a personal computer of its own. In 1981, IBM introduced the original PC, with an operating system developed by Microsoft. The IBM PC used a different microprocessor chip than the Motorola 68000 used by the Apple computers. Because the IBM PC's microprocessor had a smaller memory capacity than the Motorola 68000, it was unable to operate a memory-intensive graphical operating system like that used in the Apple computers. Confined by limited hardware capabilities, Microsoft produced the character-based MS-DOS operating system for the PC.

Eventually, computer chip manufacturers developed more-powerful microprocessors, increasing the memory capacity of personal computers. Microsoft capitalized on this increased capacity in 1985 by introducing Windows 1.0, a program designed to operate on top of MS-DOS to provide a graphical user interface.

Apple cried foul over Microsoft's introduction of Windows, claiming that Microsoft had copied the Lisa and Macintosh operating systems. Apple and Microsoft settled their dispute reasonably quickly, with Apple granting Microsoft a license to use the elements of Windows 1.0 derived from Apple. In exchange, Microsoft agreed to delay the release of any version of its Excel spreadsheet that would operate on computers other than the Macintosh, and to release an enhanced version of Microsoft Word for the Macintosh.

Before long, Microsoft introduced upgrades to its Windows software that became increasingly similar to the Apple Macintosh operating system. As Windows became more powerful, consumers began to question the comparative value of the Macintosh computers, which offered fewer and fewer technical advantages over their cheaper IBM-compatible counterparts.

APPLE v. MICROSOFT AND HEWLETT-PACKARD: THE BATTLE OVER ICONS

Apple responded to Microsoft's upgraded versions of Windows with a lawsuit alleging copyright infringement.[2] In the same lawsuit, Apple sued Hewlett-Packard, claiming its New Wave software also infringed Apple's copyrights. Apple contended that Microsoft and Hewlett-Packard had improperly copied several of the Macintosh features, including the use of icons. Apple's claims were ambitious. In addition to preventing the use of the particular icons contained in the Macintosh operating system, Apple sought to prevent Microsoft and Hewlett-Packard from using icons altogether.

The Right to Use Icons Generally

The court quickly whittled down the vast majority of Apple's claims, including Apple's attempt to prevent Microsoft and Hewlett-Packard from using icons altogether. Three primary factors led the court to reject Apple's bid to prevent others from using all icons. First, Apple had granted Microsoft a license to use many of the elements found in Windows. Because Apple had licensed Microsoft to use approximately 90 percent of what it claimed were infringing features found in Windows versions 2.03 and 3.0, Apple's claims were limited by the court to Windows features not included in the 1985 license between Apple and Microsoft.

Second, the court noted that Apple's use of icons to control a computer was not original, having been previously developed by Xerox. The lack of originality precluded Apple from obtaining copyright protection for the use of all icons, even though Apple had obtained copyright registrations for its operating system. Apple should have been more humble about the origin of its icons: Shortly after Apple sued Microsoft and Hewlett-Packard, Xerox sued Apple. In that lawsuit, Xerox requested that the court cancel Apple's copyright registrations for the Apple operating systems using icons because the idea was first developed—and copyrighted—by Xerox. Xerox's efforts failed because the law made no provision for a court to cancel a copyright registration for lack of originality.

Third, by the time of the trial, consumers had come to expect the use of icons in operating systems. The strong consumer expectations made the use of icons a virtually indispensable element in computer interfaces that was ineligible for broad copyright protection. As shown in Table 1, at least twenty-one other computer systems used iconic representations to control the computer. On the basis of this evidence, the court explained that consumer expectations made it virtually impossible to produce a marketable software interface without using icons. This concept, referred to as *scènes à faire* in copyright law, prevented Apple from protecting icons in a general sense but would still allow particular icon designs to be protected.

Based on these factors, Apple was unable to prevent Microsoft and Hewlett-Packard from using icons altogether. Instead, Apple was lim-

Table 1.
Iconic operating systems

Computer Interface	Years of Release
Xerox Smalltalk	1979
Xerox Star	1981
Tektronix Smalltalk	1984
Apollo Domain 8.0	1984
Metaphor	1984–89
Xerox Viewpoint	1985
Commodore-Amiga Workbench 1.3	1987
Digital Equipment DECwindows	1988–89
IBM/MS OS/2 1.1	1988
Apollo Domain 10.3.5	1988–91
Sun Microsystems/OSF Looking Glass	1988–90
Open Software Foundation Motif	1989–91
NeXT 2.1	1989–91
IBM/MS OS/2 1.2	1989
X Consortium Tab Window Manager	1990
Geo Works Ensemble	1990
Atari GEM	1990
X.Desktop	1990
Sun Microsystems Sun View	1990
Sun Microsystems Open Windows	1990
Commodore-Amiga Workbench 2.0	1991

Microsoft demonstrated to the court that by 1991 at least twenty-one computer interfaces or operating systems used icons to represent computer functions.

ited to attempting to prove that the icon designs chosen by Microsoft and Hewlett-Packard were so similar to Apple's icon designs that they infringed Apple's copyrights.

Icon Titles

First, Apple argued that its icon design that placed the icon's title centered below the icon was a design feature improperly copied by Microsoft. (See Figure 3.) In response, the court explained that there were few places to locate a title around an icon. For example, the title could be placed above, below, or to either side of an icon. Apple's selection was a natural choice that contained little, if any, creativity. Because there were so few places to locate an icon title, it was not possible to copyright Apple's particular chosen location.

Page and Folder Icons

Next, Apple asserted that its icon designs for an image shaped like a page with a turned-down corner to indicate a file, and for an image shaped like a folder to indicate a directory, were copied by Microsoft. (See Figure 3.) But the court noted that these images had previously been used by Xerox. As a result, the court denied Apple's claim, holding that these designs lacked originality and were therefore not protected under copyright law.

Figure 3. The Macintosh icons. Early court battles fought over the right to use icons such as the Apple Macintosh icons shown here.

The Trash Can Icon

Apple also argued that its trash can icon and "Waste Basket" and "Trash" labels were copied by the New Wave software. The court found the trash can icon design to be original and capable of protection, but the labels "Waste Basket" and "Trash" were phrases too short to be protected by copyright.

In the end, very little was left of Apple's icon claims. According to an old Spanish proverb, "He who goes to the law for a sheep loses his cow." In Apple's case, both the sheep and the cow were lost. Most of Apple's icons were either standard or common representations or were nearly inseparable from the ideas they represented. As the court made quite clear, icon designs will not be protected at all if the designs are not original, if they are purely functional, if they are incapable of being expressed differently, or to the extent that they include certain essential design features. The strength of copyright protection for icon designs is directly related to their originality and creativity. If a design is particularly original and creative, the design owner will be entitled to broad protection. If not, the design owner will only be able to prevent others from making nearly exact copies of the icon design.

ICON DESIGN PATENTS

Although the icon designs at issue in the *Apple v. Microsoft and Hewlett-Packard* case were not patented, it is possible to obtain an icon design patent. This was not always the case. Until recently, whether icons could be protected by a design patent was a source of confusion.

In the 1980s, Xerox became the first to submit patent applications for icon designs. Some of Xerox's patented icon designs are shown in Figure 4 (next page). When the Patent and Trademark Office began issuing design patents to Xerox for its icon designs, the public took notice. Members of the legal and software communities debated whether an icon was an "ornamental design for an article of manufacture" as required by the design patent statute. Although a design patent protects ornamental designs, it does not protect artistic or aesthetic features in the abstract. Many people argued that icon designs were abstract artistic designs that were not part of an article of manufacture. While the public debated whether computer icons were properly the subject of design patent protection, the Patent and Trademark Office began routinely rejecting all applications for icons until the matter could be resolved.

Many of the rejected design patent applications were appealed to the Patent and Trademark Office Board of Appeals. In effect, the applicants sued the Patent and Trademark Office for improperly rejecting the applications. The Board of Appeals was slow to decide the mountain of appeals that piled up, and didn't break the logjam of pending icon design patent applications until May 18, 1992.[3] The Patent and Trademark Office concluded that icon designs qualify for design patent protection as long as the patent applications show a computer-generated icon depicted on a computer screen, monitor, or other display panel so that it is "embodied in an article of manufacture."[4] In other words, icons such as those shown in Figure 4 would not be patentable as shown, but if you drew a computer screen around them, they would be.

The availability of both patent and copyright protection should not be taken to mean that one must choose either one or the other. Although this was true at one time, it is no longer the case. Today, it is possible to obtain both copyright and design patent protection for a computer icon.

ICON LAW AND THE COMPUTER INDUSTRY

Icons were initially used and widely accepted in computer applications because users found them intuitive and easy to use. The growing use of icons, and in particular similar icons for similar functions in competing products, has been due, in part, to the narrow copyright protection available.

Before Apple's lawsuit against Microsoft and Hewlett-Packard, no one was certain whether icon designs could be protected by copyright at all. At the same time, there was concern that the court might find that Apple was entitled to broad protection for the use of icons generally. If the court had given Apple what it requested, the Apple operating system would have been the only operating system allowed to use

Figure 4. Patented icons. Although none of Apple's icon designs was patented, icons may be patented. The first icon design patents, some of which are shown here, were issued to Xerox in the late 1980s.

icons. The court's conclusion fell far short of that request, finding that copyright law does protect icon designs, but only to the extent that they are original and creative.

While Microsoft proved that many computer interfaces had used icons at the time of the lawsuit, icons are even more widely used now. Because icons must be original and somewhat creative to be protected by copyright, "ordinary," uncreative icons have frequently appeared identically in competing programs. More-sophisticated designs are also appearing, perhaps in an effort to establish sufficient originality and creativity to gain stronger copyright protection.

The rise in creative icon designs may also be due to the recent availability of icon design patents. Significantly, design patent applications for icons were denied routinely between the late 1980s and the mid-1990s—precisely the time that the industry went "icon-crazy," liberally sprinkling icons around the fringes of computer monitors. Because design patents were not available, little effort was made to produce icon designs worthy of design patents.

Now that icons clearly may be protected by copyrights or design patents, several subtle but significant changes may occur. First, software companies are likely to place a greater emphasis on developing unique icons for their software. If competing programs cannot use the same icons, consumers may be disoriented when viewing the competing program for the first time. Unless consumers are willing to invest the time to learn the meaning of each new icon, they will not switch programs.

Second, some software companies will inevitably use a "picket fence" strategy to attempt to prevent others from using icons for a given function entirely. The picket fence strategy involves obtaining copyrights or patents for as many designs as possible for the particular icon function. Using this technique, a software maker can literally corner the market, leaving others with no acceptable alternative icon designs for a given function.

Finally, the increased use of copyrights and design patents for icons will inevitably lead to litigation. Because design patents for icons have only recently been allowed, this future litigation will surely continue to shape the way that icons are used in personal computers.

ICONS: A BRIEF SUMMARY OF THE LAW

Icons are protected under copyright law as soon as they are fixed in a tangible medium of expression. Copyright protection is available for icons individually or as a part of the work in which the icons appear. Copyright law protects the unauthorized copying of the icon designs, but does not prevent others from independently developing and using similar designs. Unless a given icon design is particularly original and creative, copyright law prevents only the nearly exact copying of the icon design.

Icons may also be protected by design patents if the patent applications are directed to novel, unobvious icons shown on a computer screen, monitor, or other display panel. Design patent owners may prevent others from using the icons even if developed independently.

Notes

1. Information regarding the origin of the Xerox Smalltalk computers and the dispute between Apple and Xerox is also reported in *Xerox Corp. v. Apple Computer, Inc.*, 734 F. Supp. 1542 (N.D. Cal. 1990).

2. Most of this chapter is based on the litigation between Apple and Microsoft reported in *Apple Computer, Inc. v. Microsoft Corp.*, 24 USPQ2d 1081 (N.D. Cal. 1982).

3. Several of the early design patent cases referred to in this chapter include *Ex parte Donoghue*, 26 USPQ2d 1266 (Bd. Pat. App. Int. 1992); *Ex parte Donaldson*, 26 USPQ2d 1250 (Bd. Pat. App. Int. 1992); and *Ex parte Strijland*, 26 USPQ2d 1259 (Bd. Pat. App. Int. 1992).

4. The Guidelines for Examination of Design Patent Applications for Computer-Generated Icons are published in the *Federal Register*, 61, no. 55 (March 20, 1996).

6

Font Fights: Attempts to Own the Alphabet

For many centuries following the invention of movable type, typeface design was a slow, painstaking process that required several years to develop a single new font. Although font designers still consider a quality font to be the work of careful craftsmanship, designers can now develop a new font in a fraction of that time. In fact, with the right computer software, it is possible to generate an original font in a few seconds.

The comparative ease of creating new fonts has created a boom in the font market and sparked considerable demand among consumers. In response to the demand, the number of professional font designers has grown from a small handful at the turn of the century and about 50 during the reign of phototype to perhaps 500 today. Industry experts estimate that there are as many as 50,000–60,000 fonts now in use.[1]

While fonts have become big business, the industry is extremely competitive. Many fonts are now sold at bargain prices or bundled with hundreds of other fonts for a nominal price. Still others may be downloaded free over the Internet. Although professional font designers may criticize the quality of such cheap fonts, consumer demand for these inexpensive fonts is brisk. These market dynamics have created a competitive industry in which even the highest-quality fonts are unable to fetch high prices.

In addition to competition in the marketplace, computer hardware and software companies have waged a substantial number of legal battles related to fonts. As font purveyors have long recognized, exclusive ownership of a popular font is extremely valuable. Consequently, font makers have engaged in legal battles involving nearly every conceivable aspect of fonts and computer font technology, including typeface design, methods of rendering typefaces, computer and printer interface formats, and trademarked names for particular fonts.

COPYRIGHT PROTECTION FOR TYPEFACES

Numerous legal battles involving fonts and font technology have taken place, but perhaps the most important have involved the fundamental questions of whether a typeface may be protected under the U.S. copyright laws. If so, a font company would receive exclusive rights in the font for 95 years. Unfortunately for font designers, the Copyright Office has routinely refused to grant copyright registrations for typefaces.

Eltra Corp. v. Ringer: Typefaces Are Not Eligible for Copyright Protection

As an initial matter, typefaces do not fit within any of the specifically enumerated categories of subject matter that may be protected by copyright. These categories include literary works; musical works; dramatic works; choreographic works; pictorial, graphic, and sculptural works; motion pictures; sound recordings; and architectural works. Typefaces certainly are not literary works, because there is clearly nothing literary about them. Moreover, the alphabet is obviously not original and cannot be protected as such.

Among the remaining categories, only "pictorial, graphic and sculptural works" seems to fit. But the Copyright Office has consistently refused to register typefaces under this category, and the courts have upheld the Copyright Office's decisions. In the mid-1970s, Eltra Corporation purchased a new typeface design from a professional typeface designer for $11,000. Eltra then sought to register the typeface design with the Copyright Office as a "work of art," the category that was revised by Congress in 1976 to read, "pictorial, graphic, and sculptural works." The Copyright Office refused to register the typeface, explaining that it contained no elements that could be identified as a work of art.

After the Copyright Office rejected its application to register the typeface, Eltra filed a lawsuit in federal court in Virginia against Barbara Ringer, the Register of Copyrights.[2] Eltra sought "mandamus," an order directing the Copyright Office to properly discharge its duties by registering the typeface design. The trial court granted Ms. Ringer's motion for summary judgment, concluding that the typeface may not be registered in the Copyright Office. Eltra promptly appealed to the United States Court of Appeals for the Fourth Circuit.

The Fourth Circuit Court of Appeals affirmed the trial court's decision. The court explained that copyright protection is not available for utilitarian works. If the sole intrinsic function of an article is its utility, the fact that an article is unique and attractively shaped will not qualify it as a work of art. But if the utilitarian article incorporates features that can be identified separately and are capable of existing independently as a work of art, such features will be eligible for copyright protection.

Although Eltra agreed that works are not eligible for copyright protection if their sole intrinsic function is utilitarian, Eltra contended that its particular typeface incorporated sufficiently artistic features that it qualified as a work of art. The court, however, was not persuaded. Congress had specifically defined "typeface" as having an intrinsic utilitarian function in its use for composing text or other combinations of characters. Further, the House Report on the 1976 Copyright Act revisions declared that, "The Committee does not regard the design of a typeface, as thus defined, to be a copyrightable 'pictorial, graphic or sculptural work' within the meaning of this bill." Consequently, the court concluded that a "typeface is an industrial design in which the design cannot exist independently and separately as a work of art. Because of this, typeface has never been considered entitled to copyright" protection.

Adobe Systems, Inc. v. Southern Software Inc.: Copyright Protection for Font Software

Although it is settled that typefaces are not eligible for copyright protection by themselves, it does not necessarily follow that computerized data for typeface designs is also ineligible for copyright protection. As the *Eltra Corp.* case illustrates, the Copyright Office has concluded that mere typefaces are not protectable in any form, whether on paper or electronic media. But subsequent legal battles have concluded that software that creates scaleable typefaces or that instructs a printer to print using a particular typeface is protectable under the copyright laws.

In some cases, the line between an unprotectable electronic typeface design and a protectable computer program that manipulates that typeface can be hazy. In 1997, Adobe Systems Inc. sued Southern Software Inc., alleging that Southern Software infringed its copyrights in software used to render typefaces.[3] Adobe's font editors selected a number of coordinates representative of the outlines of each letter for each typeface in its software. The Adobe font software then used those coordinates to create the images that are displayed or printed.

Southern Software loaded a copy of Adobe's font software onto a company computer to create its software management software, called "Key Fonts Pro 1555." Using the Adobe software, Southern Software extracted information necessary to produce an electronic font. Although Southern Software did not copy the entire Adobe font images, it did copy the reference points used to generate particular typefaces. Because the Southern Software reference points were the same as Adobe's, the fonts produced by Southern Software's computer programs were substantially the same as those produced by Adobe.

Each side asked the court to resolve the matter on summary judgment. Southern Software argued that Adobe had no copyright interest in the data Southern Software used to create its font software. The Southern Software program did not copy protectable source code but rather only the reference points that define the outline of a font. Because fonts themselves are not eligible for copyright protection, Southern Software argued, the reference points that define the outline of a font should likewise be ineligible for copyright protection.

In response, Adobe argued that its editors carefully selected the particular points used to produce a font outline. Because very little creativity is required for copyright protection, the careful selection of reference points as font reference points should be protected under the copyright laws.

The court agreed with Adobe. According to the court, even if the particular font dictates to a certain extent the points the editor must choose, it does not dictate every point that must be chosen. While the editors made their choices in part based upon functional considerations, the editors exercised a degree of creativity in selecting the reference points that is sufficient to qualify the reference points as protectable works of authorship. Thus, Southern Software's substantially similar font software infringed Adobe's copyrights.

TYPEFACE DESIGN PATENTS

Although typefaces cannot be protected under U.S. copyright laws, they can be protected under the patent laws. Until recently, however, it was not certain that a typeface qualified as an ornamental design "for an article of manufacture" as required by the design patent statutes. Because of this doubt, few font designers sought design patent protection for their typefaces, and the U.S. Patent and Trademark Office rejected many of the font design patent applications it received.

In 1996 the Patent and Trademark Office specifically addressed the patentability of type fonts and computer-generated icons. As with icons, the Patent and Trademark Office guidelines now acknowledge that typefaces qualify as ornamental designs for articles of manufacture, as required by the design patent statute. (See Figure 5.) An increasing number of font designers are now turning to design patents for legal protection for their typefaces.

The scope and validity of font design patents have not yet been tested in the courts. Considering the huge number of font designs now in existence, it may be difficult to create a new font that is not obvious in view of the previously existing fonts. If a typeface design is obvious in view of the previously existing typeface designs, it is not patentable. Even if a new font design is found not to be obvious, it seems likely the scope of protection will be quite narrow, such that font design patents will only protect the font owner from exact or nearly exact copying.

TYPEFACE TRADEMARKS

In addition to the limited protection available under the copyright and patent laws, typefaces may also be protected under the trademark

Figure 5. Patented fonts. The Patent and Trademark Office has recently allowed design patents for fonts such as the typeface design shown here.

laws. Many font companies hold several well-known trademarks for particular fonts. One such company is The Monotype Corporation, which has designed, manufactured, and distributed typeface designs and related typographic products since 1897. Among Monotype's library of typefaces is one of the world's most popular typefaces, Times New Roman. Monotype sells licenses to many other companies allowing them to use Monotype's trademarks and to incorporate Monotype's digital fonts into computer hardware and software products.

Monotype holds a variety of additional trademarks for its typefaces, including "Bembo," "Gill Sans," "Perpetua," and "Rockwell." Monotype has continuously used these trademarks in conjunction with the distribution of its typefaces in a variety of formats, including Postscript and TrueType formats. Because of the popularity of these typefaces and Monotype's efforts to advertise and enforce its trademarks, the Monotype trademarks have become widely known and are closely associated with particular typeface designs.

Although many of Monotype's fonts had been copied by others, in most cases they were distributed under different names. For example, Bitstream's "Aldine" typeface is a substantial copy of Monotype's "Bembo" typeface. But because the typefaces themselves cannot be protected under U.S. copyright laws, in many cases it is legal to copy a font and sell it under a different name.

In 1995 a court analyzed the limits of how "different" a font name must be when used by a competing company for the same font.[4] URW, a Monotype competitor, marketed and sold computerized typefaces in 1992 under names that were similar to Monotype's typeface names, including URW fonts called "Bemtus," "Gill Kayo," "Giltus," "Pertus," and "Rocktus." To create these typeface names, URW began with the first three letters of Monotype's registered trademarks and added the suffix "tus." The URW typefaces sold under these names were virtually identical to the typefaces sold by Monotype.

Monotype sued URW, alleging that URW infringed its federally registered trademarks. According to the court, Monotype's trademarks were well known and recognized in the industry as trademarks owned by Monotype. Most of Monotype's trademarks were purely "fanciful," meaning that the terms suggest nothing about the products and have no descriptive value. Among the trademarks involved in the litigation between Monotype and URW, only the word "Sans" in the trademark "Gill Sans" was suggestive, referring to sans serif, a style of typeface design. Further, Monotype's federal trademark registrations for "Bembo," "Gill Sans," and "Rockwell" were more than five years old. Under U.S. trademark law, this rendered Monotype's exclusive rights to use the marks "incontestable."

The fact that URW did not directly copy Monotype's trademarks in their entirety did not save URW. As the court explained, "the purloining of the first part of a well-known trademark and the appending to it of a worthless suffix is a method of trademark poaching long condemned by the courts." There was no doubt that URW had intended to create trademarks that were reminiscent of Monotype's marks. As the court continued, "Of course, few would be stupid enough to make exact copies of another's mark or symbol. It has been well said that the most successful form of copying is to employ enough points of similarity to confuse the public with enough points of difference to confuse the courts."

The court concluded that the public was likely to be confused by URW's use of trademarks that were similar to Monotype's trademarks, when used with fonts that were identical to Monotype's fonts. The court entered an order permanently enjoining URW from further use of the infringing trademarks and ordering URW to pay the costs of the litigation.

FONT LAW AND THE COMPUTER INDUSTRY

If the courts had initially allowed fonts to be protected under the copyright laws, the industry would have taken a different shape. In all likelihood, competing fonts would have been less plentiful and original fonts would have been more expensive, at least until font-development software was created. At the same time, competitors may have directed their attention toward creating unique fonts rather than copying pre- viously existing ones. In addition, there would be a reduced need to turn to trademarks to protect fonts if they could be protected by stronger copyright laws.

Despite the efforts of font designers to protect their typeface designs, the courts and the Copyright Office have consistently concluded that fonts may not be protected under U.S. copyright law. Thus, anyone may freely copy a typeface design without risking copyright infringement. Although the typeface itself can be freely copied without infringing any copyrights, some copiers have run afoul of the copyright laws by copying the computer code used to produce the copied typefaces. Likewise, patents covering font-rendering techniques or particular typefaces, and trademarks for particular font names serve as additional impediments to typeface copiers.

Despite the mixed bag of intellectual property rights, savvy copiers are generally able to find a legal way to copy a desirable typeface. This result has led to rampant copying throughout the industry, with iden- tical or virtually identical fonts being offered for sale by numerous competing companies or available to be downloaded for free over the Internet. Consequently, the market is rich with fonts, many of which are similar or identical to one another.

FONTS: A BRIEF SUMMARY OF THE LAW

A font, in itself, is not protectable under copyright law. Copyright protection is available, however, for a computer program used to produce a particular typeface. If a font is new and not an obvious design in view of the previously existing font designs, it may be protected for a term of fourteen years under the design patent laws. In addition, trademarks for particular typefaces cannot be used by others if consumers are likely to be confused by the use of the appropriated trademark.

Notes

1. Many of the statistics regarding the number of fonts and font designers in existence are contained in an article by Caitlin Liu, "Creating a New Generation of Vivid Typefaces," *New York Times*, August 5, 1996, sec. D, p. 5, col. 1.

2. The litigation between Eltra and Ringer is reported in *Eltra Corp. v. Ringer*, 579 F.2d 294 (4th Cir. 1978).

3. The litigation between Adobe and Southern Software is reported at *Adobe Systems Inc. v. Southern Software Inc.*, DC N. Cal. No. C95-20710RMW(PVT) February 2, 1998.

4. The Monotype trademark litigation is reported at *Monotype Corp. PLC v. International Typeface Corp.*, 43 F.3d 443 (9th Cir. 1994).

User Interface Battles

The Big Deal with Look and Feel

The "look and feel" of a computer program is an elusive concept. In general, the look and feel of a computer program is comprised of the various elements of the user interface. These elements might include stylistic aspects such as fonts, menu arrangements, color choices, icon designs and placements, presentation formats, and a host of other visual elements. It may also include aspects that are more functional or active, such as the keystrokes or mouse clicks required to perform certain operations. The look and feel of a program is the collection of these elements as a whole rather than any of them singly. Because the look and feel of a program is the aggregation of many elements, the look and feel of a particular program cannot easily be distilled down to a few brief terms.

The legal definition of "look and feel" is equally indistinct. The term is not included in copyright or any other statutory law. Rather, it is primarily a popular label for the collective user interface elements of a computer program. Because it has no foundation in the copyright statutes, few court decisions have actually used the term. Nevertheless, some decisions have expressly used it, and many others have analyzed a program's user interface without actually calling it look and feel.

The ambiguity in the law regarding look and feel is hardly unique. Many other areas of the law defy the creation of bright lines and handy definitions. Perhaps the most famous is in the area of obscenity, in which Supreme Court Justice Potter Stewart once wrote that only "hard-core" pornography could be banned. In doing so, he added, "I shall not today attempt to further define the kind of materials I understand to be embraced within that shorthand definition; and perhaps I could never succeed in doing so. But I know it when I see it." Before ruling on an obscenity case, members of the Supreme Court and their clerks sometimes view the allegedly offensive film together, to evaluate whether it is obscene. In the darkened viewing room, clerks often poke fun at Justice Stewart's vague rule by calling out, "That's it, I see it!"[1]

As if the intangible definition and the absence of an express statutory basis weren't enough to complicate the issue, the circumstances leading to a legal battle involving look and feel adds to the complexity. Typically, when a party asserts that its look and feel has been copied, it is only because very little, if anything, has been copied exactly. The plaintiff must then argue that, even though the allegedly copied program is different, it is close enough to infringe. Alternatively, the accused copier may have closely copied several elements, but the copied elements separately are in the public domain. In such cases, the plaintiff must argue that even though it owns no rights in the individual elements, it does have rights in the particular collection of them.

THE ORIGIN OF LOOK AND FEEL

Because of the relative youth of software law, many of the copyright law concepts that are applied to software were previously developed for other media. The same is true of look and feel, which was first applied in a handful of copyright lawsuits involving works such as greeting cards and television commercials. One of the first major cases to actually use the term "total concept and feel" was *Sid & Marty Krofft Television Productions, Inc. v. McDonald's Corporation*.[2] In 1969 the Kroffts introduced a Saturday morning children's television show called *H.R. Pufnstuf*. The show featured several fanciful costumed characters and a boy named Jimmy who lived in a fantasy land inhabited by moving trees and talking books. The success of the television program generated an array of H.R. Pufnstuf products and endorsements.

In early 1970 the Kroffts were approached by an executive from Needham, Harper & Steers, Inc., an advertising agency. Needham explained that it wanted to get the McDonald's hamburger restaurant advertising account by proposing a series of commercials based on the H.R. Pufnstuf characters. Despite numerous conversations regarding the project, Needham ultimately developed a McDonaldland campaign without the Kroffts, based on characters that were similar to, but different from, the H.R. Pufnstuf characters. In doing so, Needham hired several former employees of the Kroffts to construct the costumes and sets. Needham also hired the same voice expert who provided all the voices for the H.R. Pufnstuf characters. The Kroffts sued Needham and McDonald's for infringing their copyrights in the H.R. Pufnstuf television show. Following a trial, the jury found that there was copyright infringement and awarded damages to the Kroffts.

On appeal, McDonald's argued that there was no copyright infringement because of the many differences between its McDonaldland characters and the H.R. Pufnstuf characters. For example, McDonald's explained that the Pufnstuf character wears a yellow and green dragon suit with a blue cummerbund festooned with a medal that reads "mayor." The allegedly similar McDonaldland character Mayor McCheese wears formal "tails" and knicker trousers with a diplomat's sash bearing the word "Mayor." McDonald's also pointed out several other differences between the Pufnstuf and McDonaldland characters.

Despite these differences, the Court of Appeals affirmed the finding of infringement. According to the court, the "Living Island" of H.R. Pufnstuf is similar to McDonaldland in that they are both fantasy worlds inhabited by anthropomorphic plants and animals and other fanciful creatures. Both worlds also contain the same dominant features, including caves, trees, a pond, a road, and a castle. Both also have mayors with large round heads and wide mouths, and both mayors are assisted by "Keystone cop" characters. Although McDonald's implemented each of these features in a manner somewhat different from the Kroffts, the court concluded that McDonald's captured the "total concept and feel" of the Pufnstuf show.

EARLY SOFTWARE LOOK AND FEEL BATTLES: VIDEO GAMES

Many of the early look and feel battles in software involved video games, such as the dispute between Data East USA and Epyx over competing karate arcade games.[3] In 1984 Data East began distributing an arcade game called Karate Champ. Data East introduced a home computer game version of Karate Champ in October 1985. In April 1986, Epyx began distributing a home computer game entitled World Karate Championship.

The two games contained many similarities. Both were audiovisual depictions of a karate match conducted by two combatants, one in a white karate uniform and the other in red. Both also include a referee who announces the beginning and end of each match. The games contain a number of other similarities, such as a bonus round in which the game character breaks bricks. Data East sued Epyx, alleging that the look and feel of World Karate Championship infringed its copyright for Karate Champ.

The trial court concluded that the two games were virtually identical except for some minor particulars such as the referee's physical appearance, part of the scoreboard, and details of the bonus round. The trial court therefore found that Epyx was liable for copyright infringement and ordered Epyx to cease infringing and to recall all its infringing computer games.

Epyx appealed the decision to the United States Court of Appeals for the Ninth Circuit. The Court of Appeals agreed that the basic idea for each of the computer games was substantially similar. Thus, each was a martial arts karate combat game that included a referee, a scoring method, a variety of background locations, and bonus rounds. Further, the court agreed that each game contained many common similarities in the manner of expression of those ideas. For example, each game contained fourteen moves, changing background scenes, one- or two-player options, thirty-second rounds, and similar bonus scoring opportunities.

Even though these many similarities gave the two programs a similar look and feel, the Court of Appeals held that there was no infringement because the idea and expression were inseparable. Copyright law protects the expression of ideas rather than the ideas themselves. When the idea and its expression are inseparable, or where certain elements are indispensable in the expression of an idea, the expression is not protectable. With regard to the karate games, the Court of Appeals concluded that features such as scoring, a variety of player moves, the use of a referee, and bonus points were indispensable to the idea of a karate video game. Consequently, they were not protectable.

The different conclusions reached by the trial court and appeals court are indicative of the difficulty in applying the concept of look and feel. Whereas the Court of Appeals focused on the inseparability between the idea and the expression of that idea, other courts have been less troubled by the idea-expression distinction. In some cases, courts have upheld copyright protection in an overall look and feel comprised of unprotectable individual elements. Thus, whether there is a protectable overall look and feel in any particular computer program is a difficult question to answer.

LOOK AND FEEL IN APPLICATION PROGRAMS

Several courts have wrestled with the question of look and feel with regard to application programs. As with video games, the concept of look and feel has proven difficult to apply. One complicating factor is that the term "look and feel" can be applied to a wide array of software elements, including all the user interface features covered in other chapters of this book. Consequently, the look and feel battles discussed in this chapter could just as easily be placed in one or more other chapters dealing with the particular user interface elements at issue.

Moreover, it is frequently difficult to tell when the court is deciding a case on the basis of look and feel. Although an occasional court will use the term "look and feel" and some will use the term "total concept and feel," most courts simply address whether there is substantial similarity in accordance with the copyright statute. This inconsistency in terminology makes it difficult to find common threads and draw conclusions regarding the state of look and feel law.

The Look and Feel of Spreadsheet Programs: *Lotus Development Corp. v. Paperback Software*

With these limitations in mind, two legal disputes are illustrative of the application of the concept of look and feel to application programs. The first involves the battle between Lotus Development Corp. and Paperback Software over the look and feel of spreadsheet software.[4] According to Lotus, Paperback Software's VP-Planner infringed its copyrights in the Lotus 1-2-3 spreadsheet program. In evaluating the strength of the copyright protection in Lotus 1-2-3, Judge Robert E. Keeton initially noted that, although the term "look and feel" has been widely used among the public, it has not been particularly helpful in distinguishing between the elements of a computer program that are protectable and those that are not. Regardless of whether two programs contain a similar look and feel, the court must first determine the elements of the program that are protectable. Only after concluding that there is a valid copyright interest may the court evaluate whether the look and feel has been copied.

In the case of Lotus 1-2-3, the court concluded that there was a protectable user interface even though Lotus did not originate the idea of a computer spreadsheet. The first commercial spreadsheet was developed by Daniel Bricklin while a student at Harvard Business School in the late 1970s. Bricklin envisioned what he termed a "magic blackboard" that would automatically recalculate numbers as changes were made to various parts of the spreadsheet. Eventually, Bricklin's idea led to the introduction of VisiCalc, the first computer spreadsheet.

Although VisiCalc was a commercial success, it offered limited features. It was originally written for use on the Apple II computer, which had a small memory, limited display, and no advanced keyboard capabilities. Even when it was later rewritten for the IBM PC, it was not substantially upgraded to take advantage of the PC's more extensive features.

When Lotus introduced its 1-2-3 spreadsheet program, it offered many new features and took advantage of the PC's enhanced memory, keyboard, and display. Lotus 1-2-3 contained many features found in VisiCalc, including a number of cells defined by numbered rows and lettered columns. Lotus also used certain keys to initiate commands and provided various mathematical functions and formulas that could be used within the cells. Although Lotus 1-2-3 contained these essential elements of an electronic spreadsheet, Lotus did not contain the same menu and command structure found in VisiCalc. Further, the Lotus 1-2-3 user interface that included features such as a particular arrangement of commands in each menu line, symbols to represent each command, the manner of presentation on the screen, and the type of menu system used (for example, moving cursors or pull-down menus) was distinctive and protectable as a whole even though it contained individual elements that were not protectable individually.

The court concluded that Paperback copied the Lotus 1-2-3 user interface. Paperback Software's predecessor, Stephenson Software, began developing its own spreadsheet independently after recognizing both the advantages and shortcomings of VisiCalc. By January 1983, Stephenson Software had developed its spreadsheet software with a user interface and menu hierarchy that was different from both Lotus 1-2-3 and VisiCalc. Stephenson Software's principals organized Paperback Software in 1984 with the intent to complete and market the spreadsheet under the name VP-Planner. But in 1984, after having seen Lotus 1-2-3, Paperback concluded that VP-Planner would have to be compatible with Lotus 1-2-3 to succeed. Paperback then changed its user interface to make it more similar to Lotus 1-2-3. Because the VP-Planner contained the same menu structure and, as Paperback admitted, worked like 1-2-3 "keystroke for keystroke," the court held that Paperback infringed Lotus's copyrights in the look and feel of its menu and command structure.

The Look and Feel of User Interfaces: *Apple Computer, Inc. v. Microsoft Corp.*

Perhaps the most widely recognized look and feel battle was filed by Apple Computer in 1988, alleging that Microsoft's versions 2.03 and 3.0 of its Windows operating system infringed Apple's copyrights in the user interface of its Lisa and Macintosh computers.[5] In the same case, Apple alleged that Hewlett-Packard's "New Wave" software also infringed Apple's copyrights by copying the look and feel of the Macintosh user interface.

Apple had previously granted Microsoft a license in 1985 to use certain visual display elements, such as the use of "tiled" windows, in Microsoft Windows 1.0 and certain other application programs. In version 2.03 of Windows, Microsoft provided several enhancements, including the ability to overlap the windows and move the windows to any location on the screen. The new versions also allowed icons to be displayed on any part of the screen rather than be confined to the bottom of the screen as in version 1.0.

Apple and Microsoft disagreed about whether the 1985 license allowed Microsoft to create its upgraded operating systems. Apple argued that the 1985 agreement was specifically limited to Windows version 1.0 and did not allow Microsoft to use the individual user interface elements in later versions or other programs. Apple further contended that Microsoft could not use the licensed display elements in combination with unlicensed elements to create a user interface that more closely resembled the Macintosh user interface. Microsoft disagreed, arguing that the license allowed Microsoft to use the individual user interface elements in later versions. In addition, Microsoft contended that any elements outside the scope of the license were not copyrightable by Apple.

Judge William Schwarzer reviewed the evidence and applied the "extrinsic-intrinsic" test used by courts in the Ninth Circuit to evaluate copyright infringement. Under the extrinsic-intrinsic test, the court must first perform an "extrinsic" comparison to evaluate the similarity of ideas from an analytic viewpoint, carefully considering the scope of protection and analytically removing unprotected features from the original work. Next, the court will perform an "intrinsic" comparison, considering the similarity of the two works as a whole from the standpoint of the ordinary reasonable observer.

When performing the "extrinsic" evaluation, Judge Schwarzer adopted Microsoft's position, concluding that the license allowed Microsoft to use the individual display elements, in whole or in part, in any subsequent product. The look and feel of a program is comprised of all its elements as a whole. Because so much of the Apple look and feel was either licensed or within the public domain, the court decided that Microsoft would infringe Apple's rights in its look and feel only if the Windows user interface was virtually identical to the combination of the licensed and unlicensed elements in the Apple user interface.

After a number of important issues had been decided, the case was reassigned to Judge Vaughn Walker. Judge Walker wrestled with many of the same issues, writing several opinions that were seemingly inconsistent regarding whether the licensed elements must be analytically extracted from Apple's user interface before comparing it with Windows to determine whether there was substantial similarity. Ultimately, Judge Walker agreed that Apple could have a protectable look and feel in a user interface that is comprised of some novel elements together with others that are licensed or taken from the public domain. Such protection is limited, however, to the extent that the look and feel necessarily follows from the use of the licensed or public domain elements. In addition, because so many of the elements in the Windows user interface were either licensed or within the public domain, Apple's copyright protection would be limited to preventing others from using a virtually identical user interface.

Apple did not dispute that the Microsoft Windows user interface was not "virtually identical" to its Macintosh interface. Instead, Apple disagreed with the "virtual identity" standard applied by Judge Walker. But in September 1994, six years after the case began, the Court of Appeals for the Ninth Circuit issued a decision agreeing with Judge Walker and finding that Microsoft had not infringed Apple's copyrights.

LOOK AND FEEL AND THE COMPUTER INDUSTRY

Although some look and feel cases have drawn substantial public attention, the doctrine of look and feel has probably had little effect on the computer industry. To the uninformed, the result in the *Apple v. Microsoft* case may have compelled the conclusion that there are very weak rights in the look and feel of a computer program. But the strength of Apple's rights in its look and feel was weakened by the license between Apple and Microsoft more than by any aspect of copyright law. If Apple had not previously licensed Microsoft, the result may well have been different and the legal battle may have produced a landmark decision, both for the law and for the computer industry.

Though there have been many look and feel battles, including a handful of highly visible ones, look and feel has not developed into a well-defined concept within copyright law. Rather, it continues to be a fragmented legal theory that is applied haphazardly. In addition, it attempts to capture all aspects of a user interface within its reach. The combination of this uncertainty in application and apparent breadth of scope has created inevitable confusion in the computer industry as well as the legal community. Nevertheless, there is little doubt that copyright law will, at a minimum, prevent others from making virtually identical copies of an original look and feel. At least in part based on this fundamental understanding, most competing software programs are written to include a somewhat distinctive look and feel.

LOOK AND FEEL: A BRIEF SUMMARY OF THE LAW

Protection for the look and feel of computer software is not expressly included in the copyright statutes. Rather, look and feel has developed as a popular term for the user interface elements of a computer program. For the most part, the test for whether there has been copyright infringement in a program's look and feel will be the same as the test for any other aspect of the program. Although the actual tests vary widely among the various federal courts, there are two essentially common steps. First, the court will evaluate the strength of the rights in the original look and feel, filtering out aspects of the program that, for example, are within the public domain or are purely functional. The court will then compare the two works to determine the similarity of expression. If the rights in the original work are particularly strong, the accused work will infringe if it is "substantially similar"; if the rights in the original work are weak, the accused work will infringe if it is "virtually identical."

Notes

1. Justice Stewart's obscenity opinion was rendered in the 1964 case of *Jacobellis v. Ohio*. The Supreme Court's routine of viewing obscene materials involved in obscenity litigation is described by Bob Woodward and Scott Armstrong in *The Brethren* (Avon Books, 1979) at page 234.

2. The H.R. Pufnstuf case is reported at *Sid & Marty Krofft Television Productions, Inc. v. McDonald's Corp.*, 1157 F.2d 1157 (9th Cir. 1977).

3. The Karate Champ litigation is reported at *Data East USA, Inc. v. Epyx, Inc.*, 862 F.2d 204 (9th Cir. 1988).

4. The Lotus 1-2-3 litigation against Paperback Software is reported at *Lotus Development Corp. v. Paperback Software Int'l*, 740 F. Supp. 37 (D. Mass. 1990).

5. The Apple litigation against Microsoft was a lengthy proceeding that produced many published decisions, including the following decisions from the trial court in the Northern District of California: *Apple Computer, Inc. v. Microsoft Corp.*, 709 F. Supp. 925 (N.D. Cal. 1989); 717 F. Supp 1428 (N.D. Cal. 1989); 759 F. Supp. 1444 (N.D. Cal. 1991); 779 F. Supp. 133 (N.D. Cal. 1991); 799 F. Supp. 1006 (N.D. Cal. 1992); and 821 F. Supp. 616 (N. D. Cal. 1993). The appellate decision from the Ninth Circuit Court of Appeals is reported at *Apple Computer, Inc. v. Microsoft Corp.*, 35 F.3d 1438 (9th Cir. 1994).

8

Keyboard Commands and Menu Arrangements

The right to control certain keyboard commands and menu arrangements is a valuable commodity. When consumers purchase a new software program, they not only invest their money in the program, but they invest their time in learning how to use it. Depending on the complexity of the software, it may take a significant amount of time to learn all the keyboard commands, such as typing "alt-s" to save or "alt-p" to print. Learning the arrangement and function of the many menu choices may require a similar effort. Once consumers understand all the keyboard commands and menu choices required to operate a particular program, they naturally prefer not to switch to a competing program if it means learning an entire new set of keyboard commands and menu choices. If software companies can prevent others from copying their keyboard commands and menu arrangements, they can reduce the appeal of the competition and retain their market share.

The value of keyboard commands is particularly important for spreadsheet software, such as Lotus 1-2-3, Borland Quattro Pro, or Microsoft Excel. Not only do spreadsheet programs typically have several hundred different commands, but users often write their own specialized commands, or "macros." A macro is a series of commands that is executable with a single keyboard command. Rather than type each of the individual spreadsheet commands each time the user wants to execute the series of commands, the user may simply type the single macro command that will cause the entire series of commands to execute.

In 1987 Borland introduced its spreadsheet program, called Quattro, after three years of development. Many consumers agreed that

Borland's Quattro spreadsheet program was superior to the competing spreadsheet products available at the time, including Lotus 1-2-3. In addition to offering many new features not found in competing spreadsheet programs, Borland hoped to lure customers away from Lotus by making Quattro's menus and keyboard commands compatible with Lotus 1-2-3. Quattro achieved its compatibility in two primary ways. First, Quattro offered a "Lotus Emulation Interface." Although the default menu command organization for Quattro differed from Lotus 1-2-3, activating the Lotus Emulation Interface would cause the Quattro menu commands to be arranged as in Lotus 1-2-3. Second, Borland's Quattro Pro program included a "Key Reader" that translated macros written for Lotus 1-2-3 into commands that were executable by Borland's spreadsheet software. Quattro users were therefore able to use macros originally written for Lotus 1-2-3.

Lotus knew about Borland's spreadsheet shortly after it was introduced in late 1987 and discussed it internally in early 1988. Nevertheless, Lotus chose not to sue Borland immediately. At the time, Lotus was involved in litigation against Paperback Software International, a lawsuit that Lotus had initiated in January 1987. In that lawsuit, Lotus claimed that Paperback's VP-Planner software was a virtual clone of Lotus 1-2-3 and, as such, infringed Lotus's copyrights. Lotus therefore chose to await the outcome of the litigation against Paperback before turning to the Borland matter.

LOTUS v. BORLAND: THE BATTLE OVER MENUS AND KEYBOARD COMMANDS

Borland watched the Lotus-Paperback litigation closely. If Lotus won its case against Paperback, Borland figured that it would be next. One thing Borland hoped to avoid was to be sued in the same court that awarded Lotus a favorable judgment in a similar copyright infringement case. In June 1990 the U.S. District Court for the District of Massachusetts in Boston handed down its decision in the Paperback case, holding that Paperback's VP-Planner spreadsheet program infringed Lotus's copyrights.[1] The next day, Borland filed a lawsuit in California, seeking a declaratory judgment that its software did not infringe Lotus's rights. Three days later, Lotus filed a copyright infringement complaint against Borland in the same Boston court that decided the Paperback case. Lotus sought $100 million in damages and an order preventing Borland from continuing to sell its spreadsheet software.

Because both Lotus and Borland had each filed a substantially similar lawsuit, two courts—one in California, one in Massachusetts—were asked to decide the identical issue between Lotus and Borland. In such cases, one of the two courts will typically dismiss the complaint or transfer it to the other court so that the matter is resolved in a single forum. Despite Borland's objections, Lotus persuaded the California court that Boston was the proper forum for the dispute. The California court dismissed the case, and Borland's fate would be decided by the same court and the same judge that had recently ruled in favor of Lotus in a case involving many of the same issues.

The Trial Court Decision

Although Borland's spreadsheet programs were quite different from those of Lotus 1-2-3, Borland did not contest that its Quattro and Quattro Pro spreadsheets included a virtually identical copy of the entire Lotus 1-2-3 menu tree, including all 469 commands arranged into more than 50 menus and submenus. Because Borland had copied the commands and menu structure, the central issue was whether those features were capable of being protected by copyright law. If so, then Borland's products infringed Lotus's copyright.

In the *Paperback* case, Judge Keeton concluded that the Lotus 1-2-3 menu structure, taken as a whole, including the choice of command terms and the structure and order of those terms, was protected expression covered by Lotus's copyrights. Not surprisingly, Judge Keeton reached the same conclusion in the Lotus litigation against Borland. Although Borland argued that the menu structure and keyboard commands were functional, and therefore not protectable by copyright law, the court disagreed. According to Judge Keeton, a "very satisfactory" spreadsheet menu tree could be constructed using different commands and a different command structure from those of Lotus 1-2-3. Every command used by Lotus could be given many different names by competitors. For example, the court suggested that "Copy" could be called "Clone," "Ditto," "Duplicate," "Imitate," "Mimic," "Replicate," and "Reproduce," among others. Borland, in fact, had created just such an alternative structure in its Quattro spreadsheets for use when running in their native, or non-Lotus Emulation Interface, mode.

The trial court also concluded that the Borland Key Reader infringed Lotus's copyrights. Borland's Key Reader, used to translate Lotus 1-2-3 macros and commands, included a virtually identical copy of the Lotus menu tree structure, but contained only the first letters of each menu command term in place of the full command terms. For example, the Borland Key Reader stored only the letter "s" for the command "save" and the letter "c" for the command "copy." Nevertheless, the district court held that the Lotus menu structure, organization, and command names, including the first letters of those command names, are protectable expression infringed by Borland. The court then entered a permanent injunction against Borland's sales of spreadsheets containing the infringing menus.

The Court of Appeals

Borland appealed the district court's ruling to the U.S. Court of Appeals for the First Circuit. Again, the issue before the Court of Appeals was solely whether the Lotus menu command hierarchy was copyrightable subject matter. The Court of Appeals noted that the issue was a "matter of first impression." In other words, the court had not previously decided a case in which the copyrightability of a menu command hierarchy was in question.

Borland argued that the Lotus menu was uncopyrightable because it was a "system, method of operation, process, or procedure" and therefore was expressly precluded from copyright protection under the Copyright Act. The relevant portion of the Copyright Act provides, "In no case does copyright protection for an original work of authorship extend to any idea, procedure, process, system, method of operation, concept, principle, or discovery, regardless of the form in which it is described, explained, illustrated, or embodied in such work." According to Borland, this provision foreclosed the Lotus menu hierarchy from receiving copyright protection.

The court agreed with Borland, reasoning that the term "method of operation" referred to the "means by which a person operates something, whether it be a car, a food processor, or a computer." Accordingly, a text describing how to operate something would be protected expression, but the scope of the protection would not extend to the method itself. Others would be free to use the method and to describe the method in their own words.

In the court's view, the Lotus command hierarchy was not merely descriptive of Lotus 1-2-3's capabilities; rather, the commands served as the means for operating the program. Although competitors could make competing spreadsheets without copying the Lotus screen displays or the software code, it was not possible to create a program that operates in the same way without copying the Lotus 1-2-3 command hierarchy.

The Court of Appeals disagreed with the district court's conclusion that the existence of numerous alternative words that could be used for each command term rendered the commands expressive. According to the Court of Appeals, the existence of alternate forms of expression simply meant that there were alternate ways to perform the operation. The commands still formed a functional method of operation even though there were many different ways of performing the same functions.

The court was also concerned with the harsh effect on consumers if menus were protectable. If menu arrangements were protectable, consumers would have to learn how to perform the same operation in a different way for each program the consumers used. Further, users who wrote macros for Lotus 1-2-3 would not be able to use their own macros in other spreadsheet programs. Users would therefore be required to write the same macros in a different way for each different spreadsheet they used. The holding that menu structures were unprotectable methods of operation would help to avoid these results and advance the cause of interoperability.

The Supreme Court Deadlocked

Lotus appealed the decision to the United States Supreme Court. Unlike the appeal to the Court of Appeals, which may be made as a matter of right, the U.S. Supreme Court has the discretion to decide whether it will hear a particular case. Signaling the importance of the issue, the Supreme Court decided to review the case by granting *certiorari*.

Members of the computer industry and the legal community quickly chose sides, with many of them filing *amicus curiae*, or "friend of the court," briefs in support.[2] The American Intellectual Property Law Association filed a brief supporting Lotus's position, along with another brief jointly filed by Digital Equipment Corporation, The Gates Rubber Company, Intel Corporation, and Xerox Corporation. Borland was supported by briefs prepared by various scientists and professors, in addition to briefs by the Software Forum, Altai, Inc., The League for Programming Freedom, and the American Committee for Interoperable Systems.

On January 8, 1996, the Supreme Court heard oral argument from attorneys representing Lotus and Borland. Considering the zealous arguments and mountain of briefs, the Supreme Court's decision one week later was anticlimactic. Justice Stevens did not participate in the decision, leaving only eight judges to vote, and the remaining eight judges were deadlocked in a 4-4 tie. As is common in such cases, the Court did not prepare a written opinion, but rather issued a terse *per curiam* order affirming the lower court's order. Consequently, the decision of the Court of Appeals was upheld and Borland's right to copy the uncopyrightable menu hierarchy was confirmed.

KEYBOARD COMMANDS, MENU ARRANGEMENTS, AND THE COMPUTER INDUSTRY

The issue presented in the *Lotus v. Borland* case is critical in the computer industry. There probably is no software today that operates without a hierarchy of menu commands. As computers have become increasingly powerful, the number of commands available in a typical program has continued to grow. At the same time, the investment required of consumers to learn the command terms and command structure has increased dramatically. In many cases, the burden of learning the new command structure used in a competing program may be sufficient to dissuade consumers from switching programs.

Prior to the *Lotus v. Borland* decision, many programs contained menu commands that were similar to those used by competitors, but few copied their competitors' command structure outright. Although the Supreme Court's decision was ambivalent, many software companies are likely to view the *Lotus v. Borland* decision as a green light that allows unfettered copying of command structures.

As with many issues in software law, the law regarding menu and command hierarchies is not cast in stone. Although the Supreme Court effectively upheld the decision of the Court of Appeals that command structures are not protectable by copyright law, the issue may again reach the Supreme Court in the future. Assuming that all nine judges participate in such a future proceeding, the result could easily be contrary to the holding in *Lotus v. Borland*. In the meantime, most software companies are likely to assume that they can freely copy command hierarchies without running afoul of the copyright laws.

KEYBOARD COMMANDS AND MENU ARRANGEMENTS: A BRIEF SUMMARY OF THE LAW

The *Lotus v. Borland* case held that menu commands and command hierarchies are methods of operation that may not be protected by copyright law. Although the *Lotus v. Borland* decision is likely to be followed by many courts, it is not a conclusive precedent in view of the 4-4 decision in the Supreme Court. Despite a reasonable presumption that menu commands and command hierarchies may be freely copied without running afoul of the copyright laws, there is considerable likelihood that a court could reach the opposite result in any particular case.

Notes

1. The litigation between Lotus and Borland was a protracted proceeding that was the subject of many reported decisions. Trial court decisions are reported at *Lotus Dev. Corp v. Borland Int'l, Inc.*, 788 F. Supp. 78 (D. Mass. 1992); *Lotus Dev. Corp v. Borland Int'l, Inc.*, 799 F. Supp. 203 (D. Mass. 1992); *Lotus Dev. Corp v. Borland Int'l, Inc.*, 831 F. Supp. 202 (D. Mass. 1993); *Lotus Dev. Corp v. Borland Int'l, Inc.*, 831 F. Supp. 223 (D. Mass. 1993). The decision of the First Circuit court of appeals is reported at *Lotus Dev. Corp v. Borland Int'l, Inc.*, 49 F.3d 807 (1st Cir. 1995).

2. Copies of the *amicus* briefs and transcripts of the oral argument before the U.S. Supreme Court are generally available through the court and several other commercial sources. The amicus briefs are reprinted in their entirety in *Computer Law Reporter* 22, no. 5 (January 1996). The transcript of oral argument is reprinted in *Computer Law Reporter* 22, no. 6 (February 1996).

9

Data Entry Formats

Many computer programs were created to enable computers to perform mathematical calculations that are too repetitive, time-consuming, or tedious to perform by hand. Such programs typically perform calculations on data that is read by the computer from an external file. The arrangement of the data in the external file is critical; the software can only perform meaningful calculations if the data is arranged in an order that the software expects.

When the data must be compiled by hand or in a manner that requires significant assembly time, the software ideally will be designed to minimize the user's effort. Otherwise, the savings gained by using the computer to perform calculations will be lost in collecting and formatting the data. Even when the formatting requirements are kept to a minimum, they still may be substantial enough to require a considerable amount of training to use the software efficiently.

The quest for compatibility has produced many disputes over data entry formats. If a competing program uses a previous program's data entry formats, the makers of the competing software can avoid the training costs incurred by the original developer. Further, users may have numerous data files created by or for the original software. The decision to switch programs may be directly related to the ability to use old data files with the competing program. Without compatibility, it is difficult or impossible for a newcomer to compete.

The contours of the legal treatment of data entry formats have been sketched by two related battles over the right to use compatible data entry formats. Both of these battles involved Engineering Dynamics, Inc. (EDI) and its software designed to perform structural analysis. In

1978, Synercom Technology, Inc. sued EDI, alleging that EDI copied Synercom's user manuals and data input formats. Fifteen years later, EDI sued Structural Software, Inc. (SSI). This time EDI was on the opposite side, alleging that SSI copied EDI's user manuals and data input formats for the same structural analysis software.

SYNERCOM v. EDI: NO PROTECTION FOR ENTRY FORMATS?

In 1969, Synercom began developing a program to perform structural analysis. Synercom's software was designed to analyze the performance of buildings under varying conditions and when constructed from a variety of materials. Prior to the development of structural analysis software, structural analysis required numerous repetitive and time-consuming calculations. For larger buildings, such calculations could require hundreds of hours to complete by hand.

Although Synercom was one of the earliest companies to produce structural analysis software, it was not the first. In fact, Synercom's software was primarily based upon a program created by IBM in the early 1960s called FRAN, an acronym for Framed Structure Analysis Program. Because IBM claimed no proprietary interest in FRAN, FRAN and its user manual were within the public domain. FRAN proved to be a useful program, but because it was designed solely to demonstrate the power of IBM computers, it was not particularly easy to use. The FRAN software accepted data that was stored on enormous decks of eighty-column keypunch cards. By punching holes in the proper locations on the keypunch cards and placing the cards in the proper order, the computer could read the data and perform the desired analysis. Synercom figured that it could make a profit if it developed a series of input formats that made FRAN easier to use. Synercom then developed an upgraded version of FRAN, which it called STRAN, along with a new user manual and many simplified eighty-column data input formats. By 1970 the Synercom STRAN software and user manuals were offered for sale

In 1975, EDI introduced a structural analysis program of its own, called SACS II, for Structural Analysis Computer System. SACS II included all the same data input formats that were used by EDI's STRAN. The similarities between SACS II and STRAN were not coincidental. EDI believed that its software must be wholly compatible with the STRAN data entry formats in order to be successful. Whereas Synercom had spent $500,000 training consumers to use the STRAN input formats, EDI could avoid this cost—enabling a lower retail price—by using the STRAN input formats. In addition, an internal EDI memorandum stressed that identical input formats would enable users to use their old data files and easily switch programs, making the structural analysis software market easy for EDI to capture.

With this compatibility objective in mind, EDI developed a suite of programs that was completely compatible with the Synercom input formats. EDI also created a user manual that contained mirror-image depictions of some eighty-column data cards, along with instructions to enable STRAN users to use the STRAN input formats with the SACS II software. EDI then combined with University Computing Company (UCC)—a company that had previously marketed the STRAN software for Synercom—to market the SACS II software.

After the SACS II software hit the market, Synercom sued UCC and EDI in federal court in Texas, alleging that UCC and EDI infringed its copyrights in both the user manuals and the data input formats.[1] Extensive evidence at trial established that EDI intentionally copied both the EDI manuals and input formats. Accordingly, the court's inquiry focused mainly on whether data input formats could be protected by copyright law.

Judge Patrick Higginbotham evaluated the issue in view of the classic idea-expression dichotomy. If a data format amounts to an "idea" regarding the sequencing and ordering of data, then it cannot be protected by copyright. But if the data format is the expression of an idea, it may be protected. Weighing against copyright protection was the fact that blank forms are generally thought to convey an idea with little or no expression and are accordingly given little, if any, copyright protection. In addition, input formats may be considered to be a method of operation that cannot be protected by copyright. On the other hand, the presence of numerous alternative ways to convey the "idea" or perform the method of operation militates in favor of protection. As the court observed, there were hundreds of structural analysis programs in existence at the time of the lawsuit, and all but STRAN and SACS II had different input formats.

In the end, the court concluded that the data input formats could not be protected by copyright. According to the court, the idea behind the data input formats was indistinguishable from the expression of that idea. Further, the data input formats contained no "stylistic creativity" that is the essence of expression. Consequently, the input formats were not protectable and not infringed by EDI.

Although the input formats were not protected, the user manuals were protected under copyright law and were infringed by EDI and UCC. EDI objected that because Synercom had used substantial portions of the public-domain FRAN user manual, its STRAN user manual should not be protected by copyright law. But at least 70 percent of the

STRAN manual was the original work of Synercom. In addition, Synercom's copyright protection for its user manual extended to the work as a whole rather than the separate parts. Even though the FRAN manual remained in the public domain and could be freely copied, the STRAN manual was a protected work that was copied by EDI.

Based on its finding that EDI had copied the Synercom user manuals, the court ordered EDI to produce no further infringing manuals and to issue a recall request to all customers who had received the EDI user manuals. The court also expressed its distaste for certain tactics used by EDI during the litigation. While Synercom had alleged a claim for copyright infringement against EDI, EDI asserted allegations of fraud, unfair competition, and antitrust violations against Synercom. According to the court, many of EDI's claims against Synercom were so baseless that EDI presented no evidence in support of them at trial. Explaining that EDI conducted the litigation in a manner calculated to delay the trial and increase costs as much as possible, the court ordered EDI and UCC to pay costs and attorney's fees to Synercom. As part of a subsequent settlement agreement between the parties, EDI prepared a new edition of its user manual, entitled SACS III, that did not infringe Synercom's copyrights.

EDI v. STRUCTURAL SOFTWARE, INC.: ARE ENTRY FORMATS PROTECTED AFTER ALL?

EDI continued to refine its SACS structural analysis software, eventually leading to the development of SACS IV. Although keypunch cards were not required, SACS IV retained the eighty-column data input format from SACS II and SACS III. EDI reasoned that old users of its software would be familiar with these formats and less training would be necessary. Although EDI did not seek copyright registrations for its software, it obtained four registrations for its user manuals containing 51 of its 200 different data input formats.

In 1986, Structural Software, Inc. (SSI) developed its own structural analysis program, using a similar eighty-column format. In developing and marketing its StruCAD★3D software, SSI's objectives in 1986 mirrored those of EDI in 1975. Many of StruCAD's potential users were already familiar with EDI's SACS interface. SSI could minimize training requirements and encourage users to switch programs if the data formats were compatible. While the StruCAD software was based on a public domain structural analysis program that differed from SACS, StruCAD borrowed heavily from the SACS user interface and data entry formats.

EDI sued SSI and the StruCAD software developer, Rao Guntur, in federal court in Louisiana, claiming that they copied fifty-six of EDI's data entry formats.[2] EDI also asserted that SSI and Guntur copied various output formats and portions of EDI's user manuals. Guntur and SSI admitted that they copied EDI material when they developed StruCAD, but they argued that the copied input formats were not copyrightable in the first place. After all, ten years earlier the Texas court had agreed with EDI's argument that they were not copyrightable. Even if they were copyrightable, SSI pointed out that EDI had copied many of its formats from Synercom and therefore could not possibly own the copyright interest itself.

After a four-day trial, the trial court dismissed EDI's claims against Guntur individually and dismissed EDI's input format-related copyright claims against SSI. The trial court was persuaded by the previous decision in *Synercom v. EDI* holding that input formats were not copyrightable. At the same time, the trial court agreed that SSI infringed EDI's copyrights in its user manuals and ordered SSI to pay damages of $250,000.

EDI appealed the trial court decision, contending that data input formats may be protected by copyright law. Before turning to the merits of whether data input formats are copyrightable, the Court of Appeals observed that many aspects of copyright law remain unresolved. Thus far, the courts have agreed that both the source code and object code are protectable. There is also a consensus that at least some of the "nonliteral" aspects of a computer program, such as its structure, sequence of operation, organization, and user-interface, are also protectable. But the distinction between protectable expression and an unprotectable idea is hazy at best, and it becomes increasingly obscure as one moves from the literal code to the various nonliteral elements. As Judge Edith Jones explained in her appellate decision, "Court decisions are, generously described, in a state of creative ferment concerning the methods by which nonliteral elements of a computer program may be identified and analyzed for copyrightability."

The Court of Appeals had little trouble dismissing the notion that its ruling was in any way controlled by the previous ruling in the *Synercom v. EDI* dispute. The *Synercom* case was decided in 1978, before Congress passed the 1980 amendments to the Copyright Act expressly declaring that computer programs are within the scope of copyright law. While this difference was probably reason enough to disregard the *Synercom* court's position, Judge Jones also believed that at least one difference between the two cases was fundamental. In *Synercom v. EDI*, Synercom sought copyright protection for each of its data input formats, individually. But in the *EDI v. SSI* case, EDI argued that its collection of fifty-six data input formats, taken as a whole, constituted protectable expression without regard to whether any input format may be protectable standing alone. The Court of Appeals found it easier to find copyright protection in a larger work than in a smaller one.

Ultimately, the Court of Appeals reversed the trial court's ruling that EDI's data input formats were not protectable under copyright law. Because the trial court had concluded that data input formats were not protectable at all, it did not consider the factual questions of whether EDI's particular data formats were infringed by SSI. The Court of Appeals therefore "remanded" the case back to the trial court to consider the matter in view of its holding that data input formats may be protected under copyright law.

The appeals court also considered whether Guntur would be personally liable for the copyright infringement. Although both Guntur and SSI were named as defendants, the trial court dismissed the case against Guntur because there was insufficient evidence of corporate impropriety or disregard of the corporate form to "pierce the corporate veil." Judge Jones reversed the trial court's ruling, explaining that individuals are liable for their own torts even if they are acting in their corporate capacity. Consequently, Guntur was liable along with SSI for any infringement damages.

DATA INPUT LAW AND THE COMPUTER INDUSTRY

Litigation over data input formats has likely had little effect on the computer industry. There have been few cases actually litigated, so it is difficult to accurately gauge the real impact. Nevertheless, the *Synercom* decision was viewed by many as the probable state of the law for more than a decade. Software companies undoubtedly relied on the assumption that the *Synercom* decision was good law and, based on that assumption, freely copied any desirable data input formats without concern that it might constitute copyright infringement. The dearth of litigation over data input formats provides at least some evidence of the public's acquiescence in the *Synercom* ruling.

The advance of technology has likely had a far greater effect on data input formats. The use of eighty-column keypunch cards created a unique opportunity for input formats to be visible at the user level. The replacement of keypunch cards with magnetic disks and CD-ROMs reduced the user's awareness of data formats and the likelihood of related litigation. Although there are still issues related to the manner in which data is entered from a keyboard or other sources, decisions regarding particular input formats appear to be driven more by market and technological considerations than legal ones. In addition, the trend today is toward standardization of such formats, in the interest of compatibility. Though disputes still arise, the mutually beneficial goal of achieving interoperability among software programs has done much to reduce them.

DATA ENTRY FORMATS: A BRIEF SUMMARY OF THE LAW

There have been few decisions addressing whether data input formats may be copyrightable, making it difficult to confidently predict whether any particular court would conclude that they are protectable. Nevertheless, it seems more likely than not that data entry formats are protectable under copyright law to the same extent as any other non-literal element of a computer program.

Notes

1. The *Synercom* cases are reported at *Synercom Tech v. University Computing Co.*, 462 F. Supp. 1003 (N.D.Tex. 1978) and *Synercom Tech v. University Computing Co.*, 474 F. Supp. 37 (N.D.Tex. 1979).

2. The later *EDI* case is reported at *Engineering Dynamics, Inc. v. Structural Software, Inc.*, 26 F.3d 1335 (5th Cir. 1994).

Clashes over Code

Copying Operating Systems

One of the more interesting aspects of the computer industry today is the plethora of "IBM-compatible" or "clone" computers that are available in contrast with the dearth of Apple Macintosh-compatible machines. Until 1996, there were no Macintosh-compatible computers at all (see Figure 6); the only way to obtain a truly Macintosh-compatible computer was to buy a Macintosh from Apple.

Figure 6. Many clones but few Apples. Legal rights in operating systems are the primary reason that, prior to 1996, there were no Apple-compatible or Macintosh-compatible computers, but there were countless IBM-compatible machines.

This phenomenon raises the question: What is it that makes a computer IBM-compatible or Macintosh-compatible? As recently as a decade ago, most people probably would have answered that it is the hardware that defines a computer. After all, different computers are made from different hardware, aren't they? At the dawn of the personal computer age, in the mid-1970s, the answer would have been a resounding yes. The original Apple I computer, for instance, was quite different from other computers available at the time. Featuring a microprocessor and 8K (kilobytes) of memory, it was a computer only in a technical sense. Unlike today's typical computers, it offered no disk drive, no monitor, no CD-ROM, no hard drive, no keyboard, and no mouse. Yet in many ways it was far more advanced than its competition, which consisted largely of mail-order machines that required tedious assembly by the consumer. In addition, there was virtually no software available for these early computers. Instead, consumers were expected to develop their own software programs to make use of the computer. Because there was little software, the hardware initially defined the differences among computers.

THE SEEDS OF CONFLICT

Over time, software in general and the operating system in particular began to play an increasingly important role in defining the differences among computers. The Apple II computer helped lay the foundation for both the legal and technical importance of the operating system. The Apple II was a quantum leap from the Apple I, offering 64K of memory, a monitor, a keyboard, and a floppy disk drive. By 1981, Apple was an industry leader, with 3,000 employees and annual sales of $335 million.

The booming personal computer industry and the near-overnight success of Apple drew the attention of consumers and competitors alike. Investors and competitors are drawn to a booming industry like shoppers to a grand opening sale. During an industry's early boom period, almost everyone makes money. The key to long-term success is often simply to jump into the industry early enough and solidly enough to become entrenched as a player by the time the market approaches saturation.

Perhaps the easiest way to jump into a new market is simply to copy a successful product. One newcomer that tried to jump into the personal computer market this way was Franklin Computer Corporation. Founded in 1981, Franklin's mission was to develop and sell computers that would be compatible with the Apple II.

The reasoning behind Franklin's desire to make a computer compatible with the Apple II was clear. By 1981, consumers could choose from a substantial array of software to run on the Apple II. Virtually every day, the list of available software titles for the Apple II increased. If Franklin were to develop a completely new computer, it would be faced with the daunting task of trying to sell a computer for which there was no software. Even in a booming industry, Franklin would have had a slim chance of success. If, on the other hand, Franklin could manufacture a computer that would run software designed for the Apple II, Franklin's computer might be successful from the beginning.

To capitalize on the large and growing market for Apple software, Franklin designed a computer, the Ace 100, that copied nearly all of the Apple II operating system. There was no doubt that Franklin had copied Apple's operating system. Although the Franklin operating system differed in a few places, Franklin's master disk holding the Ace 100 operating system contained the word "Applesoft" and the name of James Huston, an Apple systems programmer who wrote much of the Apple operating system. On the strength of this evidence, Franklin had no choice but to admit that it had copied Apple's operating system.

Franklin's entry into the personal computer industry presented Apple with a marketing risk. By 1982, Franklin's Apple II-compatible Ace 100 had sales approaching 1,000 computers. Compared to Apple, Franklin was a tiny player presenting no immediate challenge to Apple's market share. But the industry was growing rapidly, and Apple itself barely existed five years earlier. Although Franklin was unlikely to cut deeply into Apple's sales in the short run, Apple was concerned about the long run.

APPLE v. FRANKLIN: **THE BATTLE OVER OPERATING SYSTEMS**

As an alternative to beating Franklin on the market playing field, Apple could pursue legal action. Here, too, there was risk. In 1981 there was sharp debate whether the courts would or should protect operating systems under the copyright laws. Given the legal uncertainties, Apple faced a very real possibility that it could lose in court, even though Franklin had unabashedly copied Apple's operating system. A loss in the courts would be catastrophic: Countless companies were surely eager to follow Franklin's lead if the court gave its approval.

Ultimately, Apple decided to pursue litigation.[1] Apple's primary claim was that Franklin violated Apple's rights under the copyright law by copying Apple's operating system. To hasten its legal remedy, Apple sought a preliminary injunction ordering Franklin to stop selling computers containing the copied operating system. An "injunction" is a court order that stops, or "enjoins," the other party from taking or continuing a particular action. It is "preliminary" if a party obtains such an order prior to trial, enjoining the other party's actions between the time the order is issued and the date of the trial. If Apple could show the court that it was likely to succeed if its case went to trial and that the injury it was suffering exceeded any legitimate injury to Franklin that would result from the injunction, Apple could obtain an order directing Franklin to stop making or selling computers containing the copied operating system.

The Trial Court's Decision

Apple's fears were realized when the court ruled on Apple's request for a preliminary injunction in July 1982. The trial court judge denied Apple's motion for a preliminary injunction, concluding that it did not believe that Apple's operating system was copyrightable.

The trial court was troubled by two primary aspects of Apple's request to extend copyright protection to operating systems. First, operating systems, like most software, are initially developed using instructions to the computer in languages generally referred to as source code. Although any language may be used to produce source code, programmers typically use one of many "high-level" languages based on programming commands that may be quickly understood by humans. For efficiency, source code is compiled into object code, a language that computers can understand but that humans can decipher only with great difficulty. In the view of the trial court, programs written in source code are "expressive" because they contain instructions that may be understood by humans. Once compiled into object code, the expressive nature is lost because humans often have great difficulty understanding the code. In the trial court's view, programs compiled into object code are functional rather than expressive. Because copyright law protects "expression" and does not protect the functional portion of a work of authorship, the court concluded that operating systems are not protected by the copyright laws.

Second, the court was bothered by the form in which operating systems are stored. Operating systems are embedded in read-only memory, or "ROM," rather than stored on paper or some other medium that humans can read. The copyright laws require that a work of authorship must be "fixed in a tangible medium of expression" to be afforded protection. Some other very early court decisions held that expression in a medium that cannot be visually understood by humans is not a form that may be protected. Following these decisions, the court concluded that computer programs stored in ROM were not protected by copyright and denied Apple's requested preliminary injunction.

The Appellate Court's Decision

Apple promptly appealed the trial court's decision. Unlike the trial court, the Court of Appeals was particularly interested in the extent to which Franklin had copied Apple's operating system. Franklin should have listened to its namesake, Benjamin Franklin, who advised, "He that goes a borrowing goes a sorrowing." The evidence showed that Franklin had copied nearly all of Apple's operating system. Testimony also indicated that Franklin probably could have successfully developed an Apple-compatible operating system on its own, without copying. Franklin was therefore able to take advantage of the forty-six person-months and $740,000 that Apple had spent developing the Apple II operating system, with very little additional expense of its own.

To most people, it seems wrong to allow one company to directly copy the fruits of another company's effort and investment. Unfortunately for Franklin, if it seems wrong to most people, it generally also seems wrong to the court.

The Court of Appeals reversed the trial court's decision in August 1983, granting Apple the preliminary injunction it requested. Unlike the trial court, the Court of Appeals had little trouble concluding that object code should be protected under the copyright laws. The copyright statutes had been amended in 1976 and again in 1980 to address the application of the copyright laws to computer programs. Nowhere did the copyright statutes distinguish between object and source code. Instead, it defined a "computer program" as a "set of statements or instructions to be used directly or indirectly in a computer in order to bring about a certain result." Whether in object code or in source code, computer programs were to be given copyright protection.

Nor did the Court of Appeals have difficulty concluding that storage in ROM met the copyright statute's "fixed in a tangible medium of expression" requirement. The 1976 and 1980 amendments to the copyright laws were intended to extend copyright protection to computer programs. Unless software was also protected in magnetic storage media, copyright protection would be virtually worthless. Although storage in ROM is certainly unlike a traditional writing on paper, it is still "fixed" and intended to be protected by the copyright laws. Today, the copyright statute clearly intends to provide protection for computer programs stored in ROM. It is sufficient if the work of authorship is fixed in a medium from which it can be perceived or communicated, "either directly or with the aid of a machine or device."

The Court of Appeals also rejected Franklin's argument that an operating system is a "process" or "method of operation" that cannot be protected by copyright. Franklin acknowledged that application programs were properly protected by copyright. Yet application programs also contain processes and methods of operation. Franklin therefore had to persuade the court that the processes or methods in operating systems were somehow different. Franklin's argument was essentially that operating systems were *purely* functional. Because an operating system is embedded in the machine and defines, at the most basic level, the way the computer will function, Franklin asserted that an operating system, unlike an application program, was part of the machine itself rather than a true work of authorship. The court disagreed, concluding that all computer programs are functional and that the copyright laws make no distinction between operating systems and application programs.

Finally, Franklin argued that Apple's operating system was an "idea" that could not be protected by copyright rather than a form of "expression" capable of copyright protection. Under copyright law, if there is only one way to express an idea, the expression is not copyrightable. Although Franklin could possibly have developed an Apple-compatible operating system on its own, Franklin contended that it would still have been remarkably similar or identical to Apple's operating system in many respects. As such, Franklin urged, Apple's operating system should not be protected.

The Court of Appeals reframed the question to address Franklin's argument. Whereas Franklin argued that there was only one way to construct an Apple-compatible operating system (an argument that is suspect at best), the court noted that there were numerous ways to construct an operating system without regard to whether it was compatible with Apple II software. The "idea," according to the Court of Appeals, was a program that would enable a computer to function rather than a program that would enable a computer to run software designed for the Apple II. Framed in this manner, Apple's operating system was one of many possible forms of expression that reflected the "idea" of an operating system, and therefore was copyrightable.

Eventually, Apple and Franklin settled their dispute rather than continue with an appeal to the United States Supreme Court. Because it was unable to legally manufacture computers that were compatible with Apple II software, Franklin shifted gears and tried to sell IBM-compatible machines. Franklin's attempt to sell IBM-compatible computers, however, was probably doomed from the beginning. As a result of its legal losses to Apple, Franklin's finances were simply too depleted to mount an effective entry into what had already become a cutthroat market. Shortly after switching to IBM clones, Franklin filed for Chapter 11 bankruptcy protection.

After reorganizing, Franklin managed to recover from bankruptcy. Changing its focus yet again, Franklin concentrated on a variety of single-function hand-held electronic devices. Probably the most successful of Franklin's products was the Spelling Ace, which sold 350,000 units in the Christmas season of 1986.[2]

OPERATING SYSTEM PROTECTION AND THE COMPUTER INDUSTRY

Perhaps based on its victory against Franklin, Apple continued its corporate policy of refusing to license its operating system to other computer manufacturers. Apple apparently believed that consumers would be willing to pay a premium to purchase a computer from Apple, the only source for computers that contained the Apple operating system. As a result of this policy, prior to 1996 there were no Apple II-compatible or Macintosh-compatible computers.

IBM, on the other hand, decided very early to purchase a license for the operating system in its computers from Microsoft. Because Microsoft owned the copyright to its operating system, MS-DOS, Microsoft was able to sell licenses to allow other computer manufacturers to use the operating system. Compared to Apple's policy, IBM's policy of licensing its operating system from a third party has created a virtual explosion of IBM-compatible computers.

If Franklin had won and operating systems were held not to be protected by the copyright laws, countless others surely would have followed Franklin's lead and copied the Apple operating system. Though we can only speculate about what the industry would look like today, it seems likely that the market share for Apple-compatible computers would be greater than it currently is. At the same time, the direct competition might have made Apple's share of the Apple-compatible market smaller than it currently is.

In 1996, Apple reversed course and began to allow other computer manufacturers to use the Apple Macintosh operating system to make Macintosh-compatible computers. Several major manufacturers, including IBM, have taken a license from Apple. Ironically, IBM's computers that use the Macintosh operating system will no longer be "IBM-compatible."

Whether Apple's recent change in operating system licensing strategy is a sound decision is a matter that will be determined over time. Regardless of the soundness of Apple's policy to license or not to license its operating system, Apple's ability to prevent others from using its operating system without a license is a matter of copyright law—a law that Apple helped to define.

OPERATING SYSTEMS: A BRIEF SUMMARY OF THE LAW

An operating system, whether in object code or source code, is protected under copyright law. It likewise makes no difference whether the operating system software is stored in ROM, on a floppy disk, or on paper. One who directly copies or distributes an operating system without permission has infringed the owner's copyright.

Notes

1. The litigation between Apple and Franklin is reported at *Apple Computer, Inc. v. Franklin Computer Corp.*, 545 F. Supp. 812 (E.D. Penn. 1982), *rev'd*, 714 F.2d 1240 (3rd Cir. 1983).

2. A summary of Franklin's postlitigation activities is summarized in Paul M. Eng, "The Latest Word from the Spelling-Ace Maker," *Business Week* (April 19, 1993): 110.

11

Code Structure, Sequence, and Organization

Many computer legal battles have addressed the scope of intellectual property rights in particular aspects of computer software that can be perceived by users, such as user interfaces and data input formats. Other legal battles have confirmed that copyright law protects software code from being copied exactly, line-by-line, by others. This chapter addresses the extent to which a software company may claim rights to "nonliteral" computer code, including aspects sometimes referred to as the structure, sequence, and organization of the software. Protection for these nonliteral elements is of vital importance: If copyright law does not protect them, then a competitor can simply gain access to the original code, study the structure, sequence, and organization, and use the original program as a recipe for developing a competing program.

The original developer typically would prefer strong rights in nonliteral elements—as copyright law increasingly covers nonliteral elements, it reaches more and more functional aspects of software and begins to look a lot like the protection afforded under patent law without the same rigorous application process. Obviously a company has exclusive rights to certain functional aspects of its software if the company holds a patent covering the software. But to what extent does copyright law give the same rights?

Before turning to the case of *Whelan v. Jaslow*, the first major legal battle addressing this question, it is important to keep in mind an essential requirement under copyright law that is not required by patent law. Because copyright law prevents others from *copying* the original work, there must be at least some access to the original program. If the competing program has been created completely independently, it cannot constitute copyright infringement of the original work.

Assuming that there has been some access to the original program or its code, the ability to create a competing program without committing copyright infringement is determined primarily by the placement of the line separating idea from expression. As more and more aspects of a program are considered to be protectable expression rather than unprotectable idea, copyright protection is increasingly extended to cover functional or nearly functional elements.

THE HIGH-WATER MARK FOR COPYRIGHT PROTECTION: *WHELAN v. JASLOW*

Among the countless court decisions that have analyzed the idea-expression dichotomy, few courts have given as much territory to expression as the court in *Whelan Associates, Inc. v. Jaslow Dental Laboratories, Inc.*[1] In 1978, Rand Jaslow attempted to write a computer program to handle many of the business operations of the Jaslow Dental Laboratory, including billing and accounting, inventory, cost controls, customer lists, and related functions. With no experience or training in computer programming, Rand Jaslow purchased a TRS-80 from Radio Shack and began coding. After a few months of effort, Jaslow failed to create a program that would perform the desired tasks.

Despite the lack of success in developing a program on his own, Jaslow still believed that the company would benefit by having software to perform many of its business functions. Jaslow hired Strohl Systems to develop the desired automation software. In exchange for approximately $18,000, Strohl was to develop software for use on an IBM Series 1 computer that Jaslow Laboratories was to acquire. Strohl retained ownership of the software and could market it to other dental laboratories. Jaslow Laboratories earned a 10 percent royalty on sales of the software to other companies.

Elaine Whelan, an officer and half-owner of Strohl, designed the software for Jaslow. In the course of her development work, she frequently conferred with Rand Jaslow regarding the operation of Jaslow Laboratories and the features and functions that Jaslow wanted to be included in the software. Whelan also gathered a significant amount of similar information from other laboratories so that the software could be written in a manner that would make it adaptable for other laboratories. By March 1979 the software was completed and delivered to Jaslow.

Whelan left Strohl in November 1979 to form her own business, Whelan Associates, Inc. Whelan Associates acquired Strohl's interest in the software that Strohl had begun marketing under the name "Dentalab." Whelan Associates then entered an agreement with Jaslow

Laboratories in which Jaslow would be the exclusive sales representative for the Dentalab software. In exchange for 35 percent of the gross sales price and 5 percent of any modification work, Jaslow agreed to use its best efforts to diligently market the software. Likewise, Whelan Associates agreed to use its best efforts to make improvements to the software.

For two years, the marketing arrangement between Whelan and Jaslow went reasonably well. Nevertheless, Jaslow apparently wanted a larger share of the profits. Jaslow also believed that the potential market for the software could be increased if it were written in BASIC rather than Event Driven Language (EDL), because EDL would not run on many of the smaller personal computers that were becoming increasingly popular. In late 1982 Jaslow began to create a new version of the Dentalab software in BASIC, closely copying the functionality, user interfaces, and other aspects of the Dentalab software. To do so, Jaslow gained access to the Dentalab source code without the consent of Whelan or Strohl.

As Jaslow's BASIC version of the dental laboratory software was nearing completion, Jaslow terminated the contract with Whelan Associates. At the same time, Jaslow alleged that the software contained valuable Jaslow trade secrets and suggested that Whelan should not continue to sell the software to others. Meanwhile, Jaslow was again unsuccessful in developing the dental laboratory software on his own. This time he hired Jonathan Novak to help him finish the version for the IBM-PC. Jaslow then formed a new company, called Dentcom, to market the IBM-PC version of the software. Dentcom's version of the software, called "Dentlab," was sold to twenty-three customers by 1984, earning gross profits of slightly over $100,000.

On June 30, 1983, Jaslow filed a lawsuit in state court in Pennsylvania, alleging that Whelan Associates had misappropriated its trade secrets. Whelan responded by filing a lawsuit in federal court in Pennsylvania, alleging that Dentcom's Dentlab software infringed Whelan's copyrights in its Dentalab software. Whelan Associates also asserted other claims, including trademark infringement, unfair competition, and interference with contractual relations.

After a three-day "bench" trial—one before a judge rather than a jury—the court ruled for Whelan Associates on all counts. The court was persuaded by evidence showing that the Dentcom version contained nearly identical file structures and screen displays and had several substantially similar subroutines. Although Dentcom's version was not a direct transliteration of Whelan's version, its structure and overall organization were substantially similar (see Figure 7). The trial court awarded damages to Whelan in an amount equal to Dentcom's profits of $101,269 and enjoined Dentcom from any further sales of its infringing version.

Dentcom appealed the decision to the U.S. Court of Appeals for the Third Circuit. The Court of Appeals began its analysis by rejecting the "extrinsic-intrinsic" test for copyright infringement that is frequently used by other circuit courts of appeals. Under the extrinsic-intrinsic test, the court is required to perform two separate analyses. First, it must determine whether the two works in question are substantially similar, using expert testimony if available to make a technical assessment of similarity. Second, the court must question whether the two works are similar to the "lay observer," without expert testimony or the same careful, detailed scrutiny. The Third Circuit Court of Appeals preferred to collapse these tests into one, asking simply whether the works are substantially similar using all available evidence.

APPENDIX A
ORDER ENTRY PROGRAMS

Dentcom PC Systems	*Dentalab System*
Primary Menu, choose [1] Production MENU	Primary Menu, choose [1] Production SCHEDULING
Production menu choose [1] ORDER ENTRY ORDER ENTRY program	Production Menu, choose [1] ORDER ENTRY DL1000 program (Order entry)
"ENTER ACCOUNT NAME KEY:	"ENTER ACCOUNT OR NAMEKEY" "Check CUSTMAST for valid customer.
Check CUSTMAST for valid customer. If valid, read CUSTMAST file for this customer.	Read CUSTMAST file on this customer.
If yes, increment order # in ORDERS	Increment sequential order no. in ORDERS. Display customer name, address.
Display entry screen, patient shade, mould, remake, call Dr.? Dr.? case/span #, Drs. request date, final case statut T, F, B, R.	Display entry screen (6.6), patient shade, remake, call Pan #, Dr's. request date.
IS THIS SCREEN CORRECT?	
If yes ask for first department number. Display dept. order screen (P10) (list of item in this dept. from ITEMMAST)	Ask for first department number. Display dept. order screen (6.8–6.11) (list of items in this dept. from ITEMMAST)
User entry choices	User entry choices
System adds days in dept. from COMPANY to present date to find due out date. Time is of AM. "Noon" or PM. System accumulates case load by product of item load factor × quantity.	System adds days in dept. [DAYVAL] to present date to find due out date. System computes workload for dept/day out by product of load factor × quantity.
ITEMMAST	ITEMMAST
Adds this to load already in DEPTLOAD for date out.	Add this to load already in DAYVAL for date out.

Figure 7. Competing dental lab software. Portions of the Dentcom and Dentalab software appear quite similar in this side-by-side comparison.

Next came the difficult question of separating idea from expression. The court noted that the famous Judge Learned Hand once observed that the distinction between idea and expression is inevitably an *ad hoc* analysis. Many courts have recited similar remarks made by Judge Hand in an apparent effort to justify the subjectivity of their opinions. According to the Third Circuit in the *Whelan* case, the purpose or function of the utilitarian work is the work's idea, and everything not necessary to that purpose or function is part of the expression of the idea. If there are several means to achieve the desired purpose, then the particular means chosen is unnecessary to the purpose and is expression rather than idea.

Applying this rule to the Dentalab software, the "idea" was the creation of a program to automate dental laboratory business functions, and the "expression" was everything in the software that carried out that idea. The court therefore concluded that Whelan's copyrights extended to the "manner in which the software operates, controls, and regulates the computer in receiving, assembling, calculating, retaining, correlating, and producing useful information, either on a screen, printout, or by audio communication." Thus, the detailed structure of the Dentalab program, including many nearly functional aspects, was protected under copyright law. In view of this broad reach of Whelan's copyrights and the many similarities between Dentalab and Dentlab, the Court of Appeals upheld the decision of the trial court.

STRUCTURE, SEQUENCE, AND ORGANIZATION AND THE COMPUTER INDUSTRY

The decision by the Third Circuit Court of Appeals in *Whelan* is as far as the courts have gone in extending copyright protection to the functional aspects of computer software. Although *Whelan* stops far short of holding that copyright law allows a software company to prevent others from using the same functionality in competing application programs, *Whelan* clearly extended copyright protection to features well beyond the literal software code, including the program structure, sequence, organization, and many functional or nearly functional elements. Many commentators have criticized the approach used by the *Whelan* court and the scope of copyright law it creates. Likewise, most other courts of appeals have devised different tests for infringement that provide substantially narrower rights. Nevertheless, the approach used by the *Whelan* court is still the law in the Third Circuit Court of Appeals.

The *Whelan* decision created an expectation in the computer industry that software would enjoy broad rights under copyright law. Under

Whelan, it would be difficult to create a computer program after seeing an original program's source code without violating the copyrights in that original program. *Whelan*, then, provided a strong incentive for independent development, contributing significantly to the use of "clean rooms" and other devices to ensure that competing software is developed without access to original works. Although subsequent court decisions have slowly retreated from *Whelan's* breadth, the software industry still relies on strong copyright laws as the foundation of its intellectual property protection.

The *Whelan* decision and others reaching similar holdings probably led many software companies to believe that copyrights provided a strong and sufficient measure of protection and that patents were therefore unnecessary (assuming they were available). Following the retreat from *Whelan* and the recent acceptance of software patents, many software companies now find themselves a step behind their competitors that began filing patent applications years earlier. Although this dynamic likely has had no effect on innovation, it has created a marketplace in which some large companies are holding weak copyrights and no patents while some smaller companies hold valuable patent portfolios.

PROGRAM STRUCTURE, SEQUENCE, AND ORGANIZATION: A BRIEF SUMMARY OF THE LAW

Many court decisions have extended copyright protection to the "nonliteral" aspects of computer software, including its structure, sequence, and organization. By extending protection to these nonliteral elements, copyright law protects many nearly functional aspects of application programs. Perhaps more than any other aspect of copyright law, the law regarding nonliteral elements varies greatly among the various federal courts.

Note

1. The litigation between Whelan and Jaslow is reported in several decisions, including *Whelan Associates v. Jaslow Dental Labs., Inc.*, 609 F. Supp. 1307 (D.C. Pa. 1985); *Whelan Associates v. Jaslow Dental Labs., Inc.*, 609 F. Supp. 1325 (D.C. Pa. 1985); and *Whelan Associates v. Jaslow Dental Labs., Inc.*, 797 F.2d 1222 (3rd Cir. 1986).

12

Who Owns Programming Languages?

Languages are the tools of the trade, both for lawyers and for programmers. Although progress is being made, there's no mistaking the sesquipedalian writings of a real lawyer. Lawyers are famous for turning the familiar English language into something unrecognizable, using ten words when one will do, and adding qualifiers to cover every foreseeable possibility, no matter how remote. In many cases, the English language isn't recognizable because it isn't English at all. Lawyers love to insert Latin wherever possible to demonstrate their grasp of complex concepts and continue to keep the law beyond the reach of non-lawyers. Wherefore, *res ipsa loquitur*.

Of course, programmers are no different from lawyers in their language habits. They simply use different languages, acronyms, and terms of art. A lawyer might say, "Your cause of action would be precluded by, *inter alia*, laches, if it had not already been barred by estoppel or *res judicata*," and a programmer might be overheard saying, "Your TN3270 data stream must be directed through the server before it can reach the legacy host over a persistent TCP/IP socket connection."

Language is important; programming languages are critical. Obviously, every software program is written in a particular programming language. Considering the size of the computer industry, the ability to control or own a popular computer language could be extremely valuable.

EARLY ASSUMPTIONS AND PERIPHERAL BATTLES

Until fairly recently, conventional wisdom within the computer industry was that programming languages could not be owned by anyone. Although this belief was based on no authority whatsoever, it was so widely held that few people even thought about it at all. The general assumption has been that programming languages contain no elements of expression. Rather, languages exist solely to serve the functional purpose of allowing functional software to be developed. Consequently, languages cannot be protected under the copyright laws because they are pure ideas rather than expressions of ideas.

This conclusion is analogous to spoken and written languages. For example, the alphabet is not expressive by itself and cannot be protected by copyright laws. As discussed in Chapter 6, the inability to protect the alphabet is so well established that fonts are also precluded from copyright protection even if they appear to be unique and expressive. Likewise, individual words are not capable of protection under the copyright laws. Under a doctrine sometimes referred to as the "short words and phrases doctrine," single words and strings of only a few words are considered to be too brief and fundamental to contain the expression necessary for copyright protection. Consequently, many have assumed that just as the English language cannot be protected by copyright law, a computer language may be freely used by anyone.

The notion that languages could not be owned is likely also a product of the late development of laws governing software in general. By the time the courts were finally applying copyright laws to software with regularity in the late 1970s and early 1980s, the industry had been using numerous languages without any doubt that they could be freely used without violating any intellectual property laws. There simply were no claims that Basic, Fortran, or Cobol were owned by others and could only be used by paying licensing fees.

The manner in which most languages have been developed has also prevented ownership battles. During the early period, languages were often developed in a manner that precluded claims to ownership. For example, many languages were developed in a quasi-public setting by industry working groups, with the assumption that they would be "open" languages that could be freely used by anyone. Other languages, such as Ada, were developed primarily by the U.S. government, which cannot own copyrights in the work product it develops. In still other cases, languages were created by computer manufacturers who hoped that the languages would be widely used to develop software that would fuel demand for their computers. Because of the manner in which many of these early languages were developed, there simply was no possibility for anyone to claim to own them.

Whereas there were no real language battles through the 1980s, recent disputes have raised doubt over the ownership assumption. Unfortunately, most of these disputes have dealt with fringe issues that shed light on language ownership only by analogy. Among these peripheral battles, the lawsuits filed by Lotus against Borland[1] and Paperback[2] appear to be the closest to the mark.

In *Lotus Development Corp. v. Paperback Software International*, Lotus accused Paperback of copying the Lotus 1-2-3 user interface and command structure when it developed its competing spreadsheet software. Judge Robert E. Keeton of the Massachusetts District Court held that Paperback was liable for copying the Lotus user interface and command structure. In doing so, Judge Keeton rejected the notion that computer languages cannot be protected by copyright law. At the same time, he explained that he did not consider the Lotus 1-2-3 user interface and command structure to constitute a programming language.

Some commentators have disagreed with Judge Keeton, opining that the Lotus 1-2-3 command structure should be considered a programming language. After all, a computer programming language is generally defined as a set of terms, syntax rules for combining the terms, and the assignment of meaning to statements that combine terms according to the syntax rules. The Lotus 1-2-3 command structure meets this definition. Lotus 1-2-3 included command terms such as "Print," "Move," and "Copy" that may also be triggered with the initial letters of the command terms, in this case, P, M, or C. When the command terms are combined using the proper syntax, the result is a statement that has a defined meaning.

Debating whether the Lotus 1-2-3 command structure constitutes a programming language may generate more noise than light. Even if the command structure meets the definition of a programming language, because the court did not consider it to be a language, the opinion is not persuasive precedent that languages should be protected under copyright law. Perhaps most importantly, the *Paperback* decision is merely one district court opinion and carries no mandatory weight of authority.

Judge Keeton rendered a similar opinion in a subsequent lawsuit filed by Lotus against Borland International, Inc. When Borland developed its Quattro Pro spreadsheet program, it included a feature called the "Key Reader," designed to allow Quattro Pro to interpret and run macros written in the 1-2-3 macro language. Many Lotus 1-2-3 users had created libraries of macros for use with the 1-2-3 spreadsheet. The Key Reader deciphered Lotus 1-2-3 macros "on the fly," and translated them into commands that would be understood by Quattro Pro. By using the

Key Reader, former Lotus 1-2-3 users could switch to Borland Quattro Pro without having to re-create all their macros in the Quattro Pro macro language.

According to Judge Keeton, the Lotus 1-2-3 macro language was protected under the copyright law and was copied by Borland's Key Reader. Although a programming language obviously serves a functional purpose, Judge Keeton reasoned that the particular terms and syntax chosen to perform the command functions were not dictated by function alone. Thus, because there were many other possible terms and syntax rules that could have been used by Lotus to define its macro language, the macro language was expression that could be protected under the copyright laws.

HOT JAVA: A LANGUAGE BATTLE BREWS

While the Lotus lawsuits offer hints at the way courts may approach the question of programming language ownership, they still leave plenty of room for doubt. The question of whether a programming language may be protected under the copyright laws will likely remain unanswered until a new programming language is developed by an independent company and copied by another.

The Java programming language developed by Sun Microsystems may provide an opportunity to test whether it is possible to own programming languages under the copyright laws. Sun's Java language, introduced on the Internet in March 1995, was billed as a programming language for developing applets that could be downloaded over the Internet and would run under a browser. Java's promise is to provide cross-platform compatibility. The computer industry today includes many different operating systems and numerous microprocessor designs that are incompatible with one another. Application programs designed for one system, or platform, often do not run on other platforms. For example, programs written for the Microsoft Windows environment do not run on an Apple Macintosh system without extensive and often time-consuming modifications.

Software companies are often faced with a difficult choice. Because a separate version of each program must be developed for each platform, software companies must either commit the resources necessary to develop and support a version for each platform or must choose to develop software for certain platforms and not others. Companies with limited resources may be forced to confine their products to a limited number of platforms.

Java aims to solve this problem by creating a common programming environment that may be used on any platform. Though it is often referred to as a programming language, Java is both a programming language and a platform. As a programming language, Java can be used to develop software applications and applets that can be downloaded over the Internet to run under a Web browser. But as with any other language, Java applets or applications only run on a platform capable of interpreting Java instructions. Consequently, the Java technology specifies a platform, or "virtual machine," that interprets Java code and allows it to run on the particular platform. By providing a virtual machine that is tailored to each system, the same Java code can run on any system. Because Java is aimed at the Internet, Java platforms are commonly included in Web browsers. Thus, companies such as Microsoft and Netscape have licensed the Java technology from Sun and include Java platforms within their browser products.

Sun's Java technology is protected by a variety of intellectual property rights, including patents and copyrights. Nevertheless, Sun has openly published its Java specifications and application program interfaces (APIs) to allow software developers and system manufacturers to develop their products in accordance with the Sun standards. At the same time, Java has retained at least some control over its Java language. Java's licensing program requires Java products developed by others to pass a set of tests to ensure that they comply with published Java standards. In addition, Sun generally requires systems manufacturers and browser developers that distribute Java-compatible products to do so in a manner that fully conforms to Java standards, without adding or deleting any requirements.

According to Sun, Java has become "the most rapidly adopted programming language environment in the history of the software industry." Over 70 million users own platforms (primarily in the form of Web browsers) that are capable of running programs written in the Java programming environment. In addition, an estimated 750,000 programmers are developing programs using the Java language. By any measure, Java is a success.

THE LANGUAGE BATTLE: *SUN MICROSYSTEMS v. MICROSOFT*

Like most of the rest of the computer industry, Microsoft desired to produce products that incorporate the Java technology. In March 1996 Sun and Microsoft entered into two licensing agreements—one allowing use of the Java technology, and one allowing use of the Java trademarks and logos. According to Sun, the license granted Microsoft a right to use the Java technology, subject to certain terms and conditions. Among other things, Microsoft's Java-compatible products were required to fully conform to the Java specifications and to pass Sun's test suites to ensure such conformance. Microsoft must, under the contract, distribute products that add value to the Java technology, but it may not do so in a manner that affects Java's platform independence.

In October 1997 Sun sued Microsoft over Microsoft's use of the Java technology.[3] According to Sun, Microsoft selectively incorporated only portions of the Java Developer's Kit in its products, "intentionally and deliberately attempting to fragment" the Java programming environment by causing programs written by other Java developers to fail to operate on Microsoft products, including its Internet Explorer browser and Windows operating system. By including the "Java compatible" logo on such products, Sun claims that Microsoft has breached its contract with Sun and committed trademark infringement.

Sun believes that Microsoft feels threatened by the Java technology. In 1996, approximately 85 percent of the personal computers around the world ran a Microsoft operating system. Because of Microsoft's market dominance, Sun asserts, other independent software makers are likely to create their first—or only—version of their program code to operate on a Microsoft operating system, such as Windows 95 or Windows NT. The vast supply of software, in turn, creates even stronger demand for the Microsoft operating systems. Java poses a threat to Microsoft's dominance by creating a platform-independent programming environment. With Java, software developers can create one version of their software that will operate within any browser or operating system. If an ample supply of software is written in Java, consumers would have greater freedom to choose competing operating systems and Web browsers. According to Sun's complaint, this fear motivated Microsoft to intentionally thwart Java's ability to run on any platform.

Sun's complaint initially alleged a variety of claims, including breach of contract, trademark infringement, false advertising, and others. But in its initial and first amended complaints, Sun did not allege copyright infringement. Without an allegation that Microsoft infringed Sun's copyrights in the Java source code, the Sun-Microsoft litigation would not resolve the open question of programming language ownership. Sun later added a claim for copyright infringement, contending that Microsoft infringed Sun's copyrights by using the Java code in a form not expressly authorized by license.

Microsoft, of course, denies Sun's allegations. According to Microsoft, all Microsoft products comply with the contractual requirement. In fact, Microsoft contends that its Internet Explorer 4.0 Web browser is the most compatible, fastest, functional browser for running Java applications. Microsoft further contends that even Sun's own virtual machine is less compatible than Microsoft's Internet Explorer.

In answering Sun's complaint, Microsoft asserted several counter-claims of its own, including claims for breach of contract, breach of the covenant of good faith and fair dealing, and unfair competition. Among other things, Microsoft contends that Sun failed to deliver upgrades that were compatible with earlier versions, did not provide notice of planned modifications, and failed to deliver and use publicly available Java test suites. Because Microsoft contends that its products are within the scope of the license, Microsoft alleged that Sun's allegations to the contrary are false and constitute unfair competition.

In an effort to gain quick relief, Sun filed several motions seeking preliminary injunctions. Sun's first motion was filed on November 17, 1997, about a month after filing the lawsuit, seeking to bar Microsoft from using the Java Compatible logo on Microsoft products because they did not pass Sun's compatibility test and included modifications of the Java technology. Judge Ronald Whyte of the U.S. District Court in San Jose granted Sun's motion on March 24, 1998. According to Judge Whyte's order, Microsoft may not use the Java Compatible logo on its Internet Explorer or other products that contain incompatible implementations of the Java platform.

Sun filed additional motions in May 1998, asking for an order in the form of a preliminary injunction requiring Microsoft to include a fully compatible implementation of the Java platform in its Windows 98 products that include Java content. Sun also asked the court to prevent Microsoft from shipping any Java programming tools unless they generate only fully Java-compatible software. The court granted Sun's motion on November 18, 1998, giving Microsoft ninety days to cease shipping any browser or operating system software unless it contained a fully compatible version of Java that passed Sun's Java test suites. The court also ordered Sun to post a $15 million bond within ten days.

In all likelihood, the litigation between Sun and Microsoft will not answer the question of whether a company may own a programming language. Even if the lawsuit proceeds all the way to trial, the majority of the claims are related to the license agreement rather than copyright infringement. By taking a license, Microsoft at least implicitly acknowledged that Sun owns the language and its related technology. Although Microsoft challenged Sun's copyright ownership in its summary judgment opposition, Microsoft did not contend that Java was a programming language incapable of copyright protection. Further, Sun's basis for owning the Java language is not limited to the copyright laws because Sun also holds patents. Though it is pure speculation until the court issues a ruling on the matter, the language ownership issue will likely remain unresolved well after the Java litigation ends.

PROGRAMMING LANGUAGES AND THE
COMPUTER INDUSTRY

Prior to the Lotus spreadsheet cases, nearly the entire computer industry believed that programming languages were not protected by the copyright laws. Indeed, there was virtually no debate over the matter. Programming languages were simply functional tools from which expressive, protectable computer programs were written.

This fundamental belief fostered an environment in which languages were developed in industry-wide, working group settings. Because languages could not be owned, there was no advantage to any single entity spending the resources necessary to develop an advanced programming language. Consequently, better languages were developed and freely used with the consent of the developers.

But the Lotus spreadsheet cases and others like it have chipped away at the rock-solid belief that languages cannot be owned. Java was developed against this backdrop, as the courts cast doubt on the previously decided issue. If the court issues rulings in Sun's favor, particularly ruling that the Java programming language is protected under the copyright laws, then other companies are likely to focus their attention on developing innovative, proprietary languages to compete with or complement Java.

On the other hand, the Sun-Microsoft litigation could result in a holding that programming languages are not protectable under the copyright laws. If so, Sun's litigation strategy will have backfired, placing at least some aspects of its Java technology within the public domain. Even though Sun's patents and existing licenses will offer a measure of protection, they will eventually expire, allowing the industry to freely use the Java language.

PROGRAMMING LANGUAGES: A BRIEF
SUMMARY OF THE LAW

Until recently, programming languages were widely believed to be incapable of protection under the copyright laws. Recent court decisions have called that belief into question, suggesting that a programming language might constitute a work of authorship after all. But until the matter is squarely addressed by the courts or by Congress, there will still be plenty of room for doubt.

Notes

1. The litigation between Lotus and Borland was a protracted proceeding that was the subject of many reported decisions. Trial court decisions are reported at

Lotus Dev. Corp v. Borland Int'l, Inc., 788 F. Supp. 78 (D. Mass. 1992); *Lotus Dev. Corp v. Borland Int'l, Inc.,* 799 F. Supp. 203 (D. Mass. 1992); *Lotus Dev. Corp v. Borland Int'l, Inc.,* 831 F. Supp. 202 (D. Mass. 1993); *Lotus Dev. Corp v. Borland Int'l, Inc.,* 831 F. Supp. 223 (D. Mass. 1993). The decision of the First Circuit court of appeals is reported at *Lotus Dev. Corp v. Borland Int'l, Inc.,* 49 F.3d 807 (1st Cir. 1995).

2. The Lotus-Paperback decision is reported at *Lotus Development Corp. v. Paperback Software Int'l,* 740 F. Supp. 37 (D. Mass. 1990).

3. Much of the outline of the Sun-Microsoft litigation is provided by court documents filed by Sun and Microsoft. Both Sun and Microsoft maintain Internet sites containing press releases, court documents, and other information related to the litigation. Perhaps because of its close ties to the Internet, there are endless accounts on the Internet reporting the progress of the litigation.

13

Efforts to Control Data and Databases

In its most basic form, a database is simply a collection of information. Though all the data within the collection may be well known or within the public domain, the compilation may be valuable because it allows research or analysis or provides other benefits not possible without first gathering the information and organizing it in a meaningful way. Many companies have taken advantage of expanded computer capabilities and the growth of the Internet to produce electronic databases offering information such as phone numbers, financial transactions, news articles, issued patents, court decisions, and much more.

Considering the value of such databases and the effort required to produce them, those who compile databases naturally would prefer to prevent others from copying them. But will the law prevent others from copying a database when it amounts to nothing more than a collection of facts that are within the public domain and cannot be protected individually? The answer lies in the battle between Feist Publications Inc. and Rural Telephone Service Co.

FEIST PUBLICATIONS, INC. v. RURAL TELEPHONE SERVICE CO.: THE BATTLE OVER DATA

In a handful of areas, the legal battle that defines substantive computer law was waged over subject matter unrelated to computers. The battle establishing computer database law is one such area, involving the right to copy phone books in paper rather than electronic form.

Nevertheless, the rule of law is the same regardless of whether the data is stored on paper or on magnetic or other computer accessible media.

Rural Telephone Service Company, or RTSC, is a public utility that provides telephone service to local communities in northwest Kansas. Like most states, Kansas enacted regulations that required RTSC and other phone companies to annually issue an updated phone book. RTSC publishes a typical directory that includes white pages that alphabetically list the RTSC subscribers by name, town, and telephone number, along with yellow pages containing paid advertisements. RTSC registered each of its phone books with the Copyright Office and included appropriate copyright notices.

Feist Publications, Inc. is a publishing company, rather than a phone company, specializing in publishing areawide telephone directories. Unlike the RTSC directory, which covers only a single calling area, the Feist directories cover large geographic areas encompassing several local calling areas. The Feist phone books also include community interest, school, and government listing sections. With a single Feist directory, there is less need to call directory assistance or to obtain and consult multiple directories.

Beginning in 1978, Feist published annual issues of the Northwest Area-Wide directory, a directory that included the same geographic area as the RTSC directory. Because Feist was not a phone company, Feist did not have the same access to the listing data enjoyed by RTSC and other phone companies. To obtain the listing data, Feist entered into license agreements with each of the local telephone companies serving the area covered by the Northwest Area-Wide directory. Through the license agreements, the local phone companies agreed to sell Feist the right to include the white page listings in its directory each year.

RTSC was the only local phone company among the eleven companies within the Northwest Area-Wide directory coverage area that refused to license its listings to Feist. Both Feist and RTSC recognized that the Feist directory would be left with a gaping hole without the listings from the RTSC phone book, making it far more difficult for Feist to compete for yellow pages advertising revenue. Because it could not successfully publish the Northwest Area-Wide directory without the RTSC listings, Feist used the listings without RTSC's consent.

Feist began with the RTSC phone book, removing several thousand listings that fell outside the intended range of its Northwest Area-Wide coverage area. Feist hired employees to telephone each of the remaining 5,000 listings to verify the accuracy of the information. The verifiers also collected street address information that was not provided in the RTSC directory. Despite Feist's additions and verification efforts, 1,309 listings in the 1983 Northwest Area-Wide directory were identical to listings in RTSC's 1982–83 white pages, including four fictitious listings that RTSC had placed in its directory to detect copying.

The Trial Court Opinion

RTSC sued Feist in federal court in Kansas, contending that Feist infringed its copyrights by using portions of the 1982–83 white pages.[1] In response, Feist argued that its copying was a fair use under the copyright laws. Feist also charged that RTSC violated antitrust laws by attempting to exclude Feist as a competitor in the yellow pages advertising market.

The trial court had little trouble finding that telephone directories are copyrightable subject matter. Feist argued that the phone book listings were simply facts that were neither original nor creative, and therefore were unprotectable under the copyright laws. But the court cited numerous previous court decisions that had disagreed with Feist's position, concluding that telephone directories are copyrightable.

The court had equally little trouble concluding that Feist had copied the RTSC directory. In many copyright infringement cases, proof of copying is made by evidence of access to the original work plus a showing that the accused work is substantially similar to the original. Feist argued that its listings contained additional information and were therefore not substantially similar to the RTSC listings. But Feist had also admitted that it extensively used the RTSC directory to prepare its own phone book. Because there was direct evidence of copying, the court did not need to resort to the "substantially similar" test, which is only used in the absence of direct evidence of copying. The presence of 1,309 identical listings, including four fictitious ones, confirmed Feist's admission that it copied the RTSC directory in preparing its own areawide directory.

Finally, Feist argued that even if it had copied portions of the RTSC directory, its use was a "fair use" under the copyright laws. The fair use doctrine is a statutory provision that allows others to use copyrighted materials in a reasonable manner without the owner's consent. The statute lists several examples of fair uses, such as criticism, comment, news reporting, teaching, scholarship, or research. In other cases, whether the use is fair is to be guided by several factors, including (1) the purpose and character of the use, including whether it is of a commercial nature or is for nonprofit educational purposes; (2) the nature of the copyrighted work; (3) the amount and substantiality of the portion used in relation to the copyrighted work as a whole; and (4) the effect of the use upon the potential market for or value of the copyrighted work.

The fair use defense necessarily involves a case-by-case inquiry. With regard to databases, the trial court opined that fair uses are limited to cross-checking an independent work. Thus, a competitor that has independently gathered its own information may compare it to an original compilation to verify accuracy. But the competitor cannot escape infringement if it begins by copying the original work, even if it later verifies the compilation by checking with original sources. Because Feist did not begin by independently compiling its directory, its use of the RTSC directory was not a fair use. Consequently, the trial court held that Feist infringed RTSC's copyrights in its 1982–83 phone book.

Feist appealed the trial court's decision to the Tenth Circuit Court of Appeals. The Tenth Circuit affirmed the trial court's ruling in an unpublished opinion, "for substantially the reasons given by the district court." After losing twice, Feist again appealed, to the U.S. Supreme Court.

The Supreme Court Opinion

The Supreme Court addressed the single issue of whether data compilations may be protected under copyright law. As the court explained, the issue concerned the interaction of two well-established propositions. The first is that facts alone are not copyrightable; the second is that compilations of facts generally are. Individual uncopyrightable facts cannot magically change their status simply by gathering them together in one place. But copyright law contemplates that they are protectable if they are assembled in certain ways.

The reconciliation of these competing propositions requires an understanding of what it is that makes such compilations copyrightable. To qualify for copyright protection, all works must be original to the author. As the Supreme Court repeated no fewer than thirteen times in its opinion, this originality requirement is a constitutional mandate that cannot be ignored either by the courts or by Congress. At the same time, the originality standard is not demanding. Under copyright law, "original" means only that the work was independently created and that it contains at least a modicum of creativity.

Obviously, facts themselves are not original works; facts are discovered, not created. Likewise, the first to find and report particular facts has not created the facts and has no copyright interest in them. Others may freely use the facts and include them in their own writings. Although facts are not original by themselves, factual compilations may possess the requisite originality. By independently selecting which facts to include and deciding how to arrange them, the author may create a work that is worthy of copyright protection.

Though a data compilation may have sufficiently original selection and arrangement to qualify for copyright protection, the protection is necessarily thin. As the Supreme Court explained, the mere fact that the work is copyrighted does not mean that every element of the work is protected. Copyright protection extends only to those elements of the work that are original to the author. Even though others may not copy the precise words used to present facts, they may copy the facts and restate them or reorganize them in subsequent works.

Previously, many courts rewarded the "sweat of the brow," giving copyright protection to databases on the theory that the effort of compilation warranted protection. The development of the doctrine extended as far back as the late 1800s, in which several courts held that "industrious collection" was sufficient for copyright protection. But the Supreme Court believed that the "sweat of the brow" doctrine went too far, effectively extending copyright protection beyond the original contributions to the facts themselves. The primary objective of copyright is not to reward the labor of authors but rather to protect expression while encouraging others to build freely upon the ideas and information conveyed in the expression. Copyright law does not prevent others from copying those elements of a work that are not original as long as such copying does not unfairly appropriate the author's original contributions.

With regard to databases, copyright protection is limited to the original contribution to the collection; that is, the original selection, coordination, or arrangement of the data. Though the originality standard is extremely low, not every database will pass muster. In RTSC's case, the selection, coordination, and arrangement of its white pages was such an obvious and mechanical alphabetical arrangement of names, towns, and phone numbers that the Supreme Court found it devoid of any creativity at all. Indeed, the alphabetical arrangement is so commonplace that it is practically inevitable. Because RTSC's phone book was not protected by copyright law, Feist could freely copy it without infringing RTSC's rights.

NEW LAWS TO PROTECT DATABASES

Many companies reacted to the *Feist* decision by lobbying Congress to develop a new law to restore protection to databases. The most recent proposal is the "Collections of Information Antipiracy Act," a bill intended to revive the "sweat of the brow" theory for database protection.[2] The new law would prohibit copying of databases that required a substantial investment of resources to collect and that the collector offers or potentially would offer for sale. To be liable for misappropriation, the copier must take all or a substantial part of the database, sufficient to cause harm to the actual or potential market for the original collection. The law allows uses of the original data that are akin to "fair use" under copyright law. It also leaves in the public domain collections gathered by governmental entities or their agents.

Although the Supreme Court ruled that it was unconstitutional to protect databases under copyright law, the new law would likely survive most constitutional challenges. In the *Feist* opinion, the Supreme Court hinted that data collections may be protected under theories of unfair competition. Because the collections antipiracy law is drafted to prevent unfair competition rather than mere copying, it is likely to be upheld when applied to stop competitors from copying an original collection and selling it as their own.

The reach of any such database law will not be known for many years, assuming that Congress passes a law and the president signs it. Nevertheless, the scope of the law will likely closely resemble copyright law prior to the *Feist* decision. One possible act that may not be constitutionally prohibited, and therefore may lie outside the reach of the new law, is the copying of an unoriginal collection for private, home use. Such acts presumably do not involve use of the collection in commerce, as required under the proposed new law. Because the potentially wrongful act is the mere copying of the collection, it should be unconstitutional to enforce the collections antipiracy law in such cases.

DATABASES AND THE COMPUTER INDUSTRY

Prior to the *Feist* decision, it was widely believed that data collections were protected by copyright law under the "sweat of the brow" theory. Indeed, the "sweat of the brow" theory was a firmly established basis for copyright protection. For more than a century, data gatherers relied on court rulings holding that the labor required to gather and organize data should be rewarded in the form of copyright protection. While many companies also turned to other legal or technical forms of protection, copyright was assumed to provide substantial legal rights.

The uncertainty surrounding the ability to protect computerized databases after the *Feist* decision caused data gatherers to place a greater reliance on other forms of protection. Most commonly, database companies have used strong language in shrink-wrap licenses in an effort to contractually bind their customers not to use the data in a competitive manner. Unfortunately, few courts have enforced shrink-wrap licenses, potentially leaving databases with no protection at all.

Even though the collections antipiracy law offers hope for legal protection, data gatherers have been forced to develop technical devices as an additional form of protection. For example, the data may be encrypted and sold with a computer program that is able to decrypt the data as well as to access and search it. By using a combination of technical and legal measures, data gatherers are able to obtain a level of protection sufficient to make the sweat of the brow worthwhile.

DATABASES: A BRIEF SUMMARY OF THE LAW

Databases may be protected under copyright law, but copyright protection does not extend to the facts contained within the database. Rather, copyright law protects databases only to the extent that they feature original selection, coordination, or arrangement of the data. Though some databases may be sufficiently original to be protected under copyright law, others will not.

Though Congress evaluates new proposed database laws nearly every session, thus far none has become law. The most recent proposal is the Collections of Information Antipiracy Act, which would prevent others from using a substantial part of a collection in a manner that harms its market value if the collector expended substantial resources to collect the data and offers or may offer it for sale.

Although courts have viewed them with mixed results, data may also be protected by using shrink-wrap licenses or other contracts.

Notes

1. The litigation between Feist and Rural Telephone Service Company is reported at *Rural Telephone Service Co. v. Feist Publications, Inc.*, 663 F. Supp. 214 (D. Kan. 1987). The Supreme Court opinion is reported at 499 U.S. 340 (1991).

2. The Collections of Information Antipiracy Act originated as H.R. 2652. For a discussion of the bill, see Jane C. Ginsburg, "An Analysis of H.R. 2652, the Collections of Information Antipiracy Act," 27 *Computer L. R.* 195 (April 1998).

V

Special Strategic Issues

14

Subversive Techniques: Reverse Engineering

Reverse engineering is the process of analyzing a computer program to determine how it is programmed and the way that it functions.[1] The reverse engineering process is often challenging. Software is typically written in a high-level "source code" that humans can understand. But computers do not understand this high-level language, which must be converted, or compiled, into an "object code" language that the computer will understand. Because most software is distributed only in object code, the reverse engineering process often requires an initial decompilation of the nearly unintelligible object code into understandable source code.

Although the mere act of decompilation may be simple, the task of deciphering the resulting source code can be quite challenging. In the original source code, programmers typically include comments to assist in understanding the code. But the reverse engineer will normally not have the benefit of these important road maps because they are generally not compiled into object code and, therefore, will not be present in the decompiled code either. In addition, the reverse engineer probably has little or no idea which of the potentially millions of lines of code contain the relevant information. Consequently, reverse engineering may be enormously expensive.

Despite the challenge and potential expense involved in reverse engineering, in many cases there is no reasonable alternative. For example, a company may desire to produce software that is compatible with another company's hardware or software products. Without knowledge of certain details about the competitor's hardware or software, development of a competing product may not be possible.[2]

SEGA ENTERPRISES, LTD. v. ACCOLADE, INC.: THE BATTLE OVER REVERSE ENGINEERING

A legal battle between Sega Enterprises and Accolade addressed whether a competitor may reverse engineer video game cartridges to learn how to develop compatible video game cartridges of its own.[3] Sega develops and markets video entertainment systems, including the Sega "Genesis" video game console and compatible video game cartridges. Sega licenses certain copyrighted computer code and the use of its Sega trademark to independent developers who make and sell games for use in the Genesis console. Though the licensees sell video game cartridges in competition with Sega, they also pay Sega royalties for the use of the copyrighted code and the Sega trademark.

Accolade is an independent video game developer that makes games for a variety of video game consoles, including the Sega Genesis. But in 1991 Accolade was not and never had been a Sega licensee. Accolade had explored the possibility of entering into a licensing agreement with Sega, but Accolade rejected the idea because it would have required that Sega be the exclusive manufacturer of all games produced by Accolade.

Because Accolade was not licensed by Sega, Accolade first had to reverse engineer Sega's video games to learn how to make compatible games of its own. Accolade purchased a Genesis console and three Sega video game cartridges, then decompiled the cartridges to study the source code. In studying the source code, Accolade engineers made printouts of the source code and loaded the disassembled code into a computer to perform experiments aimed at learning the interface specifications for the Genesis console. When the reverse engineering was finished, Accolade created a development manual containing the requirements for producing a Genesis-compatible game cartridge.

Accolade used the development manual to create its own games for the Genesis system. According to Accolade, none of the Sega game code was copied; rather, Accolade relied only on the functional interface specifications that were contained in the development manual it had created. In 1990 Accolade released a game called "Ishido" for the Sega Genesis. Ishido had previously been developed for Macintosh and IBM personal computers and was revised to create a cartridge compatible with the Sega Genesis console.

At about the same time, Sega began exploring ways to prevent others from making counterfeit games. Accordingly, Sega developed a trademark security system (TMSS) for its upgraded Genesis III console. When a game cartridge is inserted into the Genesis III console, the microprocessor searches the game program for four bytes of data consisting of the letters "S-E-G-A." If the Genesis III finds the Sega trademark initialization code in the proper location, the game will operate on the console and a message appears on the screen stating that the game was produced by Sega or under license from Sega.

Accolade learned of the release of the Genesis III console in January 1991 at a consumer electronics show. At the electronics show, Accolade also discovered that its Ishido game would not operate on the Genesis III console. Accolade then reverse engineered Sega games that were compatible with the Genesis III console and discovered the TMSS initialization code. Accolade engineers added the code segment to its development manual, with an explanation that it was a standard header file that was to be used in all games.

In 1991 Accolade released five games for use with the Genesis III console, including Star Control, Hardball!, Onslaught, Turrican, and Mike Ditka Power Football. Like Ishido, each game had previously been produced for a different hardware system. Each game also contained the header file with the TMSS initialization code. The Onslaught game, however, would not work with the Genesis III console because the header was not placed in the correct location within the program. Though Accolade understood that the TMSS initialization code was required to enable the cartridge to operate, Accolade contended that it did not learn until late 1991 that the header file triggered the display of the message that the game was licensed by Sega.

Sega sued Accolade in late 1991, alleging trademark infringement, copyright infringement, and unfair competition. Accolade filed counterclaims against Sega for unfair competition and a variety of additional claims. Each side quickly filed motions for a preliminary injunction, which the trial court considered after expedited discovery. The preliminary injunction motions presented two primary issues. First, did Accolade infringe Sega's trademark rights by including the letters "S-E-G-A" within its game code? Second, did Accolade infringe Sega's copyrights by disassembling Sega's game code to discover functional requirements for compatibility?

In support of its motion for preliminary injunction, Sega submitted a declaration from Takeshi Nagashima, one of its employees. Mr. Nagashima stated that it was simple and inexpensive to create a game cartridge that did not contain the TMSS code but would still operate on the Genesis III. Likewise, games could be modified to prevent the Sega licensing message from appearing when the cartridge was inserted. Sega even demonstrated two such modified cartridges at the hearing, but refused to allow Accolade's software engineers to examine them or to reveal the manner in which they had been modified. Based on the Nagashima declaration, the trial court determined that the TMSS code was not functional and that Sega was likely to prove trademark infringement at trial.

The trial court also ruled in Sega's favor with regard to the copyright claim. The court concluded that the act of decompiling Sega's source code was an infringement under the Copyright Act. Such disassembly was held not to be a fair use because it was performed for a commercial purpose. The court also believed that there were alternatives to disassembly that Accolade could have used that would have revealed the requirements for compatibility. Consequently, on April 3, 1992, the court enjoined Accolade from (1) disassembling Sega's copyrighted code; (2) using or modifying Sega's copyrighted code; (3) developing or selling Genesis-compatible games that were created in whole or in part based on disassembly; and (4) developing or selling any games that prompt the Sega licensing message when inserted into a Genesis console. The trial court also ordered Accolade to recall all its infringing games within ten days.

Because of the hardship imposed by the injunction and the recall order, Accolade filed an emergency appeal with the U.S. Court of Appeals for the Ninth Circuit, seeking a reversal of the injunction and a stay of the recall order pending the ruling by the Court of Appeals. Before the Court of Appeals, Accolade presented four separate arguments in support of its position that disassembly of object code does not constitute copyright infringement. The Court of Appeals rejected the first three arguments but agreed with the fourth and reversed the ruling of the trial court.

First, Accolade argued that the act of decompiling object code is an act of "intermediate copying" that is not actionable by itself. The disassembled code is not sold, but rather it facilitates the creation of another work. According to Accolade, the court should only analyze the final commercial work for copying, without regard to whether there was an intermediate work that would amount to a copy if analyzed separately. The Court of Appeals disagreed, noting that previous rulings under copyright law had not drawn a distinction between "final" works and "intermediate" works. Thus, the Court of Appeals held that intermediate copies created by decompilation may constitute copyright infringement regardless of whether any end product also infringes those rights.

Second, Accolade argued that decompilation is always permissible under the Copyright Act because it is necessary in order to gain access to those ideas and functional elements contained within the code that are not protected by copyright law. Clearly, certain aspects of Sega's game code could not be protected by copyright law. But Accolade was unable to access those unprotected elements without decompiling the code because the object code was virtually unintelligible. In essence,

Accolade contended that object code can never be fully protected because it permits the original developer to gain protection for otherwise unprotectable features.

Once again, the Court of Appeals disagreed. The Court noted that it and many other courts had previously considered the matter and concluded that object code is to be protected under the Copyright Act. Although Accolade presented persuasive arguments in support of its need to access the ideas contained within the code, the question was more appropriately addressed in the case-by-case "fair use" analysis rather than a blanket approval of reverse engineering.

Next, Accolade contended that decompilation was allowed under Section 117 of the Copyright Act. Section 117 allows the lawful owner of a copy of a computer program to modify the program if modification is an essential step in enabling the owner to use the program with particular hardware. This provision enables owners to store a copy on a hard drive or load it into RAM without fear of copyright liability. It also allows consumers to make minor modifications to software as necessary to enable the software to run on the user's hardware. But as the court explained, Section 117 is not intended to allow disassembly of object code into source code.

Finally, Accolade argued that disassembly, as a necessary step in the examination of unprotected ideas and functional elements, is a fair use under the Copyright Act. Thus, even though decompilation is an act of copyright infringement, Accolade argued that it should be a permissible one under the Copyright Act's fair use provision.

Section 107 of the Copyright Act contains several factors to be used in addressing whether a particular use is a fair one. The statutory factors include (1) the purpose of the use, particularly including whether it is for commercial or nonprofit purposes; (2) the nature of the copyrighted work, such as whether it is factual or creative; (3) the amount and substantiality of the portion used in relation to the copyrighted work as a whole; and (4) the effect of the use upon the market for the copyrighted work. The Court of Appeals addressed each of these factors, concluding that Accolade's copying was a fair use.

Under the first factor, the court noted that the use was unquestionably commercial, but cautioned that the commercial nature of the use is a matter of degree, not an absolute. Here, Accolade performed reverse engineering for the sole purpose of learning the essential requirements for compatibility. In that regard, Accolade's commercial use was intermediate and indirect. Accolade did not copy Sega's games, and never intended to avoid creating its own original works. Consequently, the commercial use factor favored Accolade.

Analysis under the second factor, the nature of the copyrighted work, also favored Accolade. In general, works of fiction receive greater protection than works that are factual or functional. Computer programs inherently contain many functional elements that are therefore entitled to lower levels of protection. In the Sega Genesis games, the TMSS code was functional and could not reasonably be examined without decompiling the object code. Because this unprotected element could not be examined without copying, the Court of Appeals afforded the video game code a lower degree of protection than more expressive, creative works.

The third factor weighed against Accolade, but only slightly. This factor evaluates the amount of the original work used in relation to the work as a whole. Obviously, Accolade used the entire original work by decompiling all of it into source code. But because Accolade used so little of the original work in its ultimate product, this factor carried little or no weight.

Finally, the fourth factor, addressing the effect of the use on the market for the copyrighted work, favored Accolade. At first blush, Accolade's copying may seem to have an adverse effect on the market for Sega's protected works. After all, Accolade's reverse engineering enabled it to enter the video game market and compete with Sega and Sega's licensees. But competition within the video game is based on qualities of the games having nothing to do with the TMSS code copied by Accolade. In addition, because consumers often purchase many games, they might well purchase games offered by both Sega and Accolade. Perhaps more importantly, it was simply inequitable for Sega to use the copyright laws to prevent others from making any competing games at all.

Based on its analysis of the fair use factors, the Court of Appeals found that Accolade's act of decompiling the Sega object code was a fair use. But the court took pains to avoid creating a broad approval of reverse engineering. It repeatedly explained that disassembly is only a fair use where the disassembly is the "only way to gain access" to the functional elements contained within the software and where there is a "legitimate reason" for seeking such access.

REVERSE ENGINEERING AND THE COMPUTER INDUSTRY

The courts have decided a handful of reverse engineering disputes, with mixed results. In one notable case, *Atari Games Corp. v. Nintendo of America, Inc.*, the Federal Circuit Court of Appeals reached essentially the same result as in *Sega*: Decompilation is permissible when it is a necessary step in the development of a compatible computer program.[4] Other court decisions have alternately approved or disapproved of reverse engineering based on a variety of different rationales.

Although the courts have been inconsistent in deciding reverse engineering cases, a slow consensus may be building in favor of allowing reverse engineering, at least for compatibility purposes. Reverse engineering generally enjoys a rich history in the United States, both in the courts and in industry. Some commentators have described reverse engineering as a "time-honored" tradition and have observed that it has long been a common practice in the industry.[5] The *Sega* decision advances this tradition and makes it likely that other courts will follow suit.

Because of the limited number of court decisions, it is difficult to gauge the effect the courts have had on reverse engineering. Nonetheless, related decisions have likely been influential. Thus, through the early 1980s, when it was unclear whether software would be given substantial copyright protection, few would have hesitated to reverse engineer a competitor's product. But as the courts published decisions providing strong copyrights, decompilation was increasingly avoided. Instead, if companies need information about a particular computer program but cannot get it from the author, they must devote long and tedious hours to studying the program without decompiling it.

REVERSE ENGINEERING: A BRIEF SUMMARY OF THE LAW

There have only been a handful of court decisions squarely addressing the propriety of reverse engineering, yielding mixed results. Although the state of the law is uncertain and may vary among different jurisdictions, the prevailing rule is that reverse engineering is permissible for scholarly purposes or when necessary for compatibility. When reverse engineering is performed for other purposes, it may constitute copyright infringement.

Notes

1. The definition of reverse engineering is loosely zx based on a definition found in the *Microsoft Press Computer Dictionary*, p. 300 (1st Ed. 1991).

2. A comprehensive article on the economic aspects of reverse engineering is Lawrence D. Graham and Richard O. Zerbe, Jr., "Economically Efficient Treatment of Computer Software: Reverse Engineering, Protection, and Disclosure," 22 *Rutgers Computer and Tech. L.J.* 61 (1996).

3. The litigation between Sega and Accolade is reported at *Sega Enterprises, Ltd. v. Accolade, Inc.*, 785 F. Supp. 1392 (N.D. Cal. 1992), *rev'd*, 977 F.2d 1510 (9th Cir. 1993).

4. The litigation between Atari and Nintendo is reported at *Atari Games Corp. v. Nintendo of America, Inc.*, 975 F.2d 832 (Fed. Cir. 1992).

5. The "time-honored" tradition quote is contained in Joel Miller, *Reverse Engineering: Fair Game or Foul?*, IEEE Spectrum (April 1993): 64.

15

Is Shrink-Wrap Licensing a Dud?

Computer software differs from other goods in that it is typically quite expensive and time-consuming to develop but can be copied and distributed cheaply and easily. Because of this wide disparity between development and copying expenses, mass-market software is licensed to consumers rather than sold. By distributing software under a license, developers can protect their investments by narrowly tailoring the specific rights that are given to consumers, expressly prohibiting them from making copies and distributing them to others.

The tool of choice for imposing the licensing terms upon consumers is the "shrink-wrap" license. Most consumer software is packaged in a cardboard box and sealed within a thin sheet of plastic that is "shrink-wrapped" around the box. The packaging often includes a notice on the outside of the box that states that opening the plastic shrink-wrap constitutes an acceptance of the terms of a license that is enclosed within the box. Alternatively, the computer disks may be contained within an envelope inside the box, with a notice on the envelope that states that opening the envelope constitutes an acceptance of the terms of a license that may be printed on the outside of the envelope. The licenses typically contain terms that prohibit copying, rental, and reverse engineering, and limit use of the software to a single computer. The licenses also generally disclaim any applicable warranties and limit the liability of the seller.

Shrink-wrap licenses have several shortcomings that raise questions about their enforceability. One of the problems with shrink-wrap licenses is that consumers do not have an opportunity to review and agree to the terms of the licenses before they purchase the software. In virtually every case, the licenses are inside the packaging and can only be reviewed by consumers after the purchase has been made. This timing raises a serious question regarding whether consumers have agreed to the license terms, even if consumers read and understand them. In addition, consumers are not given an opportunity to negotiate the terms of the license with the sellers. Instead, the licenses—no matter how reasonable—are unwaveringly offered to consumers who must take them or leave them. In some cases, the licenses contain harsh provisions that no reasonable consumer would agree to or that are contrary to the law. These and other issues have cast doubt on the enforceability of shrink-wrap licenses.

In part because of their questionable enforceability, few software makers have sought to enforce shrink-wrap licenses in the courts. Nevertheless, shrink-wrap and related forms of licenses are more ubiquitous than ever as software companies continue to find new ways to seek to impose their terms upon consumers. For example, many software makers now include their license terms on "splash screens" within the software and require users to acknowledge their consent before the software will proceed. Considering the universal use of shrink-wrap licenses and the amount of software on the market, legal disputes involving shrink-wrap licenses are inevitable.

PROCD, INC. v. ZEIDENBERG: **THE BATTLE OVER SHRINK-WRAP LICENSES**

In a handful of cases, courts have peripherally addressed the validity of shrink-wrap licenses, generally treating them with disdain. But prior to the dispute between ProCD, Inc. and Matthew Zeidenberg in 1996, no courts had squarely addressed the enforceability of consumer shrink-wrap licenses, and none had ruled that such licenses, in any context, were enforceable.[1]

ProCD is a Massachusetts company that spent millions of dollars compiling a national telephone and address database. ProCD used 3,000 publicly available phone books to create 95 million residential and commercial listings that include names, addresses, phone numbers, and industry "SIC" codes where applicable. ProCD produced several versions of its software directories, including a CD-ROM version sold under the name "Select Phone." In addition to address data, the Select Phone software included a program to search the database and return the requested information.

Like most software, Select Phone included a license agreement within the product packaging. A reference in fine print on the outside of the box mentioned the license but did not provide the specific license terms.

Inside the packaging, user documentation requested purchasers to review the license terms before using the software. ProCD also placed a reminder on its splash screen, stating that use of the software was subject to the terms of the license agreement and requiring users to indicate consent before proceeding. If purchasers did not agree to the terms of the license, purchasers were requested to return the software to the store where it was purchased.

ProCD recognized that its ability to recover its investment would be destroyed if others could freely distribute the data it had compiled or, worse yet, make it available to others over the Internet. To prevent this from happening, ProCD's shrink-wrap license contained restrictions stating that access to the data was limited to individual or personal use and that the software could not be distributed, sublicensed, or leased to others. The agreement also prohibited purchasers from making the software or its data available to others over any network.

In 1994 Matthew Zeidenberg purchased a copy of Select Phone at a retail store. Sometime in early 1995 Zeidenberg decided to use the data from Select Phone to make a commercial directory of his own, accessible over the Internet. In March 1995, Zeidenberg purchased an updated version of Select Phone for use in his Internet directory. Zeidenburg then formed a company, Silken Mountain Web Services, Inc., to assemble a telephone database that contained data from Select Phone and another commercial product. Zeidenberg wrote his own computer program to search the database, offering much less sophisticated search capabilities than those provided by ProCD.

ProCD discovered Silken Mountain's database shortly after it was placed on the Internet and demanded that Zeidenberg and Silken Mountain remove it immediately. Zeidenberg admitted that he had used listings from Select Phone but refused to remove his new Internet directory. Although Zeidenberg had seen the on-screen messages warning about license restrictions, he disregarded them because he did not believe the license to be binding. By September 1995 the Silken Mountain directory had become well-known and was receiving approximately 20,000 Internet "hits" per day.

The Trial Court Decision

ProCD sued Zeidenberg and Silken Mountain in September 1995, seeking damages for copyright infringement, breach of the shrink-wrap license agreement, and violation of the Wisconsin state computer crimes act. On the strength of the damage Silken Mountain's product was causing to ProCD's sales, ProCD immediately sought and obtained a preliminary injunction preventing Zeidenberg and Silken Mountain from offering their product over the Internet.

Shortly thereafter, both sides filed motions asking the court to resolve the matter on summary judgment. There were several issues before the court, including whether the data could be protected by copyright and whether the shrink-wrap license was valid and enforceable. The court quickly dispensed with the copyright issue, noting that ProCD obtained its data in much the same way as Zeidenberg, copying it from phone books that were compiled by others. The same Supreme Court decision that allowed ProCD to copy phone books without running afoul of the copyright laws also allowed Zeidenberg to copy the Select Phone data with impunity.

Though not protected by copyright law, ProCD asserted that its shrink-wrap license prevented others from copying its data. In analyzing the shrink-wrap issue, the court first addressed whether there was any formal law governing the interpretation of shrink-wrap licenses. As one alternative, a software transaction could be considered to be a sale of goods, invoking the laws of the Uniform Commercial Code (UCC). Alternatively, a software purchase could be a license agreement, placing it outside the reach of the UCC. Neither characterization—sale or license—is a close fit. The transaction is akin to a purchase of goods because the consumer pays for the software and receives a tangible object much like any other purchase. Further, there is no continuing royalty, no expiration date, and no security deposit often associated with licenses. On the other hand, the software contains a notice stating that the transaction is covered by a license. The ProCD court, like most courts, concluded that the enforcement of the license should be interpreted under the UCC.

Unfortunately, because the UCC was intended to govern the sale of goods, it does not address many of the issues applicable to shrink-wrap licensing. Relying on requirements imposed by the UCC, the trial court concluded that the shrink-wrap license was not enforceable. Most importantly, the court was concerned that Zeidenberg did not have an opportunity to review the license terms before purchasing the software. It did not matter that Zeidenberg bought two additional copies of Select Phone after having an opportunity to review the terms of the license contained in the first copy. In the court's view, there was no way for Zeidenberg to know whether ProCD changed the terms of the licenses in its later versions. Zeidenberg should have been given the opportunity to review the terms prior to being bound by them. Because there was no such opportunity, the license was not enforceable.

The perceived inadequacies of the UCC cemented the court's opinion. The court observed that several amendments had been proposed to add provisions to the UCC to directly govern software transactions and uphold shrink-wrap licenses. According to the court, the very existence of such proposals meant that shrink-wrap licenses were generally believed to be unenforceable under the existing version of the UCC. ProCD's license was also unenforceable, and the case was dismissed.

The Appellate Court Decision

ProCD appealed the trial court's decision to the Seventh Circuit Court of Appeals. The appeals court disagreed with the trial court, ruling that the shrink-wrap license was enforceable. Unlike the trial court, the appeals court did not believe that the inability to review the precise license terms before paying for the software was sufficient to render the license unenforceable. Because there was a notice outside the box stating that the purchase was subject to terms contained inside the box, Zeidenberg knew that his purchase was subject to a license. Zeidenberg could review the license shortly after the purchase, and was required by the software splash screens to consent to the license before proceeding. If Zeidenberg did not consent to the terms of the license, he could return the software to the seller. Thus, in the appellate court's opinion, Zeidenberg did have a full opportunity to review and reject the license terms before he was bound by them.

The court was further persuaded by the countless other consumer transactions in which consumers pay before receiving the precise language of a contract, warranty, or disclaimer. For example, insurance policies, airline tickets, and concert tickets are typically purchased before consumers have an opportunity to review the fine print that defines the terms of the agreement. Likewise, consumer electronics often include warranties, and drugs come with cautions and lists of interactions that cannot be reviewed until the packaging is opened at home. If the pay-first, read-later way of doing business works in these industries, then it should work for software as well.

Equally important, it is simply impractical to reproduce the entire license agreement on the outside of the software packaging. Even if the print would not be microscopic, it would take the place of other information that consumers might find more important, such as a description of the software's features and a listing of system requirements. According to the Court of Appeals, a notice on the outside of the box, with the terms on the inside and a right to return the software if the terms are unacceptable, is simply a reasonable way of doing business that is fair to both buyers and sellers. The court therefore reversed the trial court's decision and upheld the enforceability of the shrink-wrap license.

ELECTRONIC AND "WEB-WRAP" LICENSES

With the growth of the Internet, an increasing amount of business now takes place electronically, with no packaging and no physical shrink-wrap license. Instead, consumers visit Web sites to review and purchase software that they can download directly to their computers. Alternatively, consumers access Internet sites to gather information rather than to purchase software. Before being allowed to access certain sites or to download software, consumers are often confronted with an electronic version of the shrink-wrap license. The license, sometimes called a "Web-wrap" license, is typically similar to a shrink-wrap license or a license contained on a software splash screen.[2] Although there have not yet been any legal battles testing the enforceability of Web-wrap agreements, the popularity of such agreements and the growth of the Internet makes future Web-wrap disputes inevitable.

EFFORTS TOWARD UNIFORMITY: UCC ARTICLE 2B

With very few legal battles squarely addressing the enforceability of shrink-wrap licenses, the enforceability of shrink-wrap licenses remans in doubt, particularly for jurisdictions in which there have been no previous court decisions. In the future, courts are likely to turn to the only precedent available to them, which means using the state's contract interpretation rules and applying the rules of the Uniform Commercial Code by analogy. Because of this awkward and uncertain state of affairs, a group of lawyers is drafting a proposed new section of the UCC to address software licenses, including mass market shrink-wrap licenses. This proposed new section of the UCC, called Article 2B, attempts to standardize the law by offering a uniform provision that all state legislatures would adopt.

Because Article 2B is only in draft form, it may never be adopted by any states. In fact, there is widespread disagreement over many of the provisions of Article 2B, so it may never advance beyond a draft. If Article 2B is ever finished, it will contain core provisions dealing with shrink-wrap and other software licenses. At a minimum, Article 2B will address whether such licenses are enforceable at all and, if so, some of the essential terms they must contain. For example, Article 2B may provide that shrink-wrap licenses must allow consumers to receive a full refund after opening the packaging and reading the license, and may allow software companies to impose harsh restrictions so long as consumers have the right to a refund if they disagree. If these and other terms are ever reduced to statutory language, they will certainly change the form of software licenses and shift the rights and responsibilities of software developers and consumers.

SHRINK-WRAP LICENSES AND THE COMPUTER INDUSTRY

Shrink-wrap licenses were essential prior to the early 1980s, when it was uncertain whether copyright law would prevent others from copying software. Even after Congress amended the Copyright Act to extend protection to computer software, many software makers simply continued to include shrink-wrap licenses as an additional measure of protection. Because gaps in the protection provided by copyright law still exist, such as the ability to prevent others from copying databases, virtually all consumer software is licensed, not sold.

Even though virtually all retail software is sold under a shrink-wrap license, most consumers disregard them and believe that they are unenforceable. Consumers have not been unreasonable in their beliefs. Prior to the *ProCD* decision, very few courts faced shrink-wrap license issues, and those few that had refused to uphold them. Perhaps afraid of developing a large body of unfavorable case law, software companies have chosen not to enforce their shrink-wrap licenses in the courts. But after the *ProCD* decision, software companies may have a renewed confidence in their shrink-wrap licenses. At the very least, it is safe to say that shrink-wrap licenses are here to stay.

SHRINK-WRAP LICENSING: A BRIEF SUMMARY OF THE LAW

Shrink-wrap licenses have been the subject of few legal battles, with mixed results. Most courts seem likely to enforce them as long as there is a notice outside the software packaging, the terms of the license are reasonable, and consumers are given the opportunity to return the software if the terms are unacceptable. Ideally, "splash screens" within the software will also remind users that use of the software is subject to a license.

Notes

1. The litigation between ProCD and Zeidenberg is reported at *ProCD, Inc. v. Zeidenberg*, 908 F. Supp. 640 (W.D. Wis. 1996), *rev'd*, 86 F.3d 1447 (7th Cir. 1996).

2. For a discussion of "Web-wrap" licenses, see James A. Powers, "Beware of Pitfalls with 'Webwrap' Agreements," *Interactive Marketing News* (May 24, 1996).

16

Trademarks

For many years, Intel Corporation has been the leading manufacturer of microprocessors for personal computers, supplying as much as 75 percent of all microprocessor chips. Due at least in part to the enormous costs involved, other chip manufacturers have had difficulty loosening Intel's stranglehold on the microprocessor market. Few companies can afford to spend the $150 million that Intel spent to develop its Pentium chip. Fewer still can afford to build a new fabrication facility, which can cost in excess of $1 billion.

Following Intel's lead, microprocessor technology has advanced at a rapid pace. Each microprocessor family typically has a shelf life of two or three years before it is replaced by the next generation. Consequently, Intel spends millions of dollars each year developing the next microprocessor generation. Intel's leadership position, the significant costs involved, and the pace of development in the industry have allowed Intel to enjoy a brief monopoly on each new generation. Competing microprocessor makers typically require six months or more after the introduction of Intel's latest microprocessor before they are able to produce a compatible, competing chip of their own.

Like most electronics parts manufacturers, Intel used numerical designations for its early microprocessors, beginning with the 8086 and 8088 microprocessors. Subsequent generations included the 80186 and 80188; 80286; 80386; and 80486. Throughout the computer industry, these designations were shortened, so the microprocessors were generally referred to as the 286, 386, and 486. When competing chip makers introduced compatible microprocessors, they gave them the same designations as their Intel counterparts so that consumers would understand that they were interchangeable with the Intel chips.

Beginning with the 386, Intel planned to emphasize the designations more strongly as trademarks, linking the designations more closely to Intel as the supplier of the microprocessors bearing those designations. Intel recognized the competitive advantage it would hold if it could be the sole source for microprocessors bearing the 386 and 486 markings. Unfortunately for Intel, other chip manufacturers also recognized the advantages of using the same designations and were unwilling to abandon the designations that they, too, had been using for several years. To prevent others from using what it believed were proprietary trademarks, Intel would have to take its case to the courts.

Following the 486 family of microprocessors, Intel changed course and dropped the "x86" format for its chips. Instead, Intel named its next generation the Pentium. At the same time, Intel launched a campaign to advertise its microprocessors more directly to consumers, primarily using an "Intel Inside" logo to indicate that a personal computer contained an Intel microprocessor.

Shortly after introducing the Pentium, Intel discovered a flaw in the manner in which the chip performed floating point mathematical calculations. The flaw prompted many consumers to joke about the reasons behind Intel's decision to use the Pentium name and the Intel Inside logo. For example:

Q: Why didn't Intel call its Pentium processor the 586?
A: Because it added 100 to 486 and got 585.99985415245, and that would be too hard to remember.

Q: What do you call the Intel Inside logo?
A: A warning label.

While the timing of Intel's new trademark campaign and the discovery of the Pentium flaw provided fertile ground for jokes, the two events were completely unrelated. Rather, Intel's decision to use the Pentium trademark stemmed from a lawsuit between Intel and Advanced Micro Devices, Inc. over the right to use the 386 designation.

WHAT'S IN A NAME?

For centuries, artisans, craftsmen, manufacturers, and retailers have used trademarks to identify their wares. Although trademarks may take a variety of forms, most commonly including words or symbols, all trademarks share a common purpose: Trademarks identify a particular person or organization as the source of the goods or services bearing the mark. Assuming that a trademark properly identifies a person or organization as the source of goods, the trademark owner holds the right to prevent others from using the same mark or similar marks in a manner that is likely to confuse the public as to the source or sponsorship of the competing goods.

One common problem for trademark owners arises from improper trademark use. If a mark becomes famous, so that it is widely recognized by the consuming public, it may be quite valuable. In an effort to build trademark recognition, many companies improperly use their trademarks as names for their goods, rather than designations of source. Similarly, consumers sometimes use a mark in a generic fashion to refer to all goods of a similar type. Unfortunately, some companies later discover that their brilliant marketing efforts are rewarded with a widely recognized name that the entire world may freely use. If a court determines that a mark is understood by consumers to refer to a type of goods rather than to a source for such goods, the mark will be considered "generic" and lose its trademark status. Countless companies have lost their trademark rights in this manner. Familiar terms that were once claimed as trademarks but that have been found by the courts to be generic include *aspirin, bundt, cellophane, cola, DOS, escalator, jujubes, matchbox, murphy bed, super glue, shredded wheat, thermos, trampoline, yellow pages,* and *yo-yo.* In each case, a court held that the mark was generic and that anyone could use the mark to refer to the goods. Other companies such as Coca-Cola and Xerox are working vigilantly to police improper uses of their trademarks so that they retain their valuable trademark status.

THE BATTLE OVER CHIP NAMES: *INTEL v. ADVANCED MICRO DEVICES*

In the late 1980s, Intel found itself in precisely this position. Intel's 386 designation for computer chips had become highly recognizable, but other companies had been using the designation as well, and Intel had made little or no effort to stop such competing uses. By 1988 Intel was aware that the 386 designation was being perceived by consumers as a product description rather than a brand name. To remedy the situation, Intel began a "take back the 386 name campaign."

One of the companies that was also using the 386 designation was Advanced Micro Devices, or AMD. After Intel had used the designations 8086, 80186, and 80286, it was obvious that the 80386 was next in the progression. Consumers, the press, and others in the computer industry correctly anticipated that Intel would introduce a microprocessor designated the 386. Like other competing chip makers, AMD began using the 386 designation immediately with the introduction of its 386 microprocessors.

Intel sued AMD for trademark infringement, seeking to "enjoin," or prevent, AMD's further use of the 386 designation.[1] To prevail in its case against AMD, Intel first had to prove that the 386 designation was a trademark rather than a generic term used to describe a particular type of goods. Proof that the designation was not generic required a showing that consumers primarily associated the term with the producer and not the product. In trademark parlance, the association of a particular trademark with a particular producer is called "secondary meaning."

As is often the case, the definition of the relevant consuming public played a role in whether the mark was generic or had secondary meaning. Arguing that the computer end-users were the relevant consumers, Intel conducted surveys to show that end-users associated the 386 designation with Intel. Meanwhile, AMD argued that the original equipment manufacturers, or OEMs, were the relevant consumers and conducted a survey of OEMs. In AMD's survey, 72 percent of respondents concluded that 386 was a generic description, while only 21 percent stated that it was a brand name. The court agreed with AMD's definition of the relevant market, concluding that the consumers buy computers without paying much attention to the processors. The OEMs, on the other hand, must carefully decide which processors to buy.

Having decided that the OEMs were the relevant consumers, the court had little choice but to reject Intel's survey evidence establishing secondary meaning in the 386 designation among computer end-users. Instead, the court relied on AMD's uncontroverted survey of OEMs, which found that 72 percent of respondents thought that the term 386 was a generic product description and not a brand name or designation of source.

The court also relied on additional evidence showing that several Intel employees thought the designation was generic. For example, evidence at trial showed that at least some Intel employees, including the Intel trademark program manager, were aware that the 386 designation was perceived as a product description and not a brand name. References within the corporation to a "take back the 386 name campaign" were viewed as an admission that the name had become generic.

Finally, the court found that Intel simply had not taken steps to treat the 386 designation as a trademark. Prior to its campaign to take back the 386 name, Intel had not attempted to obtain trademark registrations for any of its microprocessors in the x86 series. Likewise, Intel had not used any x86 designations as trademarks. In sum, Intel's failure to register its designations as trademarks and the widespread generic use of the designations by others prevented Intel from enjoying trademark rights in the *x*86 designations.

TRADEMARK LAW AND THE COMPUTER INDUSTRY

Following Intel's loss to AMD in the courts, Intel dropped the *x*86 designation for its next microprocessor, which would have been the 586. Instead, Intel adopted "Pentium" as a trademark to refer to its next-generation microprocessor. Perhaps to disprove the court's conclusion that computer end-users do not make buying decisions based on the brand of the computer's microprocessor, Intel has spent a significant amount of money advertising and promoting the Pentium mark directly to computer end-users. To facilitate its end-user marketing, Intel created the "Intel Inside" logo for use on computers containing Intel microprocessors. One form of the Intel Inside and Pentium logos is shown in Figure 8.

Intel's emphasis on trademarks has led other chip makers to attempt to create brand recognition in the mind of consumers. Notably, Cyrix has sought to establish itself as a recognizable supplier of microprocessors. In 1993 Cyrix spoofed Intel's "Intel Inside" swirl logo with a similar swirl surrounding the word "ditto." The logo was part of a Cyrix

Figure 8. Computer trademarks. Intel's legal battles led to the development and promotion of the now-ubiquitous Intel Inside and Pentium trademarks, both of which are registered trademarks of the Intel Corporation.

campaign that also used the slogan "Cyrix Instead." Although Intel quickly sued Cyrix for parodying its trademarks, Cyrix may have been pleased by all the attention brought by the litigation. The lawsuit generated an enormous amount of publicity that helped to establish Cyrix as an alternative source in the mind of consumers.[2]

Meanwhile, Intel's competitors have continued to use the $x86$ family of designations. Cyrix and AMD use the designation 586 to refer to their microprocessors that compete with the Intel Pentium. Ironically, only Intel is now no longer using the $x86$ family it originated. Nevertheless, Intel's registration and widespread advertising of the Pentium and Intel Inside trademarks have created much stronger trademark rights among a much larger group of consumers.

The Intel court battle with AMD has heightened the importance of trademarks for processors. Previously, consumers had little knowledge of the source of the computer's microprocessor. Because of the lack of consumer knowledge, OEMs could make purchasing decisions purely on the basis of price and performance. Now, consumers may make computer purchasing decisions based on the particular brand of processor the computer contains.

TRADEMARKS: A BRIEF SUMMARY OF THE LAW

A trademark is one or more words or symbols that identify a source of goods or services. One may acquire trademark rights in a variety of ways, including federal and state registration, or by use in commerce sufficient to establish an association in the mind of consumers between the mark and the supplier as the source of goods. Trademark rights may be lost if the trademark becomes known in the consuming public as a name for the goods or services themselves rather than the source of goods. If a person or organization has rights in a trademark, that person or organization may prevent others from using the mark or confusingly similar marks in association with the sale of competing goods or services.

Notes

1. The Intel litigation with AMD is reported at *Intel Corporation v. Advanced Micro Devices, Inc.,* 756 F. Supp. 1292 (N.D. Cal. 1991).

2. A summary of some of the marketing by Cyrix, including the "Ditto" logo and the Cyrix Instead tagline is outlined in Gerry Khermouch, "Nipping at Intel's Heels, Others Are in the Chips," *Brandweek* (June 6, 1994): 20.

17

Stockpiling Internet Domain Names

Over the past several years, the Internet has grown at a phenomenal pace. As recently as the mid-1990s there was little, if any, business conducted on the Web. In fact, conducting business on the Internet was considered unseemly by many of the original scientific and educational users. Despite the early reticence, businesses today are scrambling for an Internet presence as if their survival depended on it. With over eight million domain names in the popular "dot com" top-level domain, there is no doubt that the Internet is here to stay as an important commercial channel.

Predictably, the headlong dash to the Web has provided fertile ground for litigation.[1] As is the case with many new technologies, there is considerable debate over the manner in which existing laws will be applied to the new medium. Consequently, a disproportionate number of lawsuits are filed, and many courts are forced to break new ground to resolve them. Though there have been many proposals to address these legal concerns, for now the courts must deal with questions of personal jurisdiction and liability in a case-by-case fashion.

INTERNET DOMAIN NAME BASICS

The Internet began as an outgrowth of U.S. government investments in communication network technology under agreements with the Defense Advanced Research Projects Agency (DARPA), the National Science Foundation (NSF), and other agencies. After a successful research and education network was established, Congress authorized the commercialization of the network that forms the foundation of today's Internet. Because of the U.S. government's role in the development of the Internet, many aspects of the domain name system are still subject to agreements with U.S. government agencies.

Every computer connected to the Internet has a unique numerical address, much like every phone has a unique phone number. The numerical addresses correspond to easier-to-remember domain names that are heirarchically organized, comprising at least a "top-level domain," or TLD, and a "second-level domain," or SLD. The top-level domains include the popular *.com* extension for commercial users, as well as the *.net* extension for Internet service providers and the *.org* extension for nonprofit organizations. There are numerous additional top-level domains corresponding to individual countries, including, for example, *.us* for the United States, *.ca* for Canada, and *.br* for Brazil.

The second-level domain uniquely identifies a particular user. For example, McDonald's restaurants uses "mcdonalds" for its second-level domain, so that its complete domain name is *mcdonalds.com*. Predictably, individuals, agencies, schools, and businesses have chosen domain names that correspond to their names in the industry or marketplace. Because of this practice, users naturally expect that domain names are associated with companies having the same names, so that *xerox.com* maps to an Internet site for the Xerox Corporation and *u.washington.edu* maps to a site for the University of Washington.

Domain names are fast, easy, and cheap to obtain. Presently, domain names in the most popular top-level domains—*.com*, *.net*, and *.org*—are registered exclusively through Network Solutions, Inc. (NSI), a private company operating under a contract with the National Science Foundation. By completing a form and submitting it over the Internet, a new domain name can be registered in a matter of a few hours or less.

NSI registers domain names on a first-come, first-served basis; as long as the exact domain name is not already registered to another entity, it will be assigned to the applicant. Although the *.com*, *.net*, and *.org* top-level domains were originally intended to identify Internet sites as commercial users, Internet service providers, and non-profit organizations, NSI makes no attempt to verify that the domain name applicant is properly categorized. As long as the applicant represents that it is seeking a domain name within the proper top-level domain, NSI will issue the requested domain name if it is available.

Originally, domain name registration was free. Because registration was fast, easy, and free, some companies and individuals obtained and stockpiled hundreds or thousands of domain names. In many cases, such stockpiling was done with the intent to sell the domain names to others, particularly those with company names corresponding to the stockpiled domain names. Most large companies have probably been targeted by such domain name "pirates" including, for example, McDonald's, Avon, Nintendo, Microsoft, MTV, Panavision, and many others. Although NSI began charging a fee of $100 to register each domain name in an attempt to reduce the stockpiles of domain names, the fee has not provided a sufficient deterrent.

DOMAIN NAME BATTLES

The ability to obtain fast, easy, and cheap domain name registrations has provided fertile ground for legal disputes. Some disputes have involved the intentional "pirating" of a domain name for competitive purposes. In one of the earliest cases, the Princeton Review Management Corp., a standardized test preparation company, registered the domain name *kaplan.com* and posted content praising the Princeton Review and disparaging the services of its competitor, Stanley H. Kaplan Educational Center, Ltd. When Kaplan complained, Princeton Review offered to give up the name for a case of beer. Kaplan refused the offer and eventually obtained the name after an arbitration with Princeton Review.

In other disputes, domain name registrants have sought to benefit from the fame of another company's trademark, but without using the Web site to disparage that company. Many of these disputes have been resolved under the federal or state trademark dilution acts, which protect "famous" trademarks from uses by others in a manner that reduces the distinctive qualities of the famous trademarks.

A substantial number of these dilution battles have involved sexually explicit "adult" sites. For example, in 1996 Hasbro, Inc. sued Internet Entertainment Group, Ltd. (IEG) over the use of the domain name *candyland.com* for a site containing sexually explicit content. Hasbro alleged that the operation of the site would infringe its trademark rights related to the famous children's board game Candy Land. The court agreed, and issued a preliminary injunction against IEG's further use of the *candyland.com* domain name.

In still other cases, legal battles have been waged over domain names registered with the obvious intent to sell them to owners of famous trademarks. The registrant's intent is particularly obvious when the registrant has stockpiled many names corresponding to famous company trademarks. Some individuals and companies have registered hundreds or even thousands of domain names, hoping to make money this way. But in virtually every case, the trademark owner has prevailed over the domain name pirate.

Though there have been many disputes involving the warehousing of domain names, several high-profile disputes have involved Dennis Toeppen. Toeppen has registered more than 100 domain names corresponding to trademarks owned by other companies, including Delta Airlines, Neiman Marcus, Eddie Bauer, Lufthansa, and others, often attempting to sell the domain names to such companies. Three times, courts have ruled against Toeppen when he was sued by large companies seeking to obtain domain names that had been first registered by Toeppen. In the first dispute, American Standard, Inc. sued Toeppen over the right to the domain name *americanstandard.com*. The federal court in the Central District of Illinois granted a preliminary injunction to American Standard, which now uses the site to promote its air-conditioning, automotive, medical systems, and plumbing businesses.

At about the same time, Intermatic, Inc. sued Toeppen over his registration of the domain name *intermatic.com*. As with the American Standard case, the federal court in the Northern District of Illinois held that Toeppen's use of the domain name *intermatic.com* constituted dilution of Intermatic's trademark rights in the Intermatic name, which had been used for its electronics business since 1941.

Considering the outcome in the first two disputes, it wasn't surprising when the federal court in the Central District of California handed Toeppen his third loss.[2] In December 1995, Panavision attempted to register the domain name *panavision.com*. But Panavision couldn't register the domain name because Toeppen had already registered it and had posted photographs of the city of Pana, Illinois, at that site.

On December 20, 1995, Panavision sent a letter to Toeppen telling him to stop using the domain name *panavision.com* because it infringed Panavision's trademark rights. Toeppen responded by mailing a letter from Illinois to Panavision in California stating that he had the right to continue using the domain name. Toeppen's letter continued:

> If your attorney has advised you otherwise, he is trying to screw you. He wants to blaze new trails in the legal frontier at your expense. Why do you want to fund your attorney's purchase of a new boat (or whatever) when you can facilitate the acquisition of "PanaVision.com" cheaply and simply instead?

Toeppen then offered to settle the matter if Panavision would pay $13,000 in exchange for the domain name. After Panavision refused Toeppen's offer, Toeppen registered the domain name *panaflex.com*, corresponding to Panavision's Panaflex trademark.

Panavision responded by filing a lawsuit against Toeppen in federal court in the Central District of California, claiming that Toeppen's registration and attempt to sell the domain names *panavision.com* and *panaflex.com* violated federal and state trademark dilution laws. Ruling on Panavision's motion for summary judgment, the district court concluded that Toeppen's actions constituted trademark dilution under both federal and state laws.

Toeppen appealed to the Court of Appeals for the Ninth Circuit. On appeal, Toeppen urged that the court in California could not exercise jurisdiction over him because he was a resident of Illinois and had not set foot in California. Before a court may exercise jurisdiction over a nonresident, there must be proof that the nonresident has had contacts with the state related to the dispute. As Toeppen pointed out, the courts had previously generally concluded that the mere ability to access a Web site in a distant location was insufficient to exercise personal jurisdiction. In other words, the ability to access Toeppen's *panavision.com* Internet site from California was not enough for California courts to exercise jurisdiction over him.

The Court of Appeals disagreed that Toeppen had insufficient contacts with the state of California. The court explained that Toeppen had engaged in a scheme to register domain names using the trademarks of California companies, including Panavision, for the apparent purpose of extorting fees from them. Toeppen knew that Panavision would suffer harm to its trademark rights in California, where its principal place of business was located. Because Toeppen's activities had the effect of harming a company in California, as he knew it would, the court there could exercise jurisdiction over him.

The Court of Appeals also confirmed that Toeppen's activities violated the Federal Trademark Dilution Act. A violation of the FTDA requires proof that (1) the trademark is famous, (2) the defendant has made a commercial use of the mark, (3) the defendant's use began after the mark became famous, and (4) the defendant's use dilutes the quality of the trademark by diminishing the capacity of the mark to identify and distinguish goods and services.

Toeppen did not dispute that Panavision was a famous trademark, but did argue that he had not made a commercial use of it. Rather, Toeppen contended, he had merely registered the domain name and posted pictures of Pana, Illinois. But the Court of Appeals disagreed that his use was not commercial. Toeppen's "business" was to register trademarks as domain names and then sell them to the rightful trademark owners. When Toeppen attempted to sell *panavision.com* to Panavision, he made a commercial use of Panavision's trademark.

Toeppen also argued that his registration of *panavision.com* did not dilute the quality of the Panavision trademark. But some members of Congress had expressly testified that the FTDA should be used in such cases. As Senator Patrick Leahy from Vermont testified, "It is my hope that this anti-dilution statute can help stem the use of deceptive Internet addresses taken by those who are choosing marks that are associated with the products and reputations of others." The court further observed that a significant purpose of domain names is to identify the entity that owns the Web site. Toeppen's registration of *panavision.com* prevented Panavision from developing its Internet presence under that name and put Panavision at Toeppen's mercy. Consequently, Toeppen violated the Federal Trademark Dilution Act and the California Anti-Dilution statute.

DOMAIN NAMES AND THE COMPUTER INDUSTRY

In an effort to reduce some of the disputes involving domain name "warehousers," NSI enacted rules limiting applicants to a single domain name and charging a $100 registration fee. Though NSI quickly withdrew the single registration limitation, it has kept the application fee. NSI also adopted an extrajudicial dispute resolution policy. Under NSI's Domain Name Dispute Policy, the owner of a federally registered trademark (or an equivalent from a foreign country) may challenge the use of an "identical" domain name by providing NSI with a copy of the trademark registration and proof that a written complaint has been sent to the domain name holder. If the trademark's effective date predates the domain name registration, the domain name holder will be given thirty days to provide proof that it also owns a federal or foreign trademark registration. If the domain name holder does not own a trademark registration, the name will be placed "on hold" so that neither party may use it until the dispute is resolved.[3]

NSI's measures stop well short of eliminating domain name disputes and have been thoroughly criticized. Some have complained that the NSI dispute policy leaves it to the parties to find their own solution to the dispute after the name has been placed on hold. Others have observed that it favors those who have obtained trademark registrations over those with valid trademark rights but no federal registrations. Even those with trademark registrations have limited rights under the policy because it only applies to domain names that are "identical" to registered trademarks. Further, many engineers and scientists objected to the fees for what had always been a free system.

In an attempt to address many of these concerns, the International Ad Hoc Committee (IAHC) developed a plan to add several new top-level domains to the existing *.com*, *.net*, and *.org* top-level domains. Ideally, the addition of new domains would create more possibilities for domain name registration and reduce the number of disputes. Initially, seven new domains were proposed:

.firm, for businesses or firms
.store, for businesses selling goods
.web, for Internet organizations
.arts, for cultural and entertainment entities
.rec, for recreational entities
.info, for information service entities
.nom, for individuals

The mere addition of new top-level domains obviously would not eliminate domain name disputes. In fact, by adding new registration possibilities, it may increase them rather than decrease them. But the IAHC proposal also contains features that would prevent the registration of domain names corresponding to famous trademarks held by others. In the event disputes were to arise, the IAHC plan contains dispute resolution measures designed to fully resolve the matter outside the courts. Though the IAHC plan is not perfect, it stands head and shoulders above the current NSI dispute policy.

Despite its many advantages, the U.S. government had thus far rejected the IAHC proposal in favor of a slower transition of the Internet from U.S. government to private control. The National Telecommunications and Information Administration (NTIA), the agency responsible for Internet matters, has instead decided to transition control of the Internet domain name system to the Internet Corporation for Assigned Names and Numbers (ICANN) a private, not-for-profit corporation that it created. In all likelihood, no new domain names and no new dispute-resolution procedures will be implemented during the transition period. The lack of attention to trademark matters likely stems, at least in part, from the NTIA's woeful misunderstanding of the current state of affairs. According to the NTIA, "trademark/domain name disputes arise very rarely on the Internet today."[4] Though this is obviously not the case, the NTIA is unlikely to address domain name dispute issues in the near term. Instead, the NTIA will leave it to ICANN to determine whether new top-level domains should be added and, if so, to implement them.

DOMAIN NAMES: A BRIEF SUMMARY OF THE LAW

Internet domain names include at least a "top-level" domain and a "second-level" domain. The top-level domain is the portion to the right of the "dot," such as *.com*, *.net*, or *.org*. The second-level domain is the portion to the left of the "dot" and often corresponds to a company's name or trademark under which it does business.

Registration and commercial use of a domain name that is similar or identical to another's trademark may constitute trademark infringement or may violate state and federal trademark dilution laws.

Notes

1. Sally M. Abel and Connie L. Ellerbach have compiled many domain name battles in "Trademark Issues in Cyberspace: The Brave New Frontier," available at *www.fenwick.com/pub/cyber.html.*

2. The litigation between Dennis Toeppen and Panavision is reported at *Panavision International, L.P. v. Toeppen,* 141 F.3d 1316 (9th Cir. 1998).

3. The current domain name dispute policy and information regarding the general domain name structure and registration system is outlined at the Network Solutions Internet site at *rs.internic.net.*

4. The white paper published by the National Telecommunications and Information Administration is published at *www.ntia.doc.gof/ntiahome/domainname/ 022098fedreg.txt.*

18

The Next Weapon: Software Patents

Everything that can be invented has been invented.
—Charles H. Duell, Commissioner, U.S. Patent Office, 1899

Charles H. Duell was apparently a man of remarkably little technological foresight, an unusual trait for the commissioner of the U.S. Patent Office. Duell certainly did not foresee the invention of computers, airplanes, television, rockets, and cell phones, just to name a few. Nor did Duell envision the more than five million other inventions that have received patents from the U.S. Patent and Trademark Office since the time of his statement. In all likelihood, there have been more inventions from the time of Duell's statement to the present than in all of history prior to his statement.

Although probably not acting upon Duell's conclusion, for many years the U.S. Patent and Trademark Office routinely denied patents for software patent applications. The Patent Office's actions regarding software patents stem in large part from the 1972 Supreme Court decision in *Gottschalk v. Benson*. In the *Gottschalk* decision, the Supreme Court upheld the Patent Office's rejection of a patent application claiming an invention in a software algorithm for converting numbers in binary-coded decimal format to binary format. The Supreme Court reasoned that because the invention was merely the incorporation of a pure mathematical algorithm into a computer program, granting a patent would virtually prevent others from using the formula.

The Patent Office interpreted the *Gottschalk* decision as the broad disapproval of software patents and implemented patent application guidelines that made it very difficult for inventors to obtain software patents. Most software companies concluded that software patents were unavailable and figured that copyright protection was sufficient in any event. Savvy patent practitioners, however, have found ways to successfully draft software patent applications. In most cases, software applications can be written with an emphasis on the electronic circuitry rather than the computer instructions, making them appear to be directed to electronic hardware inventions rather than software inventions. In this manner, a relatively small number of software patents were issued by the Patent Office despite its intentions to the contrary.

The Supreme Court slowly retreated from its extreme position in *Gottschalk* in subsequent decisions, explaining that *Gottschalk* was only intended to apply the long-standing principle that abstract physical properties (such as Einstein's law, that $E = mc^2$) or broad laws of nature (such as the concept of gravity) cannot be patented. In its 1981 decision in *Diamond v. Diehr*, the Supreme Court explained that its *Gottschalk* decision meant nothing more than that software that merely incorporates a mathematical formula cannot be patented. Though the courts and the Patent Office slowly gave more ground to software inventors each year, it was not until the 1994 Federal Circuit decision of *In re Alappat* that the patentability of software was confirmed once and for all.

THE BATTLE OVER PATENTABILITY OF SOFTWARE: *IN RE ALAPPAT*

Kuriappan Alappat, Edward Averill, and James Larson jointly invented a *rasterizer*, a device for improving the quality of the display in a digital oscilloscope. An oscilloscope screen operates much like a television picture tube, in which the screen is formed of an array of pixels that glow when illuminated by an electron beam projected from the rear of the cathode ray tube (CRT). To produce a single display picture, the electron beam is quickly scanned in a series of horizontal lines in a pattern that resembles the pattern of printed writing on a page—across from one side to the next, then down to the next line to repeat the horizontal scan. By illuminating only selected pixels during the course of a scan, the desired picture is produced.

The number of pixels on an oscilloscope screen is finite. Although the pixels are small and very close together, there is still some space between them. When horizontal or vertical lines are drawn on the screen, the discontinuities are difficult to detect. But when sloped or curved lines are displayed, the space between the pixels is more visible and the lines appear jagged. This effect is generally called "aliasing."

Alappat (and his co-inventors) invented a technique to reduce the effects of aliasing. In Alappat's invention, the illumination intensity of the electron beam is modified so that pixels lying close to but not on a desired line to be displayed glow less brightly than pixels lying directly on the intended line. Accordingly, the resulting waveform appears to be smoother.

Alappat's method for selecting whether particular pixels would be fully or partially illuminated was controlled by a mathematical formula. Quite simply, Alappat calculated the distance between each pixel and the waveform to be drawn by the oscilloscope. The illumination intensity of the pixel depended upon the calculated distance. According to the patent application, Alappat claimed the invention as

a rasterizer for converting vector list data representing sample magnitudes of an input waveform into anti-aliased pixel illumination intensity data to be displayed on a display means comprising:
  (a) means for determining the vertical distance between the endpoints of the vectors in the data list;
  (b) means for determining the elevation of a row of pixels that is spanned by the vector;
  (c) means for normalizing the distance and elevation; and
  (d) means for outputting illumination intensity data as a predetermined function of the normalized vertical distance and elevation.

Both the Patent Office and the Board of Patent Appeals and Interferences rejected Alappat's patent application for the above claim. An eight-member Board panel concluded that Alappat's claimed invention was a mathematical algorithm cloaked in language to make it appear structural. In particular, the Board held that Alappat's use of the "means for" language could not transform an unpatentable algorithm into a patentable machine. Because each step in the claimed invention was merely part of a mathematical algorithm, the invention was not patentable.

A full, or en banc, panel of the Federal Circuit Court of Appeals reviewed the decision of the Board. In most cases, federal appeals court panels are comprised of three judges. But in certain circumstances, generally when the issue is thought to be of particular importance, the entire court (12 judges) hears the appeal.

The Federal Circuit reversed the decision of the Patent Board.[1] The court held that it was improper for the Board to have considered each of the "means for" elements as algorithm steps rather than physical elements. In Alappat's case, the patent application provided examples of structures that could perform each of the steps in the claimed invention. Consequently, the claimed invention could be properly interpreted to be a combination of electronic circuit elements that could be configured to perform the steps recited in the claimed invention. As a machine, rather than as a pure mathematical algorithm, the invention was patentable.

In addition to interpreting the claimed invention as covering an electronic circuit capable of performing the recited steps, the court noted that it could be interpreted to define a software program capable of running on a general purpose computer. Nevertheless, the court affirmed the patentability of the invention, explaining that, "We have held that such programming creates a new machine, because a general purpose computer in effect becomes a special purpose computer once it is programmed to perform particular functions pursuant to instructions from program software." Thus, even if the Alappat invention were interpreted as an algorithm for a general purpose computer, it would be patentable.

The *Alappat* decision ended the confusion that persisted following previous decisions that denied patents for software inventions on the basis that they were merely mathematical algorithms. Following *Alappat*, the question is no longer whether the claimed invention appears to be a mathematical algorithm. Rather, the focus is on whether the invention claims a patentable application of a mathematical algorithm as opposed to an unpatentable algorithm by itself. As long as the algorithm is described as running on a general purpose computer or some other tangible device, the invention is patentable subject matter.

SOFTWARE PATENT CONFUSION: THE COMPTON'S MULTIMEDIA CASE

The result in *In re Alappat* was probably inevitable. Although the patentability of software remained in doubt prior to *Alappat*, patent attorneys were becoming adept at drafting patent applications in a way that would hide the true nature of the software invention. Accordingly, the number of software-related patent applications tripled from 1988 to 1994, the year of the *Alappat* decision. Whether the courts liked it or not, the simple fact was that software patents were being applied for and obtained in record numbers. Even a contrary decision in *Alappat* would not likely have reversed this trend.

The *Alappat* decision produced additional benefits not likely foreseen by the court. The Patent Office carefully categorizes every possible type of invention into one of thousands of classes. When a new patent application is filed, it is a fairly simple matter for the assigned patent examiner to retrieve previously issued patents from the classes that are generally related to the subject matter of the application. The examiner can then compare the claimed invention to previous inventions, called the "prior art," to determine whether the claimed invention is new and unobvious, making it patentable.

But at the time of the *Alappat* decision, there was no classification system adequate to deal with software inventions. Further, many software patents did not even include the words "computer" or "software" within them, in an effort to avoid a "mathematical algorithm" rejection from the Patent and Trademark Office. This practice has caused software inventions to be classified in an awkward, inconsistent manner, making it extremely difficult for patent examiners to search for the prior art necessary to properly evaluate the patentability of new software patent applications. Following the *Alappat* decision, additional classes have been added for software inventions. In addition, patent attorneys are now able to prepare software patent applications openly, using the terms "computer" and "software" that make them easier to locate in a search.

Some opportunistic software companies that have actively pursued software patent applications have reaped the benefits of the Patent Office's shortcomings. In 1993, Compton's New Media, Inc. was the beneficiary of the Patent Office's inability to thoroughly search the prior art to determine whether Compton's claimed invention was patentable.

In the 1980s, Compton's spent $8.5 million to develop computer database and retrieval technology used to produce Compton's multimedia encyclopedia that linked photos, sounds, and video animations to text. Compton's filed a patent application on October 26, 1989, for an invention called, "Multimedia search system using a plurality of entry path means which indicate interrelatedness of information." In essence, the application claimed an invention in the computerized retrieval of text, photos, audio, animation, and video information from multimedia databases.

The Patent Office issued a patent for the invention, and Compton's interpreted the patent broadly. Compton's CEO Stanley Frank asserted that the patent applied to software running on all new platforms, including "the interactive digital multimedia highway of the future and interactive television," if the software searched multiple databases and was interactive. Compton's planned to require virtually the entire industry to pay a small royalty for using the patented technology.[2] Though the industry reacted with disbelief at the alleged breadth of the patent, it was hardly the first broad, or "pioneering," patent issued by the Patent and Trademark Office.

The apparent breadth of the Compton's patent and Compton's enforcement plans caused an uproar throughout the software world.[3] The multimedia community in particular protested in unison. Tom Lopez, president of the Interactive Multimedia Association, complained that "the patent system has cast a cloud over our emerging industry, an ambitious and motivated industry which seeks to transform the way we play, learn, think, and communicate."

Many software companies and software organizations that had previously taken positions against the patentability of software viewed the Compton's patent as further proof of the dangers of software patents. According to these antipatent groups, the issuance of software patents forces innovative software companies to expend valuable resources to defend themselves against the threat of software patents.[4] Because of the perceived threat presented by the Compton's multimedia patent, many software companies and programming organizations sought to find proof that the patent was invalid.[5] These individuals and organizations flooded the Patent and Trademark Office with complaints and arguments against the patentability of the Compton's patent.

In view of the industry clamor and the evidence presented, Patent and Trademark Office Commissioner Bruce Lehman announced on December 16, 1993, that the Patent and Trademark Office would reexamine the Compton's patent. The patent statutes contain provisions that allow patents to be reexamined when the Patent and Trademark Office is presented with written materials that were not previously considered by the Patent and Trademark Office and that tend to show that the invention is not patentable. Despite the statutory authority, the reexamination by the Patent and Trademark Office was an unusual step. In most cases, patent reexaminations are formally requested by a third party that files a reexamination request and pays the required fee of several thousand dollars. Approximately 100,000 patents issue annually; the Patent and Trademark Office initiates reexaminations without a formal third-party request only about a half-dozen times each year.

The Patent and Trademark Office conducted public hearings to consider arguments and gather "prior art," documents and other evidence showing that the subject matter of the Compton's patent was in public use or otherwise known to others before Compton's filed its patent application. After gathering information, the Patent and Trademark Office rejected all the claims of the Compton's patent. Compton's responded to the rejections, presenting new claims for its invention that attempted to limit the scope of the patent to CD-ROM based encyclopedias. Nevertheless, the Patent and Trademark Office eventually rejected all of Compton's claims, citing eighteen pre-Compton's patents and thirty-three other prior art references.

SOFTWARE PATENTS AND THE COMPUTER INDUSTRY

Until the early 1990s, the computer industry, and software companies in particular, operated under the general assumption that software was not patentable. Many companies and organizations even argued that patents were unnecessary or undesirable for computer software. Few software companies sought and obtained software patents, and virtually none developed a "patent culture" that systematically sought to protect software inventions with patents.

After decades of doubt regarding the patentability of computer software, court battles in the early 1990s, particularly including *In re Alappat*, confirmed the patentability of software. The software industry has responded by filing patent applications in record numbers. Despite years of sharp criticism from some software companies and industry groups, software patents are now increasingly embraced as an important means to protect software inventions and license technology to others.

Those few companies that had previously actively pursued patents find themselves at a distinct advantage over those without a similar patent mind-set. Many companies with a strong patent culture enjoy a portfolio of patents and a new confidence that the courts will not invalidate their software patents merely because they are for software inventions. Software companies without a similar patent mentality must act quickly to develop practices to patent and protect their inventions or risk being left behind the competition.

Many software companies also lack the practices necessary to avoid patent infringement. In the absence of patents, it has been generally safe to assume that software companies could make and sell any product as long as it was not copied from another company. But patents give their owners the right to prevent others from making, using, offering for sale, or selling the patented invention regardless of whether there has been any copying. In light of the explosion of software patent applications, software companies can no longer afford to ignore patents as a source of potential liability.

Finally, as the Compton's multimedia case clearly illustrates, many of the software patents that have been granted by the U.S. Patent and Trademark Office may have been improvidently granted. Unfortunately, there is no way of knowing how many improper patents have been granted, nor how many will be granted in the future. Although many of those patents may ultimately be invalidated, they are legally presumed to be valid in the absence of clear and convincing proof to the contrary. It is reasonable to assume that the software industry will be adversely affected by companies that seek to enforce, however un-wittingly, these flimsy patents against their competitors.

SOFTWARE PATENTS: A BRIEF SUMMARY OF THE LAW

Computer software is patentable as long as it is new and unobvious and the invention is claimed as a process, machine, article of manufacture, or composition of matter, rather than a mere unapplied mathematical algorithm or law of nature. As with patents for other subject matter, a software patent owner has the right to prevent others from making, using, offering for sale, or selling the subject matter claimed in the patent for a term of twenty years after the date of the patent application.

Notes

1. The Federal Circuit decision for *In re Alappat* may be found at *In re Alappat*, 33 F.3d 1526 (Fed. Cir. 1994); the Supreme Court case in *Gottschalk* may be found at *Gottschalk v. Benson*, 409 U.S. 63 (1972).

2. Compton's intent to enforce its patent broadly and the money spent to develop the multimedia technology was published in the *San Francisco Chronicle* on November 15, 1993, and can be found on the Internet at *www.base.com/software-patents/articles/compton.html*.

3. There was substantial press coverage of the Compton's multimedia patent case, including Jim Milliot, "USPTO Again Rejects Compton's Patent Claims," *Publishers Weekly* (November 7, 1994), p. 14; Francy Blackwood, "Multimedia Multiplies Legal Issues of Patent, Copyright," *San Francisco Business Times* (October 14, 1994), sec. A, p. 2.

4. The League for Programming Freedom maintains an Internet site containing arguments against the patentability of software and condemning the Compton's patent at *ftp.sunset.se/ftp/pub/doc/lpf/corporate-handout.*

5. Many individuals and groups sought to collect prior art to invalidate the Compton's patent. One Internet posting still available is at *fhi-berlin.mpg.de/amiga/ar/ar138/p1-7html.*

Hardware Battles

VI

19

Computer Chip Wars

For many years, Intel has been the industry leader in the computer chip market, particularly including the market for microprocessors. As the industry leader, Intel has poured substantial resources into research and development, producing hundreds of Intel patents covering its computer chips. Despite Intel's extensive patent portfolio, competitors have found ways to make and sell computer chips without infringing Intel's patents. The ability to sell certain computer chips without infringing Intel patents is the result of Intel's extensive cross-licensing and the numerous court battles interpreting those cross-licenses.

PATENT LICENSING

The patent statutes provide that patent owners may prevent others from making, using, offering for sale, selling, and importing a patented invention. Although not expressly provided by statute, patent owners may also license all or any subset of these rights to others. For example, a patent holder may license another (the "licensee") to make and use a patented invention, but not to sell it to others. Likewise, a patent holder may allow the licensee to issue sublicenses to others, or may expressly prohibit such sublicensing.

Companies use patent licenses in a variety of ways and for a variety of reasons. Some companies are skilled at developing new patentable devices but lack either the finances, manufacturing resources, or marketing abilities to turn the idea into a successful product. Others may use licensing as a means for generating revenue that requires little or no overhead. Still others may use licensing as a means of gaining access to technology owned by others, licensing the right to use patented technology in exchange for rights to use patented technology owned by others. This latter form of licensing, in which two companies license each other, is called "cross-licensing."

As with other forms of licensing, cross-licensing may arise in several ways. In some cases, two companies may simply wish to share technology. In other cases, each company may hold patents that prevent the other from making and selling products without infringement. By cross-licensing, the companies each agree to allow the other to make and sell such products without fear of being sued for patent infringement. Cross-licenses frequently include clauses that grant rights under additional patents each company obtains in the future, to avoid the necessity of drafting a new cross-license with each new patent.

COMPUTER CHIP WARS: *INTEL v. ULSI*

Cross-licenses among several major computer companies—and the court battles that interpreted those cross-licenses—have played a major role in computer chip manufacturing. Many of these court battles involve cross-licenses between Intel and other companies. Intel owns many patents related to the design and operation of microprocessor chips, including math coprocessors and related devices. In January 1983, Intel and Hewlett-Packard entered in to a cross-licensing agreement with the stated objective to "increase their freedom of design." Under the agreement, each granted the other irrevocable rights under all patents and patent applications having effective filing dates prior to January 1, 2000. Intel entered into similar agreements with other major computer companies, including an agreement with IBM in October 1989.

Apparently, Intel did not anticipate the market dynamics that would enable competing chip makers to use these Intel licensees to manufacture computer chips. After a period of rapid growth in the 1970s and 1980s, the computer industry became saturated with semiconductor manufacturing capability. Considering that a typical computer chip fabrication facility, or foundry, costs more than $1 billion to construct, companies without foundries of their own were reluctant to build them. At the same time, foundry owners found themselves with excess capacity and expensive overhead. Computer chip companies without foundries of their own eagerly turned to these foundries with excess capacity.

The manufacturing capacity was not the only attractive feature of many foundries. Intel competitors such as Cyrix Corp. and ULSI System Technology, Inc. typically were not licensed to use Intel's most important patents. Consequently, these companies risked being sued for patent infringement if they made and sold microprocessors or other devices covered by Intel patents. But in some cases, the foundry owners were also licensed to use important Intel patents. By using foundries owned by Intel licensees—for example, IBM or HP—Intel competitors reasoned that they could avoid infringing Intel's patents without obtaining a license of their own.

In August 1988 ULSI entered an agreement with HP in which HP agreed to manufacture math coprocessors for ULSI. As is common in such foundry agreements, ULSI provided HP with proprietary design specifications encoded on magnetic tape. HP used the data on the tape to imprint a design pattern onto a quartz glass plate, creating a "reticle" or lithographic mask that it used to etch the circuit layout of the ULSI circuit layout into blank silicon wafers. HP then manufactured and shipped the coprocessor chips to ULSI for resale as ULSI products.

Intel became aware of ULSI's coprocessor sales in February 1991. In July 1991 Intel filed a lawsuit in the U.S. District Court for the District of Oregon, alleging that ULSI's coprocessors infringed an Intel patent.[1] Shortly after filing the complaint against ULSI, Intel filed a motion for a preliminary injunction, seeking an order preventing ULSI from continuing to sell its coprocessors pending trial of the matter by the court. The trial court granted Intel's motion, concluding that Intel was likely to succeed at trial and that the harm to Intel in not granting the injunction outweighed the harm to ULSI in granting the motion.

ULSI appealed the preliminary injunction order to the Court of Appeals for the Federal Circuit. The Court of Appeals decided that the question of infringement depended on whether there was a sale of coprocessors from HP to ULSI. Once there is an authorized sale of a patented product, the "patent exhaustion" doctrine places the product beyond the reach of the patent owner. As ULSI argued, the cross-license between HP and Intel authorized HP to manufacture coprocessors for ULSI without infringing Intel patents. Because ULSI purchased the coprocessors legally from an authorized source, ULSI was legally authorized to dispose of them in any manner, including by selling them to consumers.

Intel argued that the "patent exhaustion" doctrine did not apply because HP did not sell the coprocessors to ULSI. Rather, Intel asserted, HP provided fabrication services to ULSI. ULSI designed its coprocessor without HP's assistance, and retained ownership of the design. Accordingly, HP could not have sold a product to ULSI because HP held no ownership rights in the coprocessors.

The Court of Appeals agreed with ULSI, holding that the agreement between HP and ULSI was a sale, triggering the patent exhaustion doctrine. The HP-ULSI contract was filled with references to the sale of goods, with few references to services. Regardless of whether HP or ULSI originated the design, HP manufactured goods and sold them to ULSI.

Intel did not dispute that its cross-license with HP was broad enough to allow HP to manufacture the coprocessor chips. Intel could have limited the cross-license with HP in a manner that restricted HP's ability to serve as a foundry. Presumably, Intel received sufficient consideration in return for the patent rights it granted to HP. But because the cross-license gave HP the unfettered right to make and sell products embodying Intel's patented inventions, HP could sell coprocessors to ULSI even if ULSI originated the design. Consequently, the Court of Appeals reversed the district court's preliminary injunction order.

COMPUTER CHIP LAW AND THE COMPUTER INDUSTRY

During the past decade, industry leader Intel has been involved in many other lawsuits related to the alleged infringement of Intel's computer chip patents. For example, in 1996 the Federal Circuit Court of Appeals rendered a decision in a dispute between Intel and Cyrix Corp. that closely resembled the earlier *Intel v. ULSI* case.[2] Cyrix designs and sells microprocessors that compete with Intel's microprocessors. Like ULSI, Cyrix did not have a facility of its own in the early 1990s, so it contracted with other companies for its manufacturing. Cyrix specifically chose foundries that were licensed to use Intel's patents.

Two of the foundries used by Cyrix were IBM and SGS-Thompson Microelectronics, Inc. Both IBM and SGS-Thompson held licenses from Intel allowing them to make and sell products that were covered by Intel patents. Although the licenses differed from the license between HP and Intel, the differences did not prevent Intel or SGS-Thompson from providing foundry services to Cyrix.

To a significant extent, Intel's licensing battles shaped the computer chip industry today. Patents covering Intel's products are arguably more important than patents held by those who are chasing Intel. If Intel had not licensed many of its patents, Intel could have prevented its competitors from making or selling competing computer chips that are covered by its patents. But by licensing its patents to companies with substantial manufacturing capabilities, Intel helped to create a market in which its competitors can gain access to important Intel patents and avoid the nearly insurmountable cost of building their own fabrication facilities at the same time. As a result, companies like Cyrix, AMD, and

ULSI are able to compete with Intel without fear of infringing any Intel patents.

COMPUTER CHIPS: A BRIEF SUMMARY OF THE LAW

Computer chips are covered by a variety of laws, including patent laws and the Semiconductor Chip Protection Act. In many cases, the major computer chip manufacturers have cross-licensed one another, enabling newcomers to produce competing chips by having them manufactured by a licensed foundry.

Notes

1. The central case involving Intel and ULSI is reported at *Intel Corp. v. ULSI System Technology, Inc.*, 995 F.2d 1566 (Fed. Cir. 1993).
2. The recent Cyrix and SGS lawsuit against Intel is reported at *Cyrix Corp. v. Intel Corp.*, 77 F.3d 1381 (Fed. Cir. 1996).

20

Hardware and Software Enhancement Devices

Though some contend that the largest room in the world is the room for improvement, others disagree. After a product is introduced—even a successful product—purchasers find flaws or make suggestions for improvements or enhancements. Sometimes, the manufacturer is quick to improve its product to fill consumer demand. But in other instances, a competitor may beat the original manufacturer to the punch by marketing an enhancement device aimed at enhancing the product or overcoming its shortcomings. In such cases, the question is not whether there is room for improvement, but who may fill the room.

In the software industry, a string of cases has helped answer the question of whether a competitor may develop and market a product intended to modify or enhance an existing product. Although these legal battles provide unclear guidance, it is possible to market enhancement devices, depending on what was copied from the original work to produce them.

SPEED-UP KITS: *MIDWAY v. ARTIC INTERNATIONAL*

One of the earliest enhancement devices lawsuits focused on the enormously popular Galaxian video game, first created in 1980. Midway Manufacturing Company manufactured the Galaxian video games for sale in the United States, and sold far more Galaxian games than any other, with the sole exception of its Pac-Man games. Whereas a typical video game production run was 1,500 to 2,000 units, Midway sold 40,000 Galaxian games and 80,000 Pac-Man games in the first two years.

Artic International found a way to capitalize on Midway's success with the Galaxian games. Artic sold a "speed-up" kit that modified the Galaxian game in several ways. When the speed-up kit was installed, it increased the number of aliens that attacked the player's space ship, caused the aliens to move faster, and instructed the aliens to drop a greater number of bombs on the player's ship. As a result, the speed-up kit made the Galaxian game more difficult to play, dramatically reducing the average play time and increasing revenues. According to Artic's advertisements, the speed-up kits would double the income from a Galaxian game.

The speed-up kit was constructed on a small printed circuit board that was designed to be inserted into a socket within the Galaxian mother board that normally held a "piggyback" memory board. Once installed, the speed-up kit replaced the memory board that was included with the original machine. Programming devices called EEPROMs (electrically erasable programmable read only memory) within the speed-up kit contained the necessary code to alter the Galaxian game. Because the speed-up kit was a replacement of portions of the original Galaxian code, much of the speed-up kit's source code was identical to the source code of the board being replaced. In fact, of the 10K of source code on the original board, all but 488 bytes were the same on the replacement board.

Midway sued Artic in federal court in the Northern District of Illinois and requested a preliminary injunction preventing Artic from selling its speed-up kits during the pendency of the litigation.[1] On March 10, 1982, the court granted Midway's motion, ordering Artic to cease its sales of the speed-up kits until the dispute was finally resolved at trial.

Artic appealed the decision to the Court of Appeals for the Seventh Circuit. At the time, it was unclear whether video games qualified as "audiovisual works" and were therefore capable of copyright protection. The copyright statute defined the term as "works that consist of a series of related images which are intrinsically intended to be shown by the use of machines or devices such as projectors, viewers, or electronic equipment, together with accompanying sounds, if any, regardless of the nature of the material objects, such as films or tapes, in which the works are embodied." Artic argued that the term "audiovisual works" aimed at movies, films, and similar media in which the "series of related images" is always displayed in a fixed sequence. If so, video games would not qualify for copyright protection because the images appear on the screen in a different order virtually every time the game is played. The Court of Appeals disagreed, observing that revisions to the copyright act were intended to apply to new technologies such as video games even if video games were not expressly mentioned in the Act. Nothing in the Act expressly required audiovisual works to be displayed in the same order every time, and the court was unwilling to interpret the act that way in view of the Congressional intent to apply copyright protection to new technologies.

Undeterred, Artic next argued that screen displays did not fall within the scope of the copyright laws because the author of the video game did not create the actual screen displays, but rather the player created them while playing the game. According to Artic, the "authorship" involved in video game displays belonged to the player who manipulated the game's controls, much as an author arranges words from a dictionary to write a book or an artist selects paints from a palette to create a painting.

But the court believed that playing a video game is less like painting than it is like changing the channels on a television. When playing a video game, the player cannot select any desired arrangement of displays. Rather, the player can only influence the game by selecting from among the various display arrangements the game creator has allowed. Similarly, one watching a movie on a videotape can rewind, fast-forward, or pause, but is limited in the ability to alter the original work. Unlike an artist creating a painting, the range of choices in video game displays has been constrained by the programmer.

Finally, the court held that Artic's speed-up kits were infringing derivative works of Midway's original Galaxian game. Artic tried to persuade the court that it did not create a derivative work, but only caused the original work to be played faster. Just as there is nothing unlawful about playing a record at 45 RPM when it was designed to be played at 33 RPM, Artic contended, the use of speed-up kits should not infringe the copyrights in the original game. When a record is played faster, it simply speeds up the original work without altering it and without creating a new work. But Artic actually created a new work, altering the original source code. In addition, there was a tremendous market for the speed-up kits, evincing their status as separate, derivative works. Consequently, the speed-up kits infringed Midway's rights in its copyrighted Galaxian game.

ADD-ON DEVICES: *LEWIS GALOOB TOYS v. NINTENDO*

Several years after the speed-up kit litigation, another enhancement device dispute was brewing. In the late 1980s, Nintendo developed its extremely popular Nintendo Entertainment System, or "NES," home video game system. The NES system was designed to accept video game cartridges containing video games produced by Nintendo or by others under license from Nintendo. It included a control pad used by players to control the play of the game.

Lewis Galoob Toys manufactured the Game Genie, a device that allowed players to alter up to three features of a Nintendo game. For example, by using the Game Genie, a player could increase the number of lives of the player's character, increase the speed at which the character moves, and allow the character to float over obstacles. Players could select from among a variety of modifications by entering codes contained in the Game Genie Programming Manual and Code Book, or they could experiment with variations of those codes.

The Game Genie was designed to be inserted between a game cartridge and the NES. It functioned by blocking the values for particular data and replacing those values with new ones. For example, by entering the proper code from the Code Book, the value that controls the character's strength could be blocked and replaced with a higher value, making the character invincible. Because of the way it was designed, the Game Genie did not contain the source code from the NES games and did not alter the data stored in the game cartridges themselves.

Galoob sued Nintendo in the U.S. District Court in Los Angeles, seeking a declaratory judgment of noninfringement.[2] As with the speed-up kit dispute, the question before the court was whether the Game Genie, by altering the play of the NES games, created an infringing derivative work of the original NES games. After a "bench trial"— meaning no jury—Judge Fern Smith ruled that the Game Genie did not create a derivative work and therefore did not infringe any Nintendo copyrights.

Nintendo appealed to the Court of Appeals for the Ninth Circuit. The central issue on appeal was again whether the Game Genie was a derivative work of the original Nintendo games. Nintendo contended that the Game Genie altered the display of the Nintendo games, thereby creating a derivative work of the original games. But the court disagreed, for two primary reasons. First, the court observed that the Game Genie was incapable of producing any displays by itself, primarily because it did not include any code from original Nintendo games. The court stressed that a derivative work must incorporate some portion of the original work. Second, although the Game Genie enhanced or altered the video displays created in the NES system, those displays were transitory and not in some "concrete or permanent form."

Nintendo argued that the Game Genie was similar to the Galaxian speed-up kit, which also modified the displays of a video game. Despite this general similarity, the devices were different in the eyes of the court.

The speed-up kit, unlike the Game Genie, contained some of the original Galaxian source code and was designed to replace a Galaxian memory board. The court also expressed concern that technological advances might be chilled by finding that the Game Genie infringed. Innovations that build on previous works, without incorporating the original works in a permanent form and without replacing demand for the original works, should be encouraged and are seldom infringing derivative works.

ADDITIONAL GAME LEVELS: *MICRO STAR v. FORMGEN*

A more recent enhancement devices dispute again focused on video games, but this time in the form of games stored on CD-ROMs for personal computers. FormGen, Inc. produced the popular Duke Nukem 3D video game for personal computers. Duke Nukem 3D is a "first person" style game in which the player's character makes its way through a maze while shooting aliens and overcoming obstacles. The game comes with several maze levels, but it also allows users to create their own additional levels with tailored scenery, aliens, and obstacles.

The Duke Nukem 3D software includes three major components, including the game engine, the source art library, and "MAP" files used by the game engine to build the mazes and invoke aliens and obstacles. The MAP files contain coded descriptions of the mazes in great detail, but do not include the actual artwork for the mazes themselves. In order to build the mazes, the game engine reads instructions from the MAP files and uses them to access the corresponding artwork contained in an art library.

Many consumers used the Duke Nukem 3D build editor to create their own mazes. Under FormGen's encouragement and approval, a substantial number of user-created levels were posted on the Internet for others to download and use. Micro Star, recognizing the popularity of the user-created levels, downloaded 300 of them and sold them on a compact disk called "Nuke It." After FormGen complained that the Nuke It CD infringed its copyrights, Micro Star sued FormGen, seeking a declaratory judgment of noninfringement.[3] FormGen counterclaimed and filed a motion with the court asking for a preliminary injunction order barring the sale and distribution of the Nuke It CD.

After the trial court denied FormGen's request for a preliminary injunction, FormGen appealed to the Ninth Circuit Court of Appeals—the same court that decided the Game Genie appeal. Under its previous ruling in the Game Genie case, a derivative work must exist in a concrete or permanent form and must incorporate some protected material from the original work. Micro Star argued that it did not create a derivative work because the mazes did not meet either of these requirements.

The court concluded that the Nuke It CD met both requirements. The MAP files on the Nuke It CD were obviously in a concrete or permanent form. Micro Star conceded that the data on its CD was permanent, but countered that its CD did not contain the displays themselves but instead contained MAP files that would be used to generate the displays. As in the Game Genie case, Micro Star argued, the Nuke It CD was simply used by the Duke Nukem 3D software to modify the video displays. But the court believed that the MAP files went farther than the Game Genie. Although they did not contain the artwork themselves, the MAP files effectively contained complete descriptions of the visual displays. Just as sheet music would constitute a "concrete and permanent form" of a copyrighted sound recording, the MAP files were a concrete and permanent form of the Duke Nukem 3D mazes.

Micro Star argued that even if the MAP files amounted to visual displays in permanent form, they did not satisfy the second requirement because they did not incorporate protected material from the original Duke Nukem 3D work. Unlike the Galaxians speed-up kits, the Nuke It MAP files did not contain source code from the original work and were not intended to replace the original source code. The Ninth Circuit, however, held that a work need not incorporate lines of code from the original work in order to satisfy this requirement. A copyright owner owns more than the exact words or lines of code used. The author also owns the story itself and the right to create sequels. The MAP files amounted to sequels in the adventures of Duke Nukem, and therefore incorporated protected material from the Duke Nukem 3D game.

The Ninth Circuit Court of Appeals also concluded that Micro Star's copying was not a fair use. For some technical reasons, the Court of Appeals observed that the outcome in the *Galoob* case was not binding precedent even though it was decided by the same court. With the *Galoob* decision out of the way, the court had little difficulty finding the use was not fair. In analyzing the fair use factors, it reasoned that the use was for financial gain; the original work was fictional and entitled to strong protection; unique, expressive aspects of the original work were taken; and the amount and importance of what was taken was substantial. The Micro Star CD also hindered FormGen's ability to create and sell its own CDs containing game levels, cementing the court's conclusion that the use was unfair.

ENHANCEMENT DEVICES AND THE COMPUTER INDUSTRY

The court decisions regarding enhancement devices are confusing at best. There have been relatively few enhancement device disputes and only a handful of court decisions, and those decisions are difficult to reconcile. Although it is possible to analyze them with the benefit of hindsight and to craft rules that apparently can be followed to avoid infringement, there is little certainty and much risk. Considering the risk, the safest route has been to obtain a license from the manufacturer of the primary product allowing the sale of the enhancement device.

The industry is filled with enhancement devices of various types, but most of them are of the hardware variety, rather than software. Devices that borrow original programming code are far more likely to infringe a software copyright than those that manipulate more functional or physical attributes. While there have been many competing computer programs, including competing video games, few, if any, have attempted to create sequels or game levels for a competitor's games. Following the Micro Star decision, that industry trend is likely to continue for a long time.

HARDWARE AND SOFTWARE ENHANCEMENT DEVICES: A BRIEF SUMMARY OF THE LAW

Because the law regarding enhancement devices has been established in a handful of court decisions, there are some sketchy guidelines but no clear rules. From the decisions thus far, it appears that enhancement devices that contain original source code and that are intended to replace an original component are likely to infringe copyrights in the original program. Likewise, programs that could be considered sequels or that provide additional adventure "levels" are very likely to infringe. Other hardware and software enhancement devices that may alter the operation of the original program *may* avoid copyright infringement in certain instances, depending on how the device functions and whether the result can be considered a derivative work.

Notes

1. The Midway case is reported at *Midway Mfg. Co. v. Artic Int'l*, 704 F.2d 1009 (7th Cir. 1983).

2. The Galoob case is reported at *Lewis Galoob Toys, Inc. v. Nintendo of America, Inc.*, 964 F.2d 965 (9th Cir. 1992).

3. The Duke Nukem case is reported at *Micro Star v. FormGen, Inc.*, 9th Cir., No. 96-56426, September 11, 1998.

21

Peripheral Devices

There have been countless battles involving a virtually endless range of peripheral devices, including mice, touch pads, monitors, disk drives, CD-ROM cleaners, storage devices, and nearly every other imaginable device. The legal subject matter of such cases is similarly broad, involving both design and utility patents, copyrights, trade secrets, misappropriation, and other legal theories. But perhaps no category of peripheral battles has caused a greater stir than the litigation over devices alleged to cause repetitive stress injury (RSI).

REPETITIVE STRESS INJURY BATTLES

RSI comes in a variety of forms and is known by a variety of names. Besides RSI, some refer to it as cumulative trauma disorder (CTD), repetitive motion injury, or carpal tunnel syndrome, a particular form of RSI. RSI is a form of injury linked to the performance of specific repetitive tasks and is particularly common in assembly line, meat packing, sewing, and computer work. When such repetitive tasks are performed, soft tissues such as muscles, nerves, and tendons become irritated and inflamed. In an extreme case, the irritation can cause permanent tissue damage.[1]

Many of the risk factors for RSI apply to those who spend their days working with computers. Repetitive typing movements and awkward, static, or constrained postures associated with computer workstations have been linked to RSI. Although RSI can affect any part of the body, the most common form among computer operators appears to be associated with the arms, wrists, and hands that are continually bent or flexed over a computer keyboard. The statistics for carpal tunnel syndrome are staggering. More than one million new office visits are made to physicians each year, resulting in more than 250,000 operations for the treatment of carpal tunnel syndrome.[2]

Naturally, the lion's share of RSI litigation is aimed at the purported cause of carpal tunnel syndrome, that is, poorly designed keyboards. For the most part, the keyboard manufacturers have fared well so far. Many of the RSI lawsuits filed have been flawed for one reason or another. In many cases, plaintiffs alleging keyboard-related injuries simply wait too long to file their lawsuits. Though the length of time varies among the states, lawsuits to recover damages for personal injuries typically must be filed within three years of the time the claim "accrues." Some states define the accrual of the injury as the date of the injury; others define it as the date of the discovery of the injury or the date of the discovery of the defendant's wrongful act. Regardless of its definition, those with RSI injuries must act diligently to investigate the source of the injuries and file a lawsuit or risk being barred by the statute of limitations.

In other cases, despite diligent inquiry, some plaintiffs have been unable to determine the proper party to sue. Keyboards and other peripheral devices are sometimes manufactured without trademarks or other identifying marks that would enable an injured worker to determine the manufacturer. Injured workers have occasionally been unable to determine the manufacturer in such cases, leaving them without a legal remedy.

In other cases, injured workers simply cannot prevail on the merits of their cases. Some plaintiffs have sued their employers, rather than keyboard manufacturers, under the Americans with Disabilities Act (ADA). To prevail in such a lawsuit, the injured worker must prove that the employer did not provide "reasonable accommodations" to the known physical or mental limitations of the otherwise qualified employee with a disability, unless such an accommodation would impose an undue hardship upon the operation of the business.[3] Where the employers have responded by providing at least some accommodations such as work breaks and wrist rests, employees have generally lost.

Despite the frequent flaws in their cases, plaintiffs have not been bashful about seeking damages. Typically, injured workers have sought damages in the millions as compensation for the pain and suffering. In some cases, spouses have joined in the fray, suing their spouse's employer for loss of "services, society, and consortium" and seeking compensatory and punitive damages. Though it is difficult to put a price on loss of "services, society, and consortium," one plaintiff pegged it at $500,000 plus $10,000,000 in punitive damages.[4]

Despite the frequent flaws, many injured workers have apparently meritorious cases and some have claimed sizable jury awards. In one case against Digital Equipment Corporation, a jury reportedly awarded a former secretary $5.3 million for injuries that were allegedly incurred using DEC keyboards. At the time, hers was considered to be the largest award in the United States for injuries related to carpal tunnel syndrome.

PERIPHERAL DEVICES AND THE COMPUTER INDUSTRY

There are now a wide range of peripheral devices available to reduce the risk of RSI or other equipment-related injuries in the workplace. Perhaps most visible are the ergonomic keyboards that are increasingly popular. Other devices aimed at reducing workplace injury include chairs and desks, mice and other pointing devices, lighting and antiglare devices, and wristpads. Some companies are also incorporating software solutions such as software timers to remind workers to take a break and voice recognition software to reduce the need for keyboarding.

Presumably, many of these products would have been developed even without the threat of litigation. Nevertheless, the tens of thousands of RSI-related lawsuits filed each year have undoubtedly spurred demand for such products, hastening the pace of development. Though some may consider the RSI litigation to be a considerable waste of time and money, it has certainly helped to create safer, more comfortable workplaces.

PERIPHERAL DEVICES: A BRIEF SUMMARY OF THE LAW

Peripheral devices, particularly including keyboards and mice, have been blamed for countless repetitive stress injuries, leading to tens of thousands of lawsuits. In most cases, the lawsuits allege that the product manufacturers negligently designed the products or the employers were negligent in not providing safer products for the workers. As a relatively new area of litigation, the general rules in such cases are still being fleshed out.

Notes

1. Many of the court decisions involving RSI provide useful background summaries of RSI, carpal tunnel syndrome, and other disorders. One concise example is reported at *Rotolo v. Digital Equipment Corporation*, 1998 U.S. App. Lexis 17042 (1998).

2. Statistics on RSI are widely available in a variety of places, including several Internet sites devoted to carpal tunnel syndrome and other related disorders. One useful site is at *www.tifaq.com*.

3. In *Beck v. University of Wisconsin Board of Regents*, 75 F.3d 1130 (7th Cir. 1995), the University provided accomodations including reduced work loads and wrist rests, which were considered important in the court's ruling in favor of the University.

4. The lawsuit cited in the text for its claims of loss of consortium is reported at *McIntire v. American Telephone & Telegraph Corp.*, 1996 U.S. App. Lexis 26658 (1996).

Future Battles

The Year 2000 Problem

Though many legal battles have affected the computer industry, perhaps no category of legal battles will influence the computer industry as deeply as the coming year 2000 battles. For decades, software everywhere has used a two-digit field to store the year related to particular events. With only two digits, the year 2000 becomes "00," which would be interpreted by most software to mean the year 1900. Even though most of the computer industry recognized that two-digit year fields could not be used forever without causing severe problems, using two digits provided substantial savings in processing and memory expenses. Besides, in most cases the year 2000 seemed like a long way off.

With the day of reckoning fast approaching, programmers everywhere are now furiously scouring software for year 2000 related problems. Virtually everything electronic, from microwave ovens to automobiles to aircraft to accounting software, must be analyzed and recoded to avoid failures when the year 2000 arrives. The analysis and correction of year 2000 problems is expected to be tremendously expensive, and may exceed $1 trillion worldwide.[1] The costs associated with year 2000 failures—and there are bound to be plenty—are less predictable and could exceed the cost of repairs. Expenses of this magnitude are certain to invite litigation as customers and vendors will squabble over who should pay these costs.

THE FIRST YEAR 2000 BATTLES

The year 2000 litigation began well before the year 2000. The first year 2000 lawsuit may have been filed in July 1997 in Michigan, involving software that was unable to process credit cards with expiration dates beyond 1999. Most banks recognized early on that banks and credit card companies would likely be among the first to tackle year 2000 problems because credit cards contain expiration dates that are often several years into the future. Unless banks corrected their processing software well in advance of the year 2000, they would not be able to issue any credit cards with expiration dates after 1999.[2] Nonetheless, some banks apparently issued credit cards with post-1999 expiration dates before all processing software was able to manage them. Produce Palace sued software vendor Tec-America in 1997 after its credit card processing software was unable to handle credit cards that expired after 1999. The complaint alleged numerous claims, including breach of contract, breach of warranty, misrepresentation, and violation of the consumer protection laws.

Many future year 2000 battles will involve custom software such as that used in credit card processing, and others will involve mass market, or "shrink wrap," software. In most cases, litigation involving mass market software will be filed as a "class action." A class action is a lawsuit in which a named plaintiff files a lawsuit on behalf of many others who are situated similarly to the plaintiff, or "representative" of the class. Because mass market software is relatively inexpensive, it is seldom worthwhile for any individual consumers to sue a software developer because the maximum amount of damages may be the retail value of the software. Likewise, it is impractical to require all affected consumers to join together in a single lawsuit. But by filing a class action lawsuit, a single consumer can file a lawsuit on behalf of all other consumers that are similarly situated, without requiring the other consumers to affirmatively join the lawsuit.

The first year 2000 class action may have been filed in 1997 in California by computer equipment reseller Altaz International against software vendor BT Accounting Systems.[3] The essence of the Altaz complaint is that BT Accounting Systems and its affiliate Software Business Technologies Inc. failed to correct year 2000 problems in their SBT Pro Series accounting software for free, instead requiring consumers to purchase upgrades at a substantial cost. Altaz claims that the problem should be repaired for free and that the required upgrade amounts to a breach of warranty, fraud, and unfair business practices.

The SBT Pro Series software included a written warranty stating that the software would operate for a period of five years. Though it was first sold in March 1997, Altaz contends that it will not work properly after the year 2000. The SBT Pro Series software also claimed to include a "day" field that allowed entry of events occurring as far as 999 days into the future. But any entry corresponding to a day in the year 2000 would be interpreted as a day occurring in 1900, causing the software to function improperly. Accordingly, Altaz contends that the defendants breached their express warranty. Altaz seeks as damages the cost of acquiring, installing, and implementing replacement software.

A similar class action was filed in February 1998 against Symantec Corp.[4] According to the complaint, versions of Norton AntiVirus prior to version 4.0 were not year 2000 compliant. The only way users of earlier versions could avoid year 2000 failures was to purchase an upgrade at $49.95. Seeking an upgrade and a year 2000 fix for free, a single representative sued Symantec on behalf of all consumers who had purchased copies of Norton AntiVirus prior to version 4.0.

The list of year 2000 lawsuits continues to grow, and includes the makers of several popular software titles as defendants. For example, two separate plaintiffs sued Intuit in New York and in California, alleging that early versions of its Quicken financial software were not year 2000 compliant.[5] The complaints contend that consumers were required to purchase upgrades at a cost of $30 to $40 to achieve compliance. As with the other lawsuits, these complaints allege breach of warranty and violations of various consumer protection laws.

FUTURE YEAR 2000 BATTLES

As the litigation so far suggests, many year 2000 disputes will focus on whether a software manufacturer must repair year 2000 problems for free, perhaps in the form of a free upgrade to purchasers of earlier noncompliant versions. In most cases, the answer to that question appears to be controlled by the warranties provided with the software, as well as applicable consumer protection laws.

Besides mass market software disputes, year 2000 battles will take a variety of other forms. One possibility for litigation arises from year 2000 compliance letters. Many companies, concerned with whether any of their software contains year 2000 bugs, have written to their vendors asking for either assurances of conformance or identification of problems. Obviously, where this process uncovers year 2000 problems, the parties must resolve which of them is responsible for the repair. But the potential for disputes is compounded when the vendor, intentionally or unwittingly, responds that there are no year 2000 concerns when in fact there are. In such cases, the vendor may be liable for fraud, misrepresentation, breach of contract, or other claims. Vendors may find themselves between a rock and a hard place, facing possible liability for breach of fiduciary duty if they refuse to answer year 2000 compliance requests from their customers.

Other disputes may arise from self-help approaches by customers. Self-help typically means modification of the software by the customer or a contractor hired by the customer to make it year 2000 compliant. If the customer is merely a licensee of the software, the customer may be exposed to potential copyright infringement or breach of contract claims for modifying the licensed software to become year 2000 compliant. If any customers are sued for such activities, they will likely have strong defenses to the copyright claims based on fair use or the right to modify the software under Section 117 of the Copyright Act, which allows modification if it is an essential step in the utilization of the software. Likewise, breach of contract claims against the customer may possibly be defended on the basis that the revisions by the customer were required in view of the "anticipatory breach" by the vendor, which has stated that it will not modify the software itself.

Whereas solving year 2000 problems has been a gold mine for many software developers, some year 2000 programmers will get the shaft. In addition to possible breach of contract and copyright infringement problems, those who attempt to solve year 2000 problems risk destroying valuable data, failing to fully locate and correct year 2000 problems, and failing to complete the corrections on time. Depending on the assurances given, year 2000 contractors could face substantial liabilities.

Companies that fail to properly assess their year 2000 issues face possible liability at several levels. For example, officers and directors may be sued by shareholders for failing to carry out their fiduciary duties. Similarly, officers and directors that do not report possible year 2000 risks on Securities and Exchange Commission filings may also face lawsuits by shareholders. These liabilities, of course, are in addition to the damages caused by the uncorrected year 2000 problems themselves. The most tragic injuries, if not the greatest liability, will almost certainly come in the form of an airline, automobile, or other accident caused by a year 2000 failure.

YEAR 2000 BATTLES AND THE COMPUTER INDUSTRY

Obviously, the courts are not responsible for the year 2000 problem, and they will not solve it either. Whereas the possibility of legal liability provides an added incentive, most year 2000 problems would be solved eventually even without the liability spur. Instead, the courts will create a lasting impact on the computer industry by building a substantial body of case law defining the rights and responsibilities of software developers and customers.

In addition to the many court decisions that will flesh out the rights of vendors and consumers, state and federal legislatures are certain to respond to the year 2000 problem by enacting laws aimed at ensuring or limiting liability for year 2000 glitches. As one example, the California legislature has considered and rejected a bill that seeks to limit damages available to plaintiffs for year 2000 problems to the cost to test and replace or repair failed systems and any actual costs resulting from bodily injury. The bill's sponsors contend that the California economy relies heavily upon high-technology companies that stand to lose a lot of money—and cut a lot of jobs—as a result of year 2000 litigation.

Statutes and court decisions that result from the year 2000 problem will be much broader, and longer lasting, than the problem itself. Among a host of software quality issues, the year 2000 problem stands out because of its breadth, magnitude, and immediacy. But long before the year 2000 problem became a household topic, attorneys began working on an addition to the Uniform Commercial Code that would provide a model law for state legislatures to enact to govern software transactions and address general software quality issues.

The Uniform Commercial Code, or UCC, is a model statute drafted and revised by a working group comprised of lawyers who solicit input from industry, legal, and legislative representatives. The various "Articles" of the UCC are aimed at most commercial transactions, including, for example, banking, securities, leases, and the sale of goods. Ideally, each state will adopt the Articles of the UCC without change, so that the laws governing such basic commercial transactions are uniform from state to state. In practice, each state tweaks the model laws a bit, introducing at least minor differences in the otherwise uniform law.

Though there are Articles of the UCC governing most commercial transactions, thus far the UCC does not apply to licensing transactions. Because virtually all commercial software is licensed, not sold, the UCC—the principal set of laws governing most other consumer transactions—does not apply to software transactions. Observing that nearly 6 percent of the country's gross national product was excluded from coverage in the commercial code, the American Bar Association recommended that the National Conference of Commissioners on Uniform State Laws give consideration to drafting an Article to treat software transactions.

The result is UCC Article 2B. As of 1998, Article 2B has gone through several drafts and is nearly a final product. Many provisions of Article 2B deal with software quality issues such as the failure of a software program to perform properly as with a program affected by the year 2000 problem. The most basic aspect of Article 2B is that it confirms the enforceability of shrink-wrap and electronic or "on-line" licenses. Article 2B also establishes rules regarding warranties, damages, quality requirements, and duties of consumers to mitigate damages.

Though Article 2B attempts to address many of the software licensing and quality issues, it won't be the last word on such matters, at least as it presently exists. In fact, there are so many contested provisions of Article 2B that it may well never be enacted by any states. The flood of year 2000 litigation will verify the importance of Article 2B, provide incentives for state legislatures to enact additional laws, and establish judge-made laws not previously existing. Many of these laws will directly affect the way software is designed, sold, and used by consumers for many years to come.

THE YEAR 2000 PROBLEM: A BRIEF SUMMARY OF THE LAW

Though there are no laws aimed at the year 2000 problem itself, there are statutes and court decisions generally addressing software quality issues, including laws related to warranties, breach of contract, strict liability, negligence, and others. The strength of these laws—and others yet to be written—will be determined in the few years after the year 2000. The year 2000 litigation will likely create a substantial body of case law and statutes that will create a lasting impact on software quality.

Notes

1. Estimates of the magnitude of the cost to correct the year 2000 problem are widespread. One estimate placing the total at $1 trillion is suggested by Matthew Bender and Co., Rel.35-10/98, at p. 3E-3, n.3.

2. The Produce Palace lawsuit is Case No. 97-CK (Mich. Cir. Ct. Macomb Co.) and was filed July 11, 1997.

3. The Altaz lawsuit is Case No. 172539 (Calif. Super. Ct. Marin Co.) and was filed in December 1997.

4. The Norton AntiVirus lawsuit is *Capellan v. Symantec Corp.*, Case No. 772147 (Calif. Super. Ct. Sta. Clara Co.) and was filed on February 19, 1998.

5. The two Intuit lawsuits are *Chilelli v. Intuit Inc.*, Case No. 98-013559 (NY Supr. Ct. Nassau Co.) filed May 14, 1998, and *Issokson v. Intuit Inc.*, Case No. CV773646 (Calif. Super. Ct. Sta. Clara Co.), filed April 29, 1998.

23

Free Software

From the beginning of the computer age, programmers have developed and distributed software that is "free" in one form or another. In some cases, the software itself is not free but rather is based on a free or "open" specification. Such software, often referred to as "open source" or "open architecture," is developed so that it complies with a standard that may have been developed by an industry or government working group in an effort to facilitate standardization or interoperability.

In other cases, the software itself is given away free as a promotional device. "Freeware," as it is sometimes called, is given away by the author perhaps as a demonstration of the type of software the author is capable of producing or simply because the author receives personal satisfaction from sharing it.[1] Freeware, however, is generally only free in terms of price; the author typically retains all other rights, including the rights to copy, distribute, and make derivative works from the software.

Many developers have successfully distributed software as "shareware," in which the software is distributed free with the condition that the user must pay a price to the developer if the user wishes to continue using it after a specified time. The developer expressly retains all rights in the software, which is technically only free during the brief trial period.

Software that is in the "public domain" may be freely copied, used, modified, and distributed. By definition, public domain software is owned by the public, rather than any individual, so that there are no restrictions at all. But software that is in the public domain may be modified in a manner that creates an original, new work. An author of such a modified work holds copyrights in the new work even though it is based on a work in the public domain. Although the strength of the author's rights in the new work may be minimal, the author may nevertheless prevent others from copying or modifying the new work.

THE ORIGIN OF FREE SOFTWARE

Some members of the software community have found the various forms of "free" software, including freeware, shareware, public domain, and open software, to be unsatisfactory. In response, these developers have formed organizations such as the Free Software Foundation and the League for Programming Freedom to develop a body of "free software" and to lobby against all laws providing rights in computer software.

As the Free Software Foundation defines it, "free software" is software that others may use, modify, and redistribute to others, either in its original or modified form. The "free" in "free software" refers to intellectual property rights, rather than price; some sources will charge a price for a physical copy of free software. Unlike public domain software, free software is distributed with a license that provides that any modifications of the free software must include the copyright notices of the original and may only be distributed as free software.

The origin of the free software movement seems to coincide with the development of strong copyright laws protecting software.[2] In 1976 the Copyright Act was amended to extend copyright protection to computer programs by defining a computer program as a "set of statements or instructions to be used directly or indirectly in a computer in order to bring about a certain result." Nevertheless, as recently as the early 1980s many believed that certain categories of software, including operating systems, would not be protected under the copyright laws. Perhaps more than other types of software, operating systems are functional, residing at the core of the computer and performing much of the "heavy lifting" that is transparent to the user. Because the copyright laws protect only the expressive, nonfunctional aspects of software and other works of authorship, many believed that operating systems were "too functional" to fit under copyright laws.

That belief was dispelled in 1983 when the Apple II operating system was held to be protected by the copyright laws after it was copied by Franklin Computer for its Ace 100. During the early 1980s, many other court decisions further defined the scope of copyright protection for computer software. For the most part, the courts were favorable to programmers, extending copyright protection to virtually all aspects of computer software, including operating systems; object and source code; micro-code; program structure, sequence, and organization; and look and feel. The courts also broadly interpreted the strength of copyright protection, severely limiting the ability of competitors to evaluate software when developing competing programs.

LINUX: THE QUINTESSENTIAL FREE SOFTWARE

Although the free software groups have failed to reduce or eliminate legal protection for software, they have made respectable progress in producing a library of free software, including Linux.[3] Leading the charge for free software is the Free Software Foundation, founded by Richard Stallman in 1983 to develop software that could be freely exchanged without restrictions on the ability to make copies or modifications. In 1984, FSF began the "GNU" project to develop a complete free software system that would be upwardly compatible with UNIX. The GNU system (which stands for "GNU's Not UNIX," and is pronounced with a hard "G") is intended to be free in that users may freely use, modify, and distribute the software.

Working with donated equipment, financial contributions, and voluntary programming assistance, by the 1990s FSF had either found or written all the major components of its UNIX-like operating system except for the kernel. Meanwhile, beginning in 1991, Linus Torvalds began working on his own version of UNIX after being upset by the high prices of UNIX. Before FSF was able to finish its own kernel, Linus Torvalds developed his kernel, called "Linux." FSF is still working on its own kernel, called "Hurd." When Linux was combined with other free components, including much of the GNU system, it resulted in a complete UNIX-like operating system.

The GNU software, which comprises about 28 percent of a typical Linux operating system, is distributed under what FSF calls the General Public License (GPL). The GPL takes advantage of copyright laws to ensure that free software remains free. Under the GPL, anyone may freely copy, distribute, and modify the free software. Importantly, the GPL requires that any subsequent distributions, including distributions of modified software, must also be made under the terms of the GPL. Accordingly, when others distribute modifications of free software, such modifications are also free. The GPL itself may not be modified by adding or subtracting terms.

The Linux operating system is widely available free over the Internet and through a number of bulletin boards. Unlike most software, users may actually download and modify the source code. Though Linux is available at no charge, others have produced commercial Linux packages that are sold along with additional Linux-compatible utilities and entitle the user to technical support and other benefits.

FREE SOFTWARE AND THE COMPUTER INDUSTRY

Linux has become wildly successful, with more than two million commercial Linux packages sold and several million additional copies downloaded or shared for free in 1998 alone. Though that pales in comparison to the 150 million copies of Windows 95, Windows 98, and Windows NT sold by Microsoft, the success of Linux has hardly gone unnoticed by Microsoft.

As major companies such as Boeing, Mercedes-Benz, and Sony increasingly have turned to Linux, Microsoft is looking over its shoulder. During the high-profile Microsoft antitrust trial, the press and the anti-Microsoft segment of the industry had a field day with the "Halloween" documents, a pair of internal memoranda in which Linux and the free software movement are said to pose direct threats.[4] Although Microsoft has said that the memoranda are merely one engineer's analysis intended to spark internal discussion, it is clear that the free software threat is very real.

In addition to Linux, there is now a substantial and growing body of free software. Linux has contributed to a more organized effort to develop and promote free software. In 1997 an organization calling itself the Open Source Initiative, or OSI, formed to promote the free software movement. OSI adopted the term "open source," rather than continue to use the previous term "free software," to apply to software it considered to be free. Fundamentally, open source means that there is access to the source code. It also means that users may modify and redistribute the original software, either free or for a price. According to OSI, the GNU General Public License is an open source-compatible license. There are very few differences between "free software" and "open source" software. In fact, OSI's purpose in adopting the open source term was aimed more at eliminating past negative connotations than in defining a new category of software.

The high visibility of Linux has provided momentum to OSI, which has also obtained a certification mark registration for the term "open source." OSI intends for software developers to submit code and a distribution license for review. If it meets the OSI definition of open source software, it can be distributed using the open source mark and logo.

Now that several major corporations have embraced Linux as a viable operating system, free software is shedding its negative "hacker" image as consumers reevaluate free software. At the same time, major software developers are considering whether to make some or all of the source code for certain products available to consumers. OSI's legitimacy was boosted in April 1998 when Netscape released the source code to its Navigator software. OSI trumpeted the release, pointing out the many enhancements and fixes that users posted on various Internet sites.

Though the "free software" or "open source" movement seems certain to grow, the major software companies have weapons of their own up their sleeves. For starters, the major software companies play a primary role in developing industry protocols or standards to ensure interoperability. If major software makers set out to do so, they could push the protocol development in a direction that would favor their products over free software products. Consumers might then be forced to purchase commercial software or wait for future modifications of free software.

Software patents provide an even more powerful weapon for software companies. Though free software developers can create new software to satisfy new protocols, they may not be able to develop software that avoids patent infringement. Accordingly, large software companies with significant patent portfolios may incorporate as many patented features as possible into their software to provide functionality that free software makers cannot provide. If so, then the free software movement that was started by strong copyright laws may be stalled by strong patent laws. Time, and the courts, will provide the answers.

FREE SOFTWARE: A BRIEF SUMMARY OF THE LAW

Software that is distributed for "free" comes in a variety of forms, including open software, freeware, shareware, free software, and public domain software. More recently, the term "open source" has been coined to refer to software that is essentially the same as "free software" in that it must allow access to the source code and allow users to modify and distribute the software to others. These various types of "free" software provide different rights and restrictions under the copyright laws, and users should exercise great care to avoid violating any rights that are retained by the authors of such "free" software.

Notes

1. Definitions of the terms "freeware," "free software," and "shareware" are included in most computer dictionaries, including the *Microsoft Press Computer Dictionary*, Third Edition (Microsoft Press, 1997). The term "open source" is too new to be included in dictionaries compiled prior to 1998.

2. Because the free software movement has strong roots in the hacking community, the Internet is a rich source of information. Much of the material used to prepare this chapter was found on the Internet, including an extensive site posted by the Free Software Foundation at *www.fsf.org* and the more recent Open Source Initiative site at *www.opensource.net*.

3. There is a flood of press about the development of Linux, the open source movement, and Microsoft's reactions. Again, many of these articles are available on the Internet, including, for example, a concise article at the U.S. News site at *www.usnews.com*.

4. The Microsoft Halloween documents are available on the Internet on the Open Source Initiative Web site.

24

Conclusion

It is often difficult, if not impossible, to make sense of many legal decisions affecting the computer industry. It isn't that they are poorly reasoned or inartfully written; rather, lawyers and judges have been given awkward and inadequate tools to make clear and proper legal decisions. Court decisions involving computer-related disputes become even hazier when attempting to reconcile multiple decisions apparently involving the same basic issue. It has been said that law school teaches law students to take two identical situations and show how they are different. Countless volumes of legal reporters are filled with computer-related decisions that are seemingly identical but have different holdings or that are seemingly different but have identical holdings.

Though the law itself is difficult to reconcile, there is no doubt that litigation has affected nearly every aspect of the computer industry. Certainly, those legal disputes greatly affected the litigants themselves. As Voltaire once said, "I was never ruined but twice, once when I lost a lawsuit and once when I won one." But in the rapidly developing computer industry, other competitors and the industry itself have also been affected by litigation.

THE CONSEQUENCES OF COMPUTER BATTLES

Many conclusions may be drawn from the preceding survey of litigation affecting the computer industry. Perhaps the most obvious is that there has been a lot of litigation. Probably no aspect of computer hardware or software has been untouched by litigation. Though this conclusion is fairly obvious from the litigation discussed in this book, the sampling of lawsuits outlined here is at best the tip of the iceberg. Indeed, the quantity of computer-related lawsuits filed on an average day in the U.S. courts would outnumber all the lawsuits discussed in this book. The magnitude and importance of the industry virtually assure that the volume of computer litigation is unlikely to change in the near future.

Many lawsuits have greatly affected the industry, in a variety of ways. In some cases, dominant or industry-leading companies have sued upstarts that have either copied or taken advantage of the lessons taught by the industry leaders. The outcomes have alternately cemented the positions of the industry leaders (as in Apple's lawsuit against Franklin) or have opened the doors to broader competition (for example, in the Lotus lawsuit against Borland).

Contrary results in many of the lawsuits discussed in this book may have significantly changed the shape of the industry. For example, if Apple's lawsuit against Franklin had not been reversed on appeal, Franklin may have undercut Apple in the market and become a dominant player in the industry. Further, others may have begun selling clones containing both the Apple II and Apple Macintosh operating systems. A contrary result in the *Apple v. Franklin* lawsuit may have rendered moot the subsequent litigation between Apple and Microsoft over the Microsoft Windows operating system. Though it is impossible to predict the shape of the industry today if one or more key lawsuits had turned out differently, there is little doubt that the landscape of the industry would be different.

While many major lawsuits have a critical effect on the litigants themselves, they also provide behavioral signals to the rest of the industry. For example, litigation has provided guidance regarding acceptable acts of reverse engineering and whether input formats, menus, and fonts may be copied. Computer companies can and do use this information to design and market their products.

In addition to shaping the industry in visible, external ways, litigation has altered the manner in which computer companies conduct their businesses. For example, because of court decisions interpreting the right to decompile or otherwise reverse engineer software, many companies now have "clean rooms" staffed by employees who are not allowed to see their competitors' products. Many companies also have "technology evangelists," whose primary function is to keep an eye on the competition and understand the features and functions of their products. This administrative layer is primarily a litigation avoidance tool created from the lessons taught by previous legal battles.

The law has also affected the computer industry in its uncertain, often uneven, application. Judges presiding over computer-related disputes have spent an inordinate amount of effort trying to determine what the law is before they are able to apply it. The computer industry's rapid growth began before there were laws specifically designed to handle computer software and hardware disputes. As a result, judges have been forced to turn to laws that were developed for other purposes, leading to awkward, uneven applications of the law.

The complex nature of computer hardware and software has also contributed to the significance of the law. Software and hardware disputes are often technical, taxing the understanding of judges and lawyers. This confusion and complexity is readily demonstrated in the number of trial court decisions that have been reversed on appeal. These misunderstandings by lawyers and judges have introduced elements of randomness into the law that build on themselves as decisions in subsequent lawsuits are based on earlier, mistaken rationales.

FUTURE LITIGATION

The heyday of significant computer-related litigation is far from over. In fact, there are many aspects of the computer industry that will be shaped by the courts. Perhaps at the top of the list is the form of the computer industry following the Microsoft antitrust litigation.[1] The U.S. Department of Justice and twenty states have alleged that Microsoft has engaged in anticompetitive practices or has attempted to monopolize certain segments of the software industry. Among other things, the government alleges that Microsoft has attempted to carve up the Internet browser and audio-video markets and has attempted to monopolize the browser market by bundling its Internet Explorer with its Windows operating system and altering Sun's Java language to prevent it from working on non-Microsoft products.

The protest against Microsoft is nothing short of a crusade. Indeed, with chief crusader Ralph Nader trumpeting charges that "Microsoft must be stopped," there is plenty of hue and cry to go around.[2] According to Nader, Microsoft's agenda is the imposition of "suffocating control over choices and an ever-widening monopoly." Never one to pull punches, Nader has used harsh language and levied serious charges against Microsoft.

For its part, Microsoft has viable responses to the charges against it. For starters, Microsoft is quick to point out that the price of its software has fallen in parallel with the prices of software sold by others in the industry, contrary to what one might expect from a monopolist. Microsoft also notes that it does not presently hold the dominant market share in the browser market, and that consumers may quickly and easily obtain competing browsers such as Netscape's Navigator. While Microsoft is quickly gaining market share, Microsoft contends that it is because its Internet Explorer is a superior product, and not because it is in any way forced upon consumers. Microsoft also strongly denies attempting to fragment Java or engage in any other anticompetitive practices.

Regardless of the outcome of the Microsoft antitrust litigation, it is a legal battle of historic proportions. If Microsoft emerges victorious, it will likely continue its position as the leader in the software industry. If Microsoft loses, many options are possible. Like AT&T before it, Microsoft could be broken up. This option could take many forms—one possibility is that separate companies could be formed from Microsoft's operating systems, Internet, and other applications divisions. If this option is taken, Microsoft's status as the largest company as measured by market capitalization will be short lived.

Less-drastic remedies are also possible and probably more likely. There are very few options that the government may not take. For example, the government could require divestiture of ownership in other companies, require certain strict contracting practices, mandate that certain technical information be shared or support be given, impose strict walls between Microsoft's Internet and applications divisions, or virtually anything else it deems reasonably required to enhance competition. Any of these options would likely be felt throughout the industry for many years.

In addition to the Microsoft antitrust litigation, the future will be filled with many other critical legal battles. For example, Sun litigation with Microsoft over Java may prove to be even more important than the antitrust lawsuit. Lawsuits stemming from the year 2000 problem are certain to occur and leave a lasting impression on the industry. Likewise, the future will certainly bring many battles over "cyberspace" issues as the Internet brings more and more consumers together. The present gap in database protection is certain to be filled with more litigation, and as free or open software increases its market share, litigation won't be far behind. In sum, the computer industry has been marked by companies whose fortunes have teetered on court rulings, and the future will be shaped in exactly the same way.

Notes

1. As would be expected, the Internet is flooded with documents addressing the Microsoft Java litigation and the Microsoft antitrust lawsuit. Microsoft has its own Web site offering its press releases and other information on these and other matters at *www.microsoft.com.presspass/doj/dog.htm.*

2. One Ralph Nader article, authored with James Love in November 1998, addressing the Microsoft antitrust litigation was published by *Computer World* and is available on-line at *www.computerworld.com/home/print.nsf/all/981109740E.*

Appendix

Selected Intellectual Property Statutes

Many of the United States intellectual property laws have a statutory foundation. This appendix is intended to serve as a reference for some of the more pertinent sections of these intellectual property laws. Note, however, that this appendix *only* includes excerpts of the patent, trademark, copyright, and trade secret laws. There are certainly many other fields within intellectual property law that contain relevant statutes not included here. In addition, this appendix does not include the complete patent, trademark, copyright, and trade secret laws, but rather those portions that are the most pertinent to the concepts discussed in this book.

Selected Patent Laws

The patent laws are exclusively federal law, not state law. This appendix includes those portions of the patent laws thought to be most relevant, including background definitions and provisions related to patent applications, contents, and terms, as well as provisions related to infringement and remedies. Each section comes from chapter 35 of the United States Code.

§ 100. Definitions

When used in this title unless the context otherwise indicates—

(a) The term "invention" means invention or discovery.

(b) The term "process" means process, art or method, and includes a new use of a known process, machine, manufacture, composition of matter, or material.

(c) The terms "United States" and "this country" mean the United States of America, its territories and possessions.

(d) The word "patentee" includes not only the patentee to whom the patent was issued but also the successors in title to the patentee.

§ 101. Inventions patentable

Whoever invents or discovers any new and useful process, machine, manufacture, or composition of matter, or any new and useful improvement thereof, may obtain a patent therefor, subject to the conditions and requirements of this title.

§ 102. Conditions for patentability; novelty and loss of right to patent

A person shall be entitled to a patent unless—

(a) the invention was known or used by others in this country, or patented or described in a printed publication in this or a foreign country, before the invention thereof by the applicant for patent, or

(b) the invention was patented or described in a printed publication in this or a foreign country or in public use or on sale in this country, more than one year prior to the date of the application for patent in the United States, or

(c) he has abandoned the invention, or

(d) the invention was first patented or caused to be patented, or was the subject of an inventor's certificate, by the applicant or his legal representatives or assigns in a foreign country prior to the date of the application for patent in this country on an application for patent or inventor's certificate filed more than twelve months before the filing of the application in the United States, or

(e) the invention was described in a patent granted on an application for patent by another filed in the United States before the invention thereof by the applicant for patent, or on an international application by another who has fulfilled the requirements of paragraphs (1), (2), and (4) of section 371(c) of this title before the invention thereof by the applicant for patent, or

(f) he did not himself invent the subject matter sought to be patented, or

(g) before the applicant's invention thereof the invention was made in this country by another who had not abandoned, suppressed, or concealed it. In determining priority of invention there shall be considered not only the respective dates of conception and reduction to practice of the invention, but also the reasonable diligence of one who was first to conceive and last to reduce practice, from a time prior to conception by the other.

§ 103. Conditions for patentability; non-obvious subject matter

(a) A patent may not be obtained though the invention is not identically disclosed or described as set forth in section 102 of this title, if the differences between the subject matter sought to be patented and the prior art are such that the subject matter as a whole would have been obvious at the time the invention was made to a person having ordinary skill in the art to which said subject matter pertains. Patentability shall not be negatived by the manner in which the invention was made.

(b) (1) Notwithstanding subsection (a), and upon timely election by the applicant for patent to proceed under this subsection, a biotechnological process using or resulting in a composition of matter that is novel under section 102 and nonobvious under subsection (a) of this section shall be considered nonobvious if—

(A) claims to the process and the composition of matter are contained in either the same application for patent or in separate applications having the same effective filing date; and

(B) shall, if such composition of matter, and the process at the time it was invented, were owned by the same person or subject to an obligation of assignment to the same person.

(2) A patent issued on a process under paragraph (1)—

(A) shall also contain the claims to the composition of matter used in or made by that process, or

(B) shall, if such composition of matter is claimed in another patent, be set to expire on the same date as such other patent, notwithstanding section 154.

(3) For purposes of paragraph (1), the term "biotechnological process" means—

(A) a process of genetically altering or otherwise inducing a single- or multi-celled organism to—

(i) express an exogenous nucleotide sequence,

(ii) inhibit, eliminate, augment, or alter expression of an endogenous nucleotide sequence, or

(iii) express a specific physiological characteristic not naturally associated with said organism;

(B) cell fusion procedures yielding a cell line that expresses a specific protein, such as a monoclonal antibody; and

(C) a method of using a product produced by a process defined by subparagraph (A) or (B), or a combination of subparagraphs (A) and (B).

(c) Subject matter developed by another person, which qualifies as prior art only under subsection (f) or (g) of section 102 of this title, shall not preclude patentability under this section where the subject matter and the claimed invention were, at the time the invention was made, owned by the same person or subject to an obligation of assignment to the same person.

§ 104. Invention made abroad

(a) In General.—

(1) Proceedings.—In proceedings in the Patent and Trademark Office, in the courts, and before any other competent authority, an applicant for a patent, or a patentee, may not establish a date of invention by reference to knowledge or use thereof, or other activity with respect thereto, in a foreign country other than a NAFTA country or a WTO member country, except as provided in sections 119 and 365 of this title.

(2) Rights.—If an invention was made by a person, civil or military—

(A) while domiciled in the United States, and serving in any other country in connection with operations by or on behalf of the United States,

(B) while domiciled in a NAFTA country and serving in another country in connection with operations by or on behalf of that NAFTA country, or

(C) while domiciled in a WTO member country and serving in another country in connection with operations by or on behalf of that WTO member country, that person shall be entitled to the same rights of priority in the United States with respect to such invention as if such invention had been made in the United States, that NAFTA country, or that WTO member country, as the case may be.

(3) Use of information.—To the extent that any information in a NAFTA country or a WTO member country concerning knowledge, use, or other activity relevant to proving or disproving a date of invention has not been made available for use in a proceeding in the Patent and Trademark Office, a court, or any other competent authority to the same extent as such information could be made available in the United States, the Commissioner, court, or such other authority shall draw appropriate inferences, or take other action permitted by statute, rule, or regulation, in favor of the party that requested the information in the proceeding.

(b) Definitions.—As used in this section—

(1) the term "NAFTA country" has the meaning given that term in section 2(4) of the North American Free Trade Agreement Implementation Act; and

(2) the term "WTO member country" has the meaning given that term in section 2(10) of the Uruguay Round Agreements Act.

§ 131. Examination of application

The Commissioner shall cause an examination to be made of the application and the alleged new invention; and if on such examination it appears that the applicant is entitled to a patent under the law, the Commissioner shall issue a patent therefor.

§ 132. Notice of rejection; reexamination

Whenever, on examination, any claim for a patent is rejected, or any objection or requirement made, the Commissioner shall notify the applicant thereof, stating the reasons for such rejection, or objection or requirement, together with such information and references as may be useful in judging of the propriety of continuing the prosecution of his application; and if after receiving such notice, the applicant persists in his claim for a patent, with or without amendment, the application shall be reexamined. No amendment shall introduce new matter into the disclosure of the invention.

§ 154. Contents and term of patent

(a) In General.—

(1) Contents.—Every patent shall contain a short title of the invention and a grant to the patentee, his heirs or assigns, of the right to exclude others from making, using, offering for sale, or selling the invention throughout the United States or importing the invention into the United States, and, if the invention is a process, of the right to exclude others from using, offering for sale or selling throughout the United States, or importing into the United States, products made by that process, referring to the specification for the particulars thereof.

(2) Term.—Subject to the payment of fees under this title, such grant shall be for a term beginning on the date on which the patent issues and ending 20 years from the date on which the application for the patent was filed in the United States or, if the application contains a specific reference to an earlier filed application or applications under section 120, 121, or 365(c) of this title, from the date on which the earliest such application was filed.

(3) Priority.—Priority under section 119, 365(a), or 365(b) of this title shall not be taken into account in determining the term of a patent.

(4) Specification and drawing.—A copy of the specification and drawing shall be annexed to the patent and be a part of such patent.

(b) Term Extension.—

(1) Interference delay or secrecy orders.—If the issue of an original patent is delayed due to a proceeding under section 135(a) of this title, or because the application for patent is placed under an order pursuant to section 181 of this title, the term of the patent shall be extended for the period of delay, but in no case more than 5 years.

(2) Extension for appellate review.—If the issue of a patent is delayed due to appellate review by the Board of Patent Appeals and

Interferences or by a Federal court and the patent is issued pursuant to a decision in the review reversing an adverse determination of patentability, the term of the patent shall be extended for a period of time but in no case more than 5 years. A patent shall not be eligible for extension under this paragraph if it is subject to a terminal disclaimer due to the issue of another patent claiming subject matter that is not patentably distinct from that under appellate review.

(3) Limitations.—The period of extension referred to in paragraph (2)—

(A) shall include any period beginning on the date on which an appeal is filed under section 134 or 141 of this title, or on which an action is commenced under section 145 of this title, and ending on the date of a final decision in favor of the applicant;

(B) shall be reduced by any time attributable to appellate review before the expiration of 3 years from the filing date of the application for patent; and

(C) shall be reduced for the period of time during which the applicant for patent did not act with due diligence, as determined by the Commissioner.

(4) Length of extension.—The total duration of all extensions of a patent under this subsection shall not exceed 5 years.

(c) Continuation.—

(1) Determination.—The term of a patent that is in force on or that results from an application filed before the date that is 6 months after the date of the enactment of the Uruguay Round Agreements Act shall be the greater of the 20-year term as provided in subsection (a), or 17 years from grant, subject to any terminal disclaimers.

(2) Remedies.—The remedies of sections 283, 284, and 285 of this title shall not apply to Acts that

(A) were commenced or for which substantial investment was made before the date that is 6 months after the date of the enactment of the Uruguay Round Agreements Act; and

(B) became infringing by reason of paragraph (1).

(3) Remuneration.—The acts referred to in paragraph (2) may be continued only upon the payment of an equitable remuneration to the patentee that is determined in an action brought under chapter 28 and chapter 29 (other than those provisions excluded by paragraph (2)) of this title.

§ 171. Patents for designs

Whoever invents any new, original and ornamental design for an article of manufacture may obtain a patent therefor, subject to the conditions and requirements of this title. The provisions of this title relating to patents for inventions shall apply to patents for designs, except as otherwise provided.

§ 173. Term of design patent

Patents for designs shall be granted for the term of fourteen years from the date of grant.

§ 271. Infringement of patent

(a) Except as otherwise provided in this title, whoever without authority makes, uses, offers to sell, or sells any patented invention, within the United States or imports into the United States any patented invention during the term of the patent therefor, infringes the patent.

(b) Whoever actively induces infringement of a patent shall be liable as an infringer.

(c) Whoever offers to sell or sells within the United States or imports into the United States a component of a patented machine, manufacture, combination or composition, or a material or apparatus for use in practicing a patented process, constituting a material part of the invention, knowing the same to be especially made or especially adapted for use in an infringement of such patent, and not a staple article or commodity of commerce suitable for substantial noninfringing use, shall be liable as a contributory infringer.

(d) No patent owner otherwise entitled to relief for infringement or contributory infringement of a patent shall be denied relief or deemed guilty of misuse or illegal extension of the patent right by reason of his having done one or more of the following: (1) derived revenue from acts which if performed by another without his consent would constitute contributory infringement of the patent; (2) licensed or authorized another to perform acts which if performed without his consent would constitute contributory infringement of the patent; (3) sought to enforce his patent rights against infringement or contributory infringement; (4) refused to license or use any rights to the patent; or (5) conditioned the license of any rights to the patent or the sale of the patented product on the acquisition of a license to rights in another patent or purchase of a separate product, unless, in view of the circumstances, the patent owner has market power in the relevant market for the patent or patented product on which the license or sale is conditioned.

(e) (1) It shall not be an act of infringement to make, use, offer to sell, or sell within the United States or import into the United States a patented invention (other than a new animal drug or veterinary biological product (as those terms are used in the Federal Food, Drug, and Cosmetic Act and the Act of March 4, 1913) which is primarily manufactured using recombinant DNA, recombinant RNA, hybridoma technology, or other processes involving site specific genetic manipulation techniques) solely for uses reasonably related to the development and submission of information under a Federal law which regulates the manufacture, use, or sale of drugs or veterinary biological products.

(2) It shall be an act of infringement to submit—

(A) an application under section 505(j) of the Federal Food, Drug, and Cosmetic Act or described in section 505(b)(2) of such Act for a drug claimed in a patent or the use of which is claimed in a patent, or

(B) an application under section 512 of such Act or under the Act of March 4, 1913 (21 U.S.C. 151-158) for a drug or veterinary biological product which is not primarily manufactured using recombinant DNA, recombinant RNA, hybridoma technology, or other processes involving site specific genetic manipulation techniques and which is claimed in a patent or the use of which is claimed in a patent, if the purpose of such submission is to obtain approval under such Act to engage in the commercial manufacture, use, or sale of a drug or veterinary biological product claimed in a patent or the use of which is claimed in a patent before the expiration of such patent.

(3) In any action for patent infringement brought under this section, no injunctive or other relief may be granted which would prohibit the making, using, offering to sell, or selling within the United States or importing into the United States of a patented invention under paragraph (1).

(4) For an act of infringement described in paragraph (2)—

(A) the court shall order the effective date of any approval of the drug or veterinary biological product involved in the infringement to be a date which is not earlier than the date of the expiration of the patent which has been infringed,

(B) injunctive relief may be granted against an infringer to prevent the commercial manufacture, use, offer to sell, or sale within the United States or importation into the United States of an approved drug or veterinary biological product, and

(C) damages or other monetary relief may be awarded against an infringer only if there has been commercial manufacture, use, offer to sell, or sale within the United States or importation into the United States of an approved drug or veterinary biological product. The remedies prescribed by subparagraphs (A), (B), and (C) are the only remedies which may be granted by a court for an act of infringement described in paragraph (2), except that a court may award attorney fees under section 285.

(f) (1) Whoever without authority supplies or causes to be supplied in or from the United States all or a substantial portion of the components of a patented invention, where such components are uncombined in whole or in part, in such manner as to actively induce the combination of such components outside of the United States in a manner that would infringe the patent if such combination occurred within the United States, shall be liable as an infringer.

(2) Whoever without authority supplies or causes to be supplied in or from the United States any component of a patented invention that is especially made or especially adapted for use in the invention and not a staple article or commodity of commerce suitable for substantial noninfringing use, where such component is uncombined in whole or in part, knowing that such component is so made or adapted and intending that such component will be combined outside of the United States in a manner that would infringe the patent if such combination occurred within the United States, shall be liable as an infringer.

(g) Whoever without authority imports into the United States or offers to sell, sells, or uses within the United States a product which is made by a process patented in the United States shall be liable as an infringer, if the importation, offer to sell, sale, or use of the product occurs during the term of such process patent. In an action for infringement of a process patent, no remedy may be granted for infringement on account of the noncommercial use or retail sale of a product unless there is no adequate remedy under this title for infringement on account of the importation or other use, offer to sell, or sale of that product. A product which is made by a patented process will, for purposes of this title, not be considered to be so made after—

(1) it is materially changed by subsequent processes; or

(2) it becomes a trivial and nonessential component of another product.

(h) As used in this section, the term "whoever" includes any State, any instrumentality of a State, and any officer or employee of a State or instrumentality of a State acting in his official capacity. Any State, and any such instrumentality, officer, or employee, shall be subject to the provisions of this title in the same manner and to the same extent as any nongovernmental entity.

(i) As used in this section, an "offer for sale" or an "offer to sell" by a person other than the patentee, or any designee of the patentee, is that in which the sale will occur before the expiration of the term of the patent.

§ 281. Remedy for infringement of patent

A patentee shall have remedy by civil action for infringement of his patent.

§ 282. Presumption of validity; defenses

A patent shall be presumed valid. Each claim of a patent (whether in independent, dependent, or multiple dependent form) shall be presumed valid independently of the validity of other claims; dependent or multiple dependent claims shall be presumed valid even though dependent upon an invalid claim. Notwithstanding the preceding sentence, if a claim to a composition of matter is held invalid and that claim was the basis of a determination of nonobviousness under section 103(b)(1), the process shall no longer be considered nonobvious solely on the basis of section 103(b)(1). The burden of establishing invalidity of a patent or any claim thereof shall rest on the party asserting such invalidity.

The following shall be defenses in any action involving the validity or infringement of a patent and shall be pleaded:

(1) Noninfringement, absence of liability for infringement or unenforceability,

(2) Invalidity of the patent or any claim in suit on any ground specified in part II of this title as a condition for patentability,

(3) Invalidity of the patent or any claim in suit for failure to comply with any requirement of sections 112 or 251 of this title,

(4) Any other fact or act made a defense by this title. In actions involving the validity or infringement of a patent the party asserting invalidity or noninfringement shall give notice in the pleadings or otherwise in writing to the adverse party at least thirty days before the trial, of the country, number, date, and name of the patentee of any patent, the title, date, and page numbers of any publication to be relied upon as anticipation of the patent in suit or, except in actions in the United States Court of Federal Claims, as showing the state of the art, and the name and address of any person who may be relied upon as the prior inventor or as having prior knowledge of or as having previously used or offered for sale the invention of the patent in suit. In the absence of such notice proof of the said matters may not be made at the trial except on such terms as the court requires. Invalidity of the extension of a patent term or any portion thereof under section 156 of this title because of the material failure—

(1) by the applicant for the extension, or

(2) by the Commissioner, to comply with the requirements of such section shall be a defense in any action involving the infringement of a patent during the period of the extension of its term and shall be pleaded. A due diligence determination under section 156(d)(2) is not subject to review in such an action.

§ 283. Injunction

The several courts having jurisdiction of cases under this title may grant injunctions in accordance with the principles of equity to prevent the violation of any right secured by patent, on such terms as the court deems reasonable.

§ 284. Damages

Upon finding for the claimant the court shall award the claimant damages adequate to compensate for the infringement, but in no event less than a reasonable royalty for the use made of the invention by the infringer, together with interest and costs as fixed by the court.

When the damages are not found by a jury, the court shall assess them. In either event the court may increase the damages up to three times the amount found or assessed.

The court may receive expert testimony as an aid to the determination of damages or of what royalty would be reasonable under the circumstances.

§ 285. Attorney fees

The court in exceptional cases may award reasonable attorney fees to the prevailing party.

§ 286. Time limitation on damages

Except as otherwise provided by law, no recovery shall be had for any infringement committed more than six years prior to the filing of the complaint or counterclaim for infringement in the action.

In the case of claims against the United States Government for use of a patented invention, the period before bringing suit, up to six years, between the date of receipt of a written claim for compensation by the department or agency of the Government having authority to settle such claim, and the date of mailing by the Government of a notice to the claimant that his claim has been denied shall not be counted as part of the period referred to in the preceding paragraph.

§ 287. Limitation on damages and other remedies; marking and notice

(a) Patentees, and persons making, offering for sale, or selling within the United States any patented article for or under them, or importing any patented article into the United States, may give notice to the public that the same is patented, either by fixing thereon the word "patent" or the abbreviation "pat.", together with the number of the patent, or when, from the character of the article, this can not be done, by fixing to it, or to the package wherein one or more of them is contained, a label containing a like notice. In the event of failure so to mark, no damages shall be recovered by the patentee in any action for infringement, except on proof that the infringer was notified of the infringement and continued to infringe thereafter, in which event damages may be recovered only for infringement occurring after such notice. Filing of an action for infringement shall constitute such notice.

(b) (1) An infringer under section 271(g) shall be subject to all the provisions of this title relating to damages and injunctions except to the extent those remedies are modified by this subsection or section 9006 of the Process Patent Amendments Act of 1988. The modifications of remedies provided in this subsection shall not be available to any person who—

(A) practiced the patented process;

(B) owns or controls, or is owned or controlled by, the person who practiced the patented process; or

(C) had knowledge before the infringement that a patented process was used to make the product the importation, use, offer for sale, or sale of which constitutes the infringement.

(2) No remedies for infringement under section 271(g) of this title shall be available with respect to any product in the possession of, or in transit to, the person subject to liability under such section before that person had notice of infringement with respect to that product. The person subject to liability shall bear the burden of proving any such possession or transit.

(3) (A) In making a determination with respect to the remedy in an action brought for infringement under section 271(g), the court shall consider—

(i) the good faith demonstrated by the defendant with respect to a request for disclosure,

(ii) the good faith demonstrated by the plaintiff with respect to a request for disclosure, and

(iii) the need to restore the exclusive rights secured by the patent.

(B) For purposes of subparagraph (A), the following are evidence of good faith:

(i) a request for disclosure made by the defendant;

(ii) a response within a reasonable time by the person receiving the request for disclosure; and

(iii) the submission of the response by the defendant to the manufacturer, or if the manufacturer is not known, to the supplier, of the product to be purchased by the defendant, together with a request for a written statement that the process claimed in any patent disclosed in the response is not used to produce such product. The failure to perform any acts described in the preceding sentence is evidence of absence of good faith unless there are mitigating circumstances. Mitigating circumstances include the case in which, due to the nature of the product, the number of sources for the product, or like commercial circumstances, a request for disclosure is not necessary or practicable to avoid infringement.

(4) (A) For purposes of this subsection, a "request for disclosure" means a written request made to a person then engaged in the manufacture of a product to identify all process patents owned by or licensed to that person, as of the time of the request, that the person then reasonably believes could be asserted to be infringed under section 271(g) if that product were imported into, or sold, offered for sale, or used in, the United States by an unauthorized person. A request for disclosure is further limited to a request—

(i) which is made by a person regularly engaged in the United States in the sale of the same type of products as those manufactured by the person to whom the request is directed, or which includes facts showing that the person making the request plans to engage in the sale of such products in the United States;

(ii) which is made by such person before the person's first importation, use, offer for sale, or sale of units of the product produced by an infringing process and before the person had notice of infringement with respect to the product; and

(iii) which includes a representation by the person making the request that such person will promptly submit the patents identified pursuant to the request to the manufacturer, or if the manufacturer is not known, to the supplier, of the product to be purchased by the person making the request, and will request from that manufacturer or supplier a written statement that none of the processes claimed in those patents is used in the manufacture of the product.

(B) In the case of a request for disclosure received by a person to whom a patent is licensed, that person shall either identify the patent or promptly notify the licensor of the request for disclosure.

(C) A person who has marked, in the manner prescribed by subsection (a), the number of the process patent on all products made by the patented process which have been offered for sale or sold by that person in the United States, or imported by the person into the United States, before a request for disclosure is received is not required to respond to the request for disclosure. For purposes of the preceding sentence, the term "all products" does not include products made before the effective date of the Process Patent Amendments Act of 1988.

(5) (A) For purposes of this subsection, notice of infringement means actual knowledge, or receipt by a person of a written notification, or a combination thereof, of information sufficient to persuade a reasonable person that it is likely that a product was made by a process patented in the United States.

(B) A written notification from the patent holder charging a person with infringement shall specify the patented process alleged to have been used and the reasons for a good faith belief that such process was used. The patent holder shall include in the notification such information as is reasonably necessary to explain fairly the patent holder's belief, except that the patent holder is not required to disclose any trade secret information.

(C) A person who receives a written notification described in subparagraph (B) or a written response to a request for disclosure described in paragraph (4) shall be deemed to have notice of infringement with respect to any patent referred to in such written notification or response unless that person, absent mitigating circumstances—

(i) promptly transmits the written notification or response to the manufacturer or, if the manufacturer is not known, to the supplier, of the product purchased or to be purchased by that person; and

(ii) receives a written statement from the manufacturer or supplier which on its face sets forth a well grounded factual basis for a belief that the identified patents are not infringed.

(D) For purposes of this subsection, a person who obtains a product made by a process patented in the United States in a quantity which is abnormally large in relation to the volume of business of such person or an efficient inventory level shall be rebuttably presumed to have actual knowledge that the product was made by such patented process.

(6) A person who receives a response to a request for disclosure under this subsection shall pay to the person to whom the request was made a reasonable fee to cover actual costs incurred in complying with

the request, which may not exceed the cost of a commercially available automated patent search of the matter involved, but in no case more than $500.

§ 292. False marking

(a) Whoever, without the consent of the patentee, marks upon, or affixes to, or uses in advertising in connection with anything made, used, offered for sale, or sold by such person within the United States, or imported by the person into the United States, the name or any imitation of the name of the patentee, the patent number, or the words "patent," "patentee," or the like, with the intent of counterfeiting or imitating the mark of the patentee, or of deceiving the public and inducing them to believe that the thing was made, offered for sale, sold, or imported into the United States by or with the consent of the patentee; or

Whoever marks upon, or affixes to, or uses in advertising in connection with any unpatented article, the word "patent" or any word or number importing that the same is patented for the purpose of deceiving the public; or

Whoever marks upon, or affixes to, or uses in advertising in connection with any article, the words "patent applied for," "patent pending," or any word importing that an application for patent has been made, when no application for patent has been made, or if made, is not pending, for the purpose of deceiving the public—

Shall be fined not more than $500 for every such offense.

(b) Any person may sue for the penalty, in which event one-half shall go to the person suing and the other to the use of the United States.

Selected U.S. Trademark Laws

Unlike the patent laws, both the federal and state governments may regulate trademarks. This portion of the appendix contains excerpts of the federal trademark laws related to general trademark registration, infringement, unfair competition, and remedies. Each of the following sections is taken from chapter 15 of the United States Code. Though no state laws are listed here, most state laws are quite similar to the federal trademark laws.

§ 1051. Registration of trademarks

(a) Trademarks used in commerce

The owner of a trademark used in commerce may apply to register his or her trademark under this chapter on the principal register established:

(1) By filing in the Patent and Trademark Office—
(A) a written application, in such form as may be prescribed by the Commissioner, verified by the applicant, or by a member of the firm or an officer of the corporation or association applying, specifying applicant's domicile and citizenship, the date of applicant's first use of the mark, the date of applicant's first use of the mark in commerce, the goods in connection with which the mark is used and the mode or manner in which the mark is used in connection with such goods, and including a statement to the effect that the person making the verification believes himself, or the firm, corporation, or association in whose behalf he makes the verification, to be the owner of the mark sought to

be registered, that the mark is in use in commerce, and that no other person, firm, corporation, or association, to the best of his knowledge and belief, has the right to use such mark in commerce either in the identical form thereof or in such near resemblance thereto as to be likely, when used on or in connection with the goods of such other person, to cause confusion, or to cause mistake, or to deceive: Provided, That in the case of every application claiming concurrent use the applicant shall state exceptions to his claim of exclusive use, in which he shall specify, to the extent of his knowledge, any concurrent use by others, the goods on or in connection with which and the areas in which each concurrent use exists, the periods of each use, and the goods and area for which the applicant desires registration;

    (B) a drawing of the mark; and

    (C) such number of specimens or facsimiles of the mark as used as may be required by the Commissioner.

    (2) By paying into the Patent and Trademark Office the prescribed fee.

    (3) By complying with such rules or regulations, not inconsistent with law, as may be prescribed by the Commissioner.

(b) Trademarks intended for use in commerce

A person who has a bona fide intention, under circumstances showing the good faith of such person, to use a trademark in commerce may apply to register the trademark under this chapter on the principal register hereby established:

    (1) By filing in the Patent and Trademark Office—

    (A) a written application, in such form as may be prescribed by the Commissioner, verified by the applicant, or by a member of the firm or an officer of the corporation or association applying, specifying applicant's domicile and citizenship, applicant's bona fide intention to use the mark in commerce, the goods on or in connection with which the applicant has a bona fide intention to use the mark and the mode or manner in which the mark is intended to be used on or in connection with such goods, including a statement to the effect that the person making the verification believes himself or herself, or the firm, corporation, or association in whose behalf he or she makes the verification, to be entitled to use the mark in commerce, and that no other person, firm, corporation, or association, to the best of his or her knowledge and belief, has the right to use such mark in commerce either in the identical form of the mark or in such near resemblance to the mark as to be likely, when used on or in connection with the goods of such other person, to cause confusion, or to cause mistake, or to deceive; however, except for applications filed pursuant to section 44 of this title, no mark shall be registered until the applicant has met the requirements of subsection (d) of this section; and

(B) a drawing of the mark.

(2) By paying in the Patent and Trademark Office the prescribed fee.

(3) By complying with such rules or regulations, not inconsistent with law, as may be prescribed by the Commissioner.

(c) Amendment of application under subsection (b) to conform to requirements of subsection (a) At any time during examination of an application filed under subsection (b) of this section, an applicant who has made use of the mark in commerce may claim the benefits of such use for purposes of this chapter, by amending his or her application to bring it into conformity with the requirements of subsection (a) of this section.

(d) Verified statement that trademark is used in commerce

(1) Within six months after the date on which the notice of allowance with respect to a mark is issued under section 13(b)(2) of this title to an applicant under subsection (b) of this section, the applicant shall file in the Patent and Trademark Office, together with such number of specimens or facsimiles of the mark as used in commerce as may be required by the Commissioner and payment of the prescribed fee, a verified statement that the mark is in use in commerce and specifying the date of the applicant's first use of the mark in commerce, those goods or services specified in the notice of allowance on or in connection with which the mark is used in commerce, and the mode or manner in which the mark is used on or in connection with such goods or services. Subject to examination and acceptance of the statement of use, the mark shall be registered in the Patent and Trademark Office, a certificate of registration shall be issued for those goods or services recited in the statement of use for which the mark is entitled to registration, and notice of registration shall be published in the Official Gazette of the Patent and Trademark Office. Such examination may include an examination of the factors set forth in subsections (a) through (e) of section 2 of this title. The notice of registration shall specify the goods or services for which the mark is registered.

(2) The Commissioner shall extend, for one additional 6-month period, the time for filing the statement of use under paragraph (1), upon written request of the applicant before the expiration of the 6-month period provided in paragraph (1). In addition to an extension under the preceding sentence, the Commissioner may, upon a showing of good cause by the applicant, further extend the time for filing the statement of use under paragraph (1) for periods aggregating not more than 24 months, pursuant to written request of the applicant made before the expiration of the last extension granted under this paragraph.

Any request for an extension under this paragraph shall be accompanied by a verified statement that the applicant has a continued bona fide intention to use the mark in commerce and specifying those goods or services identified in the notice of allowance on or in connection with which the applicant has a continued bona fide intention to use the mark in commerce. Any request for an extension under this paragraph shall be accompanied by payment of the prescribed fee. The Commissioner shall issue regulations setting forth guidelines for determining what constitutes good cause for purposes of this paragraph.

(3) The Commissioner shall notify any applicant who files a statement of use of the acceptance or refusal thereof and, if the statement of use is refused, the reasons for the refusal. An applicant may amend the statement of use.

(4) The failure to timely file a verified statement of use under this subsection shall result in abandonment of the application.

(e) Designation of resident for service of process and notices
If the applicant is not domiciled in the United States he shall designate by a written document filed in the Patent and Trademark Office the name and address of some person resident in the United States on whom may be served notices or process in proceedings affecting the mark. Such notices or process may be served upon the person so designated by leaving with him or mailing to him a copy thereof at the address specified in the last designation so filed. If the person so designated cannot be found at the address given in the last designation, such notice or process may be served upon the Commissioner.

§ 1052. Trademarks registrable on principal register; concurrent registration

No trademark by which the goods of the applicant may be distinguished from the goods of others shall be refused registration on the principal register on account of its nature unless it—

(a) Consists of or comprises immoral, deceptive, or scandalous matter; or matter which may disparage or falsely suggest a connection with persons, living or dead, institutions, beliefs, or national symbols, or bring them into contempt, or disrepute; or a geographical indication which, when used on or in connection with wines or spirits, identifies a place other than the origin of the goods and is first used on or in connection with wines or spirits by the applicant on or after one year after the date on which the WTO Agreement (as defined in section 2(9) of title 19) enters into force with respect to the United States.

(b) Consists of or comprises the flag or coat of arms or other insignia of the United States, or of any State or municipality, or of any foreign nation, or any simulation thereof.

(c) Consists of or comprises a name, portrait, or signature identifying a particular living individual except by his written consent, or the name, signature, or portrait of a deceased President of the United States during the life of his widow, if any, except by the written consent of the widow.

(d) Consists of or comprises a mark which so resembles a mark registered in the Patent and Trademark Office, or a mark or trade name previously used in the United States by another and not abandoned, as to be likely, when used on or in connection with the goods of the applicant, to cause confusion, or to cause mistake, or to deceive: Provided, That if the Commissioner determines that confusion, mistake, or deception is not likely to result from the continued use by more than one person of the same or similar marks under conditions and limitations as to the mode or place of use of the marks or the goods on or in connection with which such marks are used, concurrent registrations may be issued to such persons when they have become entitled to use such marks as a result of their concurrent lawful use in commerce prior to (1) the earliest of the filing dates of the applications pending or of any registration issued under this chapter; (2) July 5, 1947, in the case of registrations previously issued under the Act of March 3, 1881, or February 20, 1905, and continuing in full force and effect on that date; or (3) July 5, 1947, in the case of applications filed under the Act of February 20, 1905, and registered after July 5, 1947. Use prior to the filing date of any pending application or a registration shall not be required when the owner of such application or registration consents to the grant of a concurrent registration to the applicant. Concurrent registrations may also be issued by the Commissioner when a court of competent jurisdiction has finally determined that more than one person is entitled to use the same or similar marks in commerce. In issuing concurrent registrations, the Commissioner shall prescribe conditions and limitations as to the mode or place of use of the mark or the goods on or in connection with which such mark is registered to the respective persons.

(e) Consists of a mark which (1) when used on or in connection with the goods of the applicant is merely descriptive or deceptively misdescriptive of them, (2) when used on or in connection with the goods of the applicant is primarily geographically descriptive of them, except as indications of regional origin may be registrable under section 4 of this title, (3) when used on or in connection with the goods of the applicant is primarily geographically deceptively misdescriptive of them, or (4) is primarily merely a surname.

(f) Except as expressly excluded in paragraphs (a), (b), (c), (d), and (e)(3) of this section, nothing in this chapter shall prevent the registration of a mark used by the applicant which has become distinctive of the applicant's goods in commerce. The Commissioner may accept as prima facie evidence that the mark has become distinctive, as used on or in connection with the applicant's goods in commerce, proof of substantially exclusive and continuous use thereof as a mark by the applicant in commerce for the five years before the date on which the claim of distinctiveness is made. Nothing in this section shall prevent the registration of a mark which, when used on or in connection with the goods of the applicant, is primarily geographically deceptively misdescriptive of them, and which became distinctive of the applicant's goods in commerce before December 8, 1993.

§ 1053. Service marks registrable

Subject to the provisions relating to the registration of trademarks, so far as they are applicable, service marks shall be registrable, in the same manner and with the same effect as are trademarks, and when registered they shall be entitled to the protection provided in this chapter in the case of trademarks. Applications and procedure under this section shall conform as nearly as practicable to those prescribed for the registration of trademarks.

§ 1111. Notice of registration; display with mark; recovery of profits and damages in infringement suit

Notwithstanding the provisions of section 22 of this title, a registrant of a mark registered in the Patent and Trademark Office, may give notice that his mark is registered by displaying with the mark the words "Registered in U.S. Patent and Trademark Office" or "Reg. U.S. Pat. & Tm. Off." or the letter R enclosed within a circle, thus (®); and in any suit for infringement under this chapter by such a registrant failing to give such notice of registration, no profits and no damages shall be recovered under the provisions of this chapter unless the defendant had actual notice of the registration.

§ 1112. Classification of goods and services; registration in plurality of classes

The Commissioner may establish a classification of goods and services, for convenience of Patent and Trademark Office administration, but not to limit or extend the applicant's or registrant's rights. The applicant may apply to register a mark for any or all of the goods or services on or in connection with which he or she is using or has a bona fide intention to use the mark in commerce: Provided, That if the Commissioner by regulation permits the filing of an application for the registration of a mark for goods or services which fall within a plurality of classes, a fee equaling the sum of the fees for filing an application in each class shall be paid, and the Commissioner may issue a single certificate of registration for such mark.

§ 1114. Remedies; infringement; innocent infringement by printers and publishers

(1) Any person who shall, without the consent of the registrant—

(a) use in commerce any reproduction, counterfeit, copy, or colorable imitation of a registered mark in connection with the sale, offering for sale, distribution, or advertising of any goods or services on or in connection with which such use is likely to cause confusion, or to cause mistake, or to deceive; or

(b) reproduce, counterfeit, copy, or colorably imitate a registered mark and apply such reproduction, counterfeit, copy, or colorable imitation to labels, signs, prints, packages, wrappers, receptacles or advertisements intended to be used in commerce upon or in connection with the sale, offering for sale, distribution, or advertising of goods or services on or in connection with which such use is likely to cause confusion, or to cause mistake, or to deceive, shall be liable in a civil action by the registrant for the remedies hereinafter provided. Under subsection (b) hereof, the registrant shall not be entitled to recover profits or damages unless the acts have been committed with knowledge that such imitation is intended to be used to cause confusion, or to cause mistake, or to deceive.

As used in this subsection, the term "any person" includes any State, any instrumentality of a State, and any officer or employee of a State or instrumentality of a State acting in his or her official capacity. Any State, and any such instrumentality, officer, or employee, shall be subject to the provisions of this chapter in the same manner and to the same extent as any nongovernmental entity.

(2) Notwithstanding any other provision of this chapter, the remedies given to the owner of a right infringed under this chapter or to a person bringing an action under section 43(a) of this title shall be limited as follows:

(A) Where an infringer or violator is engaged solely in the business of printing the mark or violating matter for others and establishes that he or she was an innocent infringer or innocent violator, the owner of the right infringed or person bringing the action under section 43(a) of this title shall be entitled as against such infringer or violator only to an injunction against future printing.

(B) Where the infringement or violation complained of is contained in or is part of paid advertising matter in a newspaper, magazine, or other similar periodical or in an electronic communication as defined in section 2510(12) of title 18, the remedies of the owner of the right infringed or person bringing the action under section 43(a) of this title as against the publisher or distributor of such newspaper, magazine, or other similar periodical or electronic communication shall be limited to an injunction against the presentation of such advertising matter in future issues of such newspapers, magazines, or other similar periodicals or in future transmissions of such electronic communications. The limitations of this subparagraph shall apply only to innocent infringers and innocent violators.

(C) Injunctive relief shall not be available to the owner of the right infringed or person bringing the action under section 43(a) of this title with respect to an issue of a newspaper, magazine, or other similar periodical or an electronic communication containing infringing matter or violating matter where restraining the dissemination of such infringing matter or violating matter in any particular issue of such periodical or in an electronic communication would delay the delivery of such issue or transmission of such electronic communication after the regular time for such delivery or transmission, and such delay would be due to the method by which publication and distribution of such periodical or transmission of such electronic communication is customarily conducted in accordance with sound business practice, and not due to any method or device adopted to evade this section or to prevent or delay the issuance of an injunction or restraining order with respect to such infringing matter or violating matter.

(D) As used in this paragraph—

(i) the term "violator" means a person who violates section 43(a) of this title; and

(ii) the term "violating matter" means matter that is the subject of a violation under section 43(a) of this title.

§ 1115. Registration on principal register as evidence of exclusive right to use mark; defenses

(a) Evidentiary value; defenses

Any registration issued under the Act of March 3, 1881, or the Act of February 20, 1905, or of a mark registered on the principal register provided by this chapter and owned by a party to an action shall be admissible in evidence and shall be prima facie evidence of the validity of the registered mark and of the registration of the mark, of the registrant's ownership of the mark, and of the registrant's exclusive right to use the registered mark in commerce on or in connection with the goods or services specified in the registration subject to any conditions or limitations stated therein, but shall not preclude another person from proving any legal or equitable defense or defect, including those set forth in subsection (b) of this section, which might have been asserted if such mark had not been registered.

(b) Incontestability; defenses

To the extent that the right to use the registered mark has become incontestable under section 15 of this title, the registration shall be conclusive evidence of the validity of the registered mark and of the registration of the mark, of the registrant's ownership of the mark, and of the registrant's exclusive right to use the registered mark in commerce. Such conclusive evidence shall relate to the exclusive right to use the mark on or in connection with the goods or services specified in the affidavit filed under the provisions of section 15 of this title, or in the renewal application filed under the provisions of section 9 of this title if the goods or services specified in the renewal are fewer in number, subject to any conditions or limitations in the registration or in such affidavit or renewal application. Such conclusive evidence of the right to use the registered mark shall be subject to proof of infringement as defined in section 32 of this title, and shall be subject to the following defenses or defects:

(1) That the registration or the incontestable right to use the mark was obtained fraudulently; or

(2) That the mark has been abandoned by the registrant; or

(3) That the registered mark is being used by or with the permission of the registrant or a person in privity with the registrant, so as to misrepresent the source of the goods or services on or in connection with which the mark is used; or

(4) That the use of the name, term, or device charged to be an infringement is a use, otherwise than as a mark, of the party's individual name in his own business, or of the individual name of anyone in privity with such party, or of a term or device which is descriptive of and used fairly and in good faith only to describe the goods or services of such party, or their geographic origin; or

(5) That the mark whose use by a party is charged as an infringement was adopted without knowledge of the registrant's prior use and has been continuously used by such party or those in privity with him from a date prior to (A) the date of constructive use of the mark

established pursuant to section 7(c) of this title, (B) the registration of the mark under this chapter if the application for registration is filed before the effective date of the Trademark Law Revision Act of 1988, or (C) publication of the registered mark under subsection (c) of section 12 of this title: Provided, however, That this defense or defect shall apply only for the area in which such continuous prior use is proved; or

(6) That the mark whose use is charged as an infringement was registered and used prior to the registration under this chapter or publication under subsection (c) of section 12 of this title of the registered mark of the registrant, and not abandoned: Provided, however, That this defense or defect shall apply only for the area in which the mark was used prior to such registration or such publication of the registrant's mark; or

(7) That the mark has been or is being used to violate the antitrust laws of the United States; or

(8) That equitable principles, including laches, estoppel, and acquiescence, are applicable.

§ 1116. Injunctive relief

(a) Jurisdiction; service

The several courts vested with jurisdiction of civil actions arising under this chapter shall have power to grant injunctions, according to the principles of equity and upon such terms as the court may deem reasonable, to prevent the violation of any right of the registrant of a mark registered in the Patent and Trademark Office or to prevent a violation under section 43(a) of this title. Any such injunction may include a provision directing the defendant to file with the court and serve on the plaintiff within thirty days after the service on the defendant of such injunction, or such extended period as the court may direct, a report in writing under oath setting forth in detail the manner and form in which the defendant has complied with the injunction. Any such injunction granted upon hearing, after notice to the defendant, by any district court of the United States, may be served on the parties against whom such injunction is granted anywhere in the United States where they may be found, and shall be operative and may be enforced by proceedings to punish for contempt, or otherwise, by the court by which such injunction was granted, or by any other United States district court in whose jurisdiction the defendant may be found.

(b) Transfer of certified copies of court papers

The said courts shall have jurisdiction to enforce said injunction, as provided in this chapter, as fully as if the injunction had been granted by the district court in which it is sought to be enforced. The clerk of the court or judge granting the injunction shall, when required to do so by the court before which application to enforce said injunction is made, transfer without delay to said court a certified copy of all papers on file in his office upon which said injunction was granted.

(c) Notice to Commissioner

It shall be the duty of the clerks of such courts within one month after the filing of any action, suit, or proceeding involving a mark registered under the provisions of this chapter to give notice thereof in writing to the Commissioner setting forth in order so far as known the names and addresses of the litigants and the designating number or numbers of the registration or registrations upon which the action, suit, or proceeding has been brought, and in the event any other registration be subsequently included in the action, suit, or proceeding by amendment, answer, or other pleading, the clerk shall give like notice thereof to the Commissioner, and within one month after the judgment is entered or an appeal is taken the clerk of the court shall give notice thereof to the Commissioner, and it shall be the duty of the Commissioner on receipt of such notice forthwith to endorse the same upon the file wrapper of the said registration or registrations and to incorporate the same as a part of the contents of said file wrapper.

(d) Civil actions arising out of use of counterfeit marks

(1) (A) In the case of a civil action arising under section 32(1)(a) of this title or section 110 of title 36 with respect to a violation that consists of using a counterfeit mark in connection with the sale, offering for sale, or distribution of goods or services, the court may, upon ex parte application, grant an order under subsection (a) of this section pursuant to this subsection providing for the seizure of goods and counterfeit marks involved in such violation and the means of making such marks, and records documenting the manufacture, sale, or receipt of things involved in such violation.

(B) As used in this subsection the term "counterfeit mark" means—

(i) a counterfeit of a mark that is registered on the principal register in the United States Patent and Trademark Office for such goods or services sold, offered for sale, or distributed and that is in use, whether or not the person against whom relief is sought knew such mark was so registered; or

(ii) a spurious designation that is identical with, or substantially indistinguishable from, a designation as to which the remedies of this chapter are made available by reason of section 110 of title 36; but such term does not include any mark or designation used on or in connection with goods or services of which the manufacture or producer was, at the time of the manufacture or production in question authorized to use the mark or designation for the type of goods or services so manufactured or produced, by the holder of the right to use such mark or designation.

(2) The court shall not receive an application under this subsection unless the applicant has given such notice of the application as is reasonable under the circumstances to the United States attorney for the judicial district in which such order is sought. Such attorney may participate in the proceedings arising under such application if such proceedings may affect evidence of an offense against the United States. The court may deny such application if the court determines that the public interest in a potential prosecution so requires.

(3) The application for an order under this subsection shall—

(A) be based on an affidavit or the verified complaint establishing facts sufficient to support the findings of fact and conclusions of law required for such order; and

(B) contain the additional information required by paragraph (5) of this subsection to be set forth in such order.

(4) The court shall not grant such an application unless—

(A) the person obtaining an order under this subsection provides the security determined adequate by the court for the payment of such damages as any person may be entitled to recover as a result of a wrongful seizure or wrongful attempted seizure under this subsection; and

(B) the court finds that it clearly appears from specific facts that—

(i) an order other than an ex parte seizure order is not adequate to achieve the purposes of section 32 of this title;

(ii) the applicant has not publicized the requested seizure;

(iii) the applicant is likely to succeed in showing that the person against whom seizure would be ordered used a counterfeit mark in connection with the sale, offering for sale, or distribution of goods or services;

(iv) an immediate and irreparable injury will occur if such seizure is not ordered;

(v) the matter to be seized will be located at the place identified in the application;

(vi) the harm to the applicant of denying the application outweighs the harm to the legitimate interests of the person against whom seizure would be ordered of granting the application; and

(vii) the person against whom seizure would be ordered, or persons acting in concert with such person, would destroy, move, hide, or otherwise make such matter inaccessible to the court, if the applicant were to proceed on notice to such person.

(5) An order under this subsection shall set forth—

(A) the findings of fact and conclusions of law required for the order;

(B) a particular description of the matter to be seized, and a description of each place at which such matter is to be seized;

(C) the time period, which shall end not later than seven days after the date on which such order is issued, during which the seizure is to be made;

(D) the amount of security required to be provided under this subsection; and

(E) a date for the hearing required under paragraph (10) of this subsection.

(6) The court shall take appropriate action to protect the person against whom an order under this subsection is directed from publicity, by or at the behest of the plaintiff, about such order and any seizure under such order.

(7) Any materials seized under this subsection shall be taken into the custody of the court. The court shall enter an appropriate protective order with respect to discovery by the applicant of any records that have been seized. The protective order shall provide for appropriate procedures to assure that confidential information contained in such records is not improperly disclosed to the applicant.

(8) An order under this subsection, together with the supporting documents, shall be sealed until the person against whom the order is directed has an opportunity to contest such order, except that any person against whom such order is issued shall have access to such order and supporting documents after the seizure has been carried out.

(9) The court shall order that a United States marshal or other law enforcement officer is to serve a copy of the order under this subsection and then is to carry out the seizure under such order. The court shall issue orders, when appropriate, to protect the defendant from undue damage from the disclosure of trade secrets or other confidential information during the course of the seizure, including, when appropriate, orders restricting the access of the applicant (or any agent or employee of the applicant) to such secrets or information.

(10) (A) The court shall hold a hearing, unless waived by all the parties, on the date set by the court in the order of seizure. That date shall be not sooner than ten days after the order is issued and not later than fifteen days after the order is issued, unless the applicant for the order shows good cause for another date or unless the party against whom such order is directed consents to another date for such hearing. At such hearing the party obtaining the order shall have the burden to prove that the facts supporting findings of fact and conclusions of law

necessary to support such order are still in effect. If that party fails to meet that burden, the seizure order shall be dissolved or modified appropriately.

(B) In connection with a hearing under this paragraph, the court may make such orders modifying the time limits for discovery under the Rules of Civil Procedure as may be necessary to prevent the frustration of the purposes of such hearing.

(11) A person who suffers damage by reason of a wrongful seizure under this subsection has a cause of action against the applicant for the order under which such seizure was made, and shall be entitled to recover such relief as may be appropriate, including damages for lost profits, cost of materials, loss of good will, and punitive damages in instances where the seizure was sought in bad faith, and, unless the court finds extenuating circumstances, to recover a reasonable attorney's fee. The court in its discretion may award prejudgment interest on relief recovered under this paragraph, at an annual interest rate established under section 6621 of title 26, commencing on the date of service of the claimant's pleading setting forth the claim under this paragraph and ending on the date such recovery is granted, or for such shorter time as the court deems appropriate.

C

Selected Copyright Laws

Copyrights are the exclusive province of the federal government and may not be regulated by the state. This portion of the appendix contains excerpts of the federal copyright laws related to general copyright definitions, registration, infringement, and remedies. Each of the following sections may be found in Title 17 of the United States Code.

§ 101. Definitions.

As used in this title, the following terms and their variant forms mean the following:

An "anonymous work" is a work on the copies or phonorecords of which no natural person is identified as author.

"Audiovisual works" are works that consist of a series of related images which are intrinsically intended to be shown by the use of machines or devices such as projectors, viewers, or electronic equipment, together with accompanying sounds, if any, regardless of the nature of the material objects, such as films or tapes, in which the works are embodied.

The "best edition" of a work is the edition, published in the United States at any time before the date of deposit; that the Library of Congress determines to be most suitable for its purposes.

A person's "children" are that person's immediate offspring, whether legitimate or not, and any children legally adopted by that person.

A "collective work" is a work, such as a periodical issue, anthology, or encyclopedia, in which a number of contributions, constituting separate and independent works in themselves, are assembled into a collective whole.

A "compilation" is a work formed by the collection and assembling of preexisting materials or of data that are selected, coordinated, or arranged in such a way that the resulting work as a whole constitutes an original work of authorship. The term "compilation" includes collective works.

A "computer program" is a set of statements or instructions to be used directly or indirectly in a computer in order to bring about a certain result.

"Copies" are material objects, other than phonorecords, in which a work is fixed by any method now known or later developed, and from which the work can be perceived, reproduced, or otherwise communicated, either directly or with the aid of a machine or device. The term "copies" includes the material object, other than a phonorecord, in which the work is first fixed.

"Copyright owner," with respect to any one of the exclusive rights comprised in a copyright, refers to the owner of that particular right.

A work is "created" when it is fixed in a copy or phonorecord for the first time; where a work is prepared over a period of time, the portion of it that has been fixed at any particular time constitutes the work as of that time, and where the work has been prepared in different versions, each version constitutes a separate work.

A "derivative work" is a work based upon one or more preexisting works, such as a translation, musical arrangement, dramatization, fictionalization, motion picture version, sound recording, art reproduction, abridgment, condensation, or any other form in which a work may be recast, transformed, or adapted. A work consisting of editorial revisions, annotations, elaborations, or other modifications which, as a whole, represent an original work of authorship, is a "derivative work."

A "device," "machine," or "process" is one now known or later developed.

To "display" a work means to show a copy of it, either directly or by means of a film, slide, television image, or any other device or processor, in the case of a motion picture or other audiovisual work, to show individual images nonsequentially.

A work is "fixed" in a tangible medium of expression when its embodiment in a copy or phonorecord, by or under the authority of the author, is sufficiently permanent or stable to permit it to be perceived, reproduced, or otherwise communicated for a period of more than transitory duration. A work consisting of sounds, images, or both, that are being transmitted, is "fixed" for purposes of this title if a fixation of the work is being made simultaneously with its transmission. The terms "including" and "such as" are illustrative and not limitative.

A "joint work" is a work prepared by two or more authors with the intention that their contributions be merged into inseparable or interdependent parts of a unitary whole.

"Literary works" are works, other than audiovisual works, expressed in words, numbers, or other verbal or numerical symbols or indicia, regardless of the nature of the material objects, such as books, periodicals, manuscripts, phonorecords, film, tapes, disks, or cards, in which they are embodied.

"Motion pictures" are audiovisual works consisting of a series of related images which, when shown in succession, impart an impression of motion, together with accompanying sounds, if any.

To "perform" a work means to recite, render, play, dance, or act it, either directly or by means of any device or process or, in the case of a motion picture or other audiovisual work, to show its images in any sequence or to make the sounds accompanying it audible.

"Phonorecords" are material objects in which sounds, other than those accompanying a motion picture or other audiovisual work, are fixed by any method now known or later developed, and from which the sounds can be perceived, reproduced, or otherwise communicated, either directly or with the aid of a machine or device. The term "phonorecords" includes the material object in which the sounds are first fixed.

"Pictorial, graphic, and sculptural works" include two-dimensional and three-dimensional works of fine, graphic, and applied art, photographs, prints and art reproductions, maps, globes, charts, technical drawings, diagrams, and models. Such works shall include works of artistic craftsmanship insofar as their form but not their mechanical or utilitarian aspects are concerned; the design of a useful article, as defined in this section, shall be considered a pictorial, graphic, or sculptural work only if, and only to the extent that, such design incorporates pictorial, graphic, or sculptural features that can be identified separately from, and are capable of existing independently of, the utilitarian aspects of the article.

A "pseudonymous work" is a work on the copies or phonorecords of which the author is identified under a fictitious name.

"Publication" is the distribution of copies or phonorecords of a work to the public by sale or other transfer of ownership, or by rental, lease, or lending. The offering to distribute copies or phonorecords to a group of persons for purposes of further distribution, public performance, or public display, constitutes publication. A public performance or display of a work does not of itself constitute publication.

To perform or display a work "publicly" means—

(1) to perform or display it at a place open to the public or at any place where a substantial number of persons outside of a normal circle of a family and its social acquaintances is gathered; or,

(2) to transmit or otherwise communicate a performance or display of the work to a place specified by clause (1) or to the public, by means of any device or process, whether the members of the public capable of receiving the performance or display receive it in the same place or in separate places and at the same time or at different times.

"Sound recordings" are works that result from the fixation of a series of musical, spoken, or other sounds, but not including the sounds accompanying a motion picture or other audiovisual work, regardless of the nature of the material objects, such as disks, tapes, or other phonorecords, in which they are embodied.

"State" includes the District of Columbia and the Commonwealth of Puerto Rico, and any territories to which this title is made applicable by an Act of Congress.

A "Transfer of copyright ownership" is an assignment, mortgage, exclusive license, or any other conveyance, alienation, or hypothecation of a copyright or of any of the exclusive rights comprised in a copyright, whether or not it is limited in time or place of effect, but not including a nonexclusive license.

A "transmission program" is a body of material that, as an aggregate, has been produced for the sole purpose of transmission to the public in sequence and as a unit.

To "transmit" a performance or display is to communicate it by any device or process whereby images or sounds are received beyond the place from which they are sent.

The "United States," when used in a geographical sense, comprises the several States, the District of Columbia and the Commonwealth of Puerto Rico, and the organized territories under the jurisdiction of the United States Government.

A "useful article" is an article having an intrinsic utilitarian function that is not merely to portray the appearance of the article or to convey information. An article that is normally a part of a useful article is considered a "useful article."

The author's "widow" or "widower" is the author's surviving spouse under the law of the author's domicile at the time of his or her death, whether or not the spouse has later remarried.

A "work of the United States Government" is a work prepared by any officer or employee of the United States Government as part of that person's official duties.

A "work made for hire" is—

(1) a work prepared by an employee within the scope of his or her employment; or

(2) a work specially ordered or commissioned for use as a contribution to a collective work, as a part of a motion picture or other audiovisual work, as a translation, as a supplementary work, as a compilation, as an instructional text, as a test, as answer material for a test, or as an atlas, if the parties expressly agree in a written instrument signed by them that the work shall be considered a work made for hire. For the purpose of the foregoing sentence, a "supplementary work" is a work prepared for publication as a secondary adjunct to a work by another author for the purpose of introducing, concluding, illustrating, explaining, revising, commenting upon, or assisting in the use of the other work, such as forewords, afterwords, pictorial illustrations, maps, charts, tables, editorial notes, musical arrangements, answer material for tests, bibliographies, appendixes, and indexes, and an "instructional text" is a literary, pictorial, or graphic work prepared for publication and with the purpose of use in systematic instructional activities.

§ 102. Subject matter of copyright: In general.

(a) Copyright protection subsists, in accordance with this title, in original works of authorship fixed in any tangible medium of expression, now known or later developed, from which they can be perceived, reproduced, or otherwise communicated, either directly or with the aid of a machine or device. Works of authorship include the following categories:

(1) literary works;
(2) musical works, including any accompanying words;
(3) dramatic works, including any accompanying music;
(4) pantomimes and choreographic works;
(5) pictorial, graphic, and sculptural works;
(6) motion pictures and other audiovisual works; and
(7) sound recordings.

(b) In no case does copyright protection for an original work of authorship extend to any idea, procedure, process, system, method of operation, concept, principle, or discovery, regardless of the form in which it is described, explained, illustrated, or embodied in such work.

§ 103. Subject matter of copyright: Compilations and derivative works.

(a) The subject matter of copyright as specified by section 102 includes compilations and derivative works, but protection for a work employing preexisting material in which copyright subsists does not extend to any part of the work in which such material has been used unlawfully.

(b) The copyright in a compilation or derivative work extends only to the material contributed by the author of such work, as distinguished from the preexisting material employed in the work, and does not imply any exclusive right in the preexisting material. The copyright in such work is independent of, and does not affect or enlarge the scope, duration, ownership, or subsistence of, any copyright protection in the preexisting material.

§ 104. Subject matter of copyright: National origin.

(a) Unpublished Works.—The works specified by sections 102 and 103, while unpublished, are subject to protection under this title without regard to the nationality or domicile of the author.

(b) Published Works.—The works specified by section 102 and 103, when published, are subject to protection under this title if—
    (1) on the date of first publication, one or more of the authors is a national or domiciliary of the United States, or is a national, domiciliary, or sovereign authority of a foreign nation that is a party to a copyright treaty to which the United States is also a party, or is a stateless person, wherever that person may be domiciled; or
    (2) the work is first published in the United States or in a foreign nation that, on the date of first publication, is a party to the Universal Copyright Convention; or
    (3) the work is first published by the United Nations or any of its specialized agencies, or by the Organization of American States; or
    (4) the work comes within the scope of a Presidential proclamation. Whenever the President finds that a particular foreign nation extends, to works by authors who are nationals or domiciliaries of the United States or to works that are first published in the United States, copyright protection on substantially the same basis as that on which the foreign

nation extends protection to works of its own nationals and domiciliaries and works first published in that nation, the President may by proclamation extend protection under this title to works of which one or more of the authors is, on the date of first publication, a national, domiciliary, or sovereign authority of that nation, or which was first published in that nation. The President may revise, suspend, or revoke any such proclamation or impose any conditions or limitations on protection under a proclamation.

§ 105. Subject matter of copyright: United States Government works.

Copyright protection under this title is not available for any work of the United States Government, but the United States Government is not precluded from receiving and holding copyrights transferred to it by assignment, bequest, or otherwise.

§ 106. Exclusive rights in copyrighted works.

Subject to sections 107 through 118, the owner of copyright under this title has the exclusive rights to do and to authorize any of the following:
   (1) to reproduce the copyrighted work in copies or phonorecords;
   (2) to prepare derivative works based upon the copyrighted work;
   (3) to distribute copies or phonorecords of the copyrighted work to the public by sale or other transfer of ownership, or by rental, lease, or lending;
   (4) in the case of literary, musical, dramatic, and choreographic works, pantomimes, and motion pictures and other audiovisual works, to perform the copyrighted work publicly; and
   (5) in the case of literary, musical, dramatic, and choreographic works, pantomimes, and pictorial, graphic, or sculptural works, including the individual images of a motion picture or other audiovisual work, to display the copyrighted publicly.

§ 107. Limitations on exclusive rights: Fair use.

Notwithstanding the provisions of section 106, the fair use of a copyrighted work, including such use by reproduction in copies or phonorecords or by any other means specified by that section, for purposes such as criticism, comment, news reporting, teaching (including multiple copies for classroom use), scholarship, or research, is not an infringement of copyright. In determining whether the use made of a work in any particular case is a fair use the factors to be considered shall include—

(1) the purpose and character of the use, including whether such use is of a commercial nature or is for nonprofit educational purposes;

(2) the nature of the copyrighted work;

(3) the amount and substantiality of the portion used in relation to the copyrighted work as a whole; and

(4) the effect of the use upon the potential market for or value of the copyrighted work.

§ 113. Scope of exclusive rights in pictorial, graphic, and sculptural work.

(a) Subject to the provisions of subsections (b) and (c) of this section, the exclusive right to reproduce a copyrighted pictorial, graphic, or sculptural work in copies under section 106 includes the right to reproduce the work in or on any kind of article, whether useful or otherwise.

(b) This title does not afford, to the owner of copyright in a work that portrays a useful article as such, any greater or lesser rights with respect to the making, distribution, or display of the useful article so portrayed than those afforded to such works under the law, whether title 17 or the common law or statutes of a State, in effect on December 31, 1977, as held applicable and construed by a court in an action brought under this title.

(c) In the case of a work lawfully reproduced in useful articles that have been offered for sale or other distribution to the public, copyright does not include any right to prevent the making, distribution, or display of pictures or photographs of such articles in connection with advertisements or commentaries related to the distribution or display of such articles, or in connection with news reports.

Section 117. Limitations on exclusive rights: Computer programs.

Notwithstanding the provisions of section 106, it is not an infringement for the owner of a copy of a computer program to make or authorize the making of another copy or adaptation of that computer program provided:

(1) that such a new copy or adaptation is created as an essential step in the utilization of the computer program in conjunction with a machine and that it is used in no other manner, or

(2) that such new copy or adaptation is for archival purposes only and that all archival copies are destroyed in the event that continued possession of the computer program should cease to be rightful. Any exact copies prepared in accordance with the provisions of this section may be leased, sold, or otherwise transferred, along with the copy from which such copies were prepared, only as part of the lease, sale, or other transfer of all rights in the program. Adaptations so prepared may be transferred only with the authorization of the copyright owner.

§ 201. Ownership of copyright.

(a) Initial Ownership. Copyright in a work protected under this title vests initially in the author or authors of the work. The authors of a joint work are coowners of copyright in the work.

(b) Works Made for Hire. In the case of a work made for hire, the employer or other person for whom the work was prepared is considered the author for purposes of this title, and, unless the parties have expressly agreed otherwise in a written instrument signed by them, owns all of the rights comprised in the copyright.

(c) Contributions to Collective Works. Copyright in each separate contribution to a collective work is distinct from copyright in the collective work as a whole, and vests initially in the author of the contribution. In the absence of an express transfer of the copyright or of any rights under it, the owner of copyright in the collective work is presumed to have acquired only the privilege of reproducing and distributing the contribution as part of that particular collective work, any revision of that collective work, and any later collective work in the same series.

(d) Transfer of Ownership.

(1) The ownership of a copyright may be transferred in whole or in part by any means of conveyance or by operation of law, and may be bequeathed by will or pass as personal property by the applicable laws of intestate succession.

(2) Any of the exclusive rights comprised in a copyright, including any subdivision of any of the rights specified by section 106, may be transferred as provided by clause (1) and owned separately. The owner of any particular exclusive right is entitled, to the extent of that right, to all of the protection and remedies accorded to the copyright owner by this title.

(e) Involuntary Transfer. When an individual author's ownership of a copyright, or of any of the exclusive rights under a copyright, has not previously been transferred voluntarily by that individual author, no action by any governmental body or other official or organization purporting to seize, expropriate, transfer, or exercise rights of ownership with respect to the copyright, or any of the exclusive rights under a copyright, shall be given effect under this title, except as provided under title 11.

§ 202. Ownership of copyright as distinct from ownership of material object

Ownership of a copyright, or of any of the exclusive rights under a copyright, is distinct from ownership of any material object in which the work is embodied. Transfer of ownership of any material object, including the copy or phonorecord in which the work is first fixed, does not of itself convey any rights in the copyrighted work embodied in the object; nor, in the absence of an agreement, does transfer of ownership of a copyright or of any exclusive rights under a copyright convey property rights in any material object.

§ 204. Execution of transfers of copyright ownership

(a) A transfer of copyright ownership, other than by operation of law, is not valid unless an instrument of conveyance, or a note or memorandum of the transfer, is in writing and signed by the owner of the rights conveyed or such owner's duly authorized agent.

(b) A certificate of acknowledgement is not required for the validity of a transfer, but is prima facie evidence of the execution of the transfer if—

(1) in the case of a transfer executed in the United States, the certificate is issued by a person authorized to administer oaths within the United States; or

(2) in the case of a transfer executed in a foreign country, the certificate is issued by a diplomatic or consular officer of the United States, or by a person authorized to administer oaths whose authority is proved by a certificate of such an officer.

§ 302. Duration of copyright: Works created on or after January 1, 1978

(a) In General. Copyright in a work created on or after January 1, 1978, subsists from its creation and, except as provided by the following subsections, endures for a term consisting of the life of the author and fifty years after the author's death.

(b) Joint Works. In the case of a joint work prepared by two or more authors who did not work for hire, the copyright endures for a term consisting of the life of the last surviving author and fifty years after such last surviving author's death.

(c) Anonymous Works, Pseudonymous Works, and Works Made for Hire. In the case of an anonymous work, a pseudonymous work, or a work made for hire, the copyright endures for a term of seventy-five years from the year of its first publication, or a term of one hundred years from the year of its creation, whichever expires first. If, before the end of such term, the identity of one or more of the authors of an anonymous or pseudonymous work is revealed in the records of a registration made for that work under subsections (a) or (d) of section 408, or in the records provided by this subsection, the copyright in the work endures for the term specified by subsection (a) or (b), based on the life of the author or authors whose identity has been revealed. Any person having an interest in the copyright in an anonymous or pseudonymous work may at any time record, in records to be maintained by the Copyright Office for that purpose, a statement identifying one or more authors of the work; the statement shall also identify the person filing it, the nature of that person's interest, the source of the information recorded, and the particular work affected, and shall comply in form and content with requirements that the Register of Copyrights shall prescribe by regulation.

(d) Records Relating to Death of Authors. Any person having an interest in a copyright may at any time record in the Copyright Office a statement of the date of death of the author of the copyrighted work, or a statement that the author is still living on a particular date. The statement shall identify the person filing it, the nature of that person's interest, and the source of the information recorded, and shall comply in form and content with requirements that the Register of Copyrights shall prescribe by regulation. The Register shall maintain current records of information relating to the death of authors of copyrighted works, based on such recorded statements and, to the extent the Register considers practicable, on data contained in any of the records of the Copyright Office or in other reference sources.

(e) Presumption as to Author's Death. After a period of seventy-five years from the year of first publication of a work, or a period of one hundred years from the year of its creation, whichever expires first, any person who obtains from the Copyright Office a certified report that the records provided by subsection (d) disclose nothing to indicate that the author of the work is living, or died less than fifty years before, is entitled to the benefit of a presumption that the author has been dead for at least fifty years. Reliance in good faith upon this presumption shall be a complete defense to any action for infringement under this title.

§ 303. Duration of copyright: Works created but not published or copyrighted before January 1, 1978

Copyright in a work created before January 1, 1978, but not theretofore in the public domain or copyrighted, subsists from January 1, 1978, and endures for the term provided by section 302. In no case, however, shall the term of copyright in such a work expire before December 31, 2002; and, if the work is published on or before December 31, 2002, the term of copyright shall not expire before December 31, 2027.

§ 401. Notice of copyright: Visually perceptible copies

(a) General Provisions. Whenever a work protected under this title is published in the United States or elsewhere by authority of the copyright owner, a notice of copyright as provided by this section may be placed on publicly distributed copies from which the work can be visually perceived, either directly or with the aid of a machine or device.

(b) Form of Notice. If a notice appears on the copies, it shall consist of the following three elements:

(1) the symbol (c) (the letter C in a circle), or the word "Copyright", or the abbreviation "Copr."; and

(2) the year of first publication of the work; in the case of compilations or derivative works incorporating previously published material, the year date of first publication of the compilation or derivative work is sufficient. The year date may be omitted where a pictorial, graphic, or sculptural work, with accompanying text matter, if any, is reproduced in or on greeting cards, postcards, stationery, jewelry, dolls, toys, or any useful articles; and

(3) the name of the owner of copyright in the work, or an abbreviation by which the name can be recognized, or a generally known alternative designation of the owner.

(c) Position of Notice. The notice shall be affixed to the copies in such manner and location as to give reasonable notice of the claim of copyright. The Register of Copyrights shall prescribe by regulation, as examples, specific methods of affixation and positions of the notice on various types of works that will satisfy this requirement, but these specifications shall not be considered exhaustive.

(d) Evidentiary Weight of Notice. If a notice of copyright in the form and position specified by this section appears on the published copy or copies to which a defendant in a copyright infringement suit had access, then no weight shall be given to such a defendant's interposition of a defense based on innocent infringement in mitigation of actual or statutory damages, except as provided in the last sentence of section 504(c)(2).

§ 408. Copyright registration in general

(a) Registration Permissive. At any time during the subsistence of the first term of copyright in any published or unpublished work in which the copyright was secured before January 1, 1978, and during the subsistence of any copyright secured on or after that date, the owner of copyright or of any exclusive right in the work may obtain registration of the copyright claim by delivering to the Copyright Office the deposit specified by this section, together with the application and fee specified by sections 409 and 708. Such registration is not a condition of copyright protection.

(b) Deposit for Copyright Registration. Except as provided by subsection (c), the material deposited for registration shall include—

(1) in the case of an unpublished work, one complete copy or phonorecord;

(2) in the case of a published work, two complete copies or phonorecords of the best edition;

(3) in the case of a work first published outside the United States, one complete copy or phonorecord as so published;

(4) in the case of a contribution to a collective work, one complete copy or phonorecord of the best edition of the collective work.

Copies or phonorecords deposited for the Library of Congress under section 407 may be used to satisfy the deposit provisions of this section, if they are accompanied by the prescribed application and fee, and by any additional identifying material that the Register may, by regulation, require. The Register shall also prescribe regulations establishing requirements under which copies or phonorecords acquired for the Library of Congress under subsection (e) of section 407, otherwise than by deposit, may be used to satisfy the deposit provisions of this section.

(c) Administrative Classification and Optional Deposit.—

(1) The Register of Copyrights is authorized to specify by regulation the administrative classes into which works are to be placed for purposes of deposit and registration, and the nature of the copies or phonorecords to be deposited in the various classes specified. The

regulations may require or permit, for particular classes, the deposit of identifying material instead of copies or phonorecords, the deposit of only one copy or phonorecord where two would normally be required, or a single registration for a group of related works. This administrative classification of works has no significance with respect to the subject matter of copyright or the exclusive rights provided by this title.

(2) Without prejudice to the general authority provided under clause (1), the Register of Copyrights shall establish regulations specifically permitting a single registration for a group of works by the same individual author, all first published as contributions to periodicals, including newspapers, within a twelve-month period, on the basis of a single deposit, application, and registration fee, under the following conditions—

(A) if the deposit consists of one copy of the entire issue of the periodical, or of the entire section in the case of a newspaper, in which each contribution was first published; and

(B) if the application identifies each work separately, including the periodical containing it and its date of first publication.

(3) As an alternative to separate renewal registrations under subsection (a) of section 304, a single renewal registration may be made for a group of works by the same individual author, all first published as contributions to periodicals, including newspapers, upon the filing of a single application and fee, under all of the following conditions:

(A) the renewal claimant or claimants, and the basis of claim or claims under section 304(a), is the same for each of the works; and

(B) the works were all copyrighted upon their first publication, either through separate copyright notice and registration or by virtue of a general copyright notice in the periodical issue as a whole; and

(C) the renewal application and fee are received not more than twenty-eight or less than twenty-seven years after the thirty-first day of December of the calendar year in which all of the works were first published; and

(D) the renewal application identifies each work separately, including the periodical containing it and its date of first publication.

(d) Corrections and Amplifications. The Register may also establish, by regulation, formal procedures for the filing of an application for supplementary registration, to correct an error in a copyright registration or to amplify the information given in a registration. Such application shall be accompanied by the fee provided by section 708, and shall clearly identify the registration to be corrected or amplified. The information contained in a supplementary registration augments but does not supersede that contained in the earlier registration.

(e) Published Edition of Previously Registered Work. Registration for the first published edition of a work previously registered in unpublished form may be made even though the work as published is substantially the same as the unpublished version.

§ 409. Application for copyright registration

The application for copyright registration shall be made on a form prescribed by the Register of Copyrights and shall include—

(1) the name and address of the copyright claimant;

(2) in the case of a work other than an anonymous or pseudonymous work, the name and nationality or domicile of the author or authors, and, if one or more of the authors is dead, the dates of their deaths;

(3) if the work is anonymous or pseudonymous, the nationality or domicile of the author or authors;

(4) in the case of a work made for hire, a statement to this effect;

(5) if the copyright claimant is not the author, a brief statement of how the claimant obtained ownership of the copyright;

(6) the title of the work, together with any previous or alternative titles under which the work can be identified;

(7) the year in which creation of the work was completed;

(8) if the work has been published, the date and nation of its first publication;

(9) in the case of a compilation or derivative work, an identification of any preexisting work or works that it is based on or incorporates, and a brief, general statement of the additional material covered by the copyright claim being registered;

(10) in the case of a published work containing material of which copies are required by section 601 to be manufactured in the United States, the names of the persons or organizations who performed the processes specified by subsection (c) of section 601 with respect to that material, and the places where those processes were performed; and

(11) any other information regarded by the Register of Copyrights as bearing upon the preparation or identification of the work or the existence, ownership, or duration of the copyright.

If an application is submitted for the renewed and extended term provided for in section 304(a)(3)(A) and an original term registration has not been made, the Register may request information with respect to the existence, ownership, or duration of the copyright for the original term.

§ 411. Registration and infringement actions

(a) Except for actions for infringement of copyright in Berne Convention works whose country of origin is not the United States and an action brought for a violation of the rights of the author under section 106A(a), and subject to the provisions of subsection (b), no action for infringement of the copyright in any work shall be instituted until registration of the copyright claim has been made in accordance with this title. In any case, however, where the deposit, application, and fee required for registration have been delivered to the Copyright Office in proper form and registration has been refused, the applicant is entitled to institute an action for infringement if notice thereof, with a copy of the complaint, is served on the Register of Copyrights. The Register may, at his or her option, become a party to the action with respect to the issue of registrability of the copyright claim by entering an appearance within sixty days after such service, but the Register's failure to become a party shall not deprive the court of jurisdiction to determine that issue.

(b) In the case of a work consisting of sounds, images, or both, the first fixation of which is made simultaneously with its transmission, the copyright owner may, either before or after such fixation takes place, institute an action for infringement under section 501, fully subject to the remedies provided by sections 502 through 506 and sections 509 and 510, if, in accordance with requirements that the Register of Copyrights shall prescribe by regulation, the copyright owner—

(1) serves notice upon the infringer, not less than ten or more than thirty days before such fixation, identifying the work and the specific time and source of its first transmission, and declaring an intention to secure copyright in the work; and

(2) makes registration for the work, if required by subsection (a), within three months after its first transmission.

§ 412. Registration as prerequisite to certain remedies for infringement

In any action under this title, other than an action brought for a violation of the rights of the author under section 106A(a) or an action instituted under section 411(b), no award of statutory damages or of attorney's fees, as provided by sections 504 and 505, shall be made for

(1) any infringement of copyright in an unpublished work commenced before the effective date of its registration; or

(2) any infringement of copyright commenced after first publication of the work and before the effective date of its registration, unless such registration is made within three months after the first publication of the work.

§ 501. Infringement of copyright

(a) Anyone who violates any of the exclusive rights of the copyright owner as provided by sections 106 through 118 or of the author as provided in section 106A(a), or who imports copies or phonorecords into the United States in violation of section 602, is an infringer of the copyright or right of the author, as the case may be. For purposes of this chapter (other than section 506), any reference to copyright shall be deemed to include the rights conferred by section 106A(a). As used in this subsection, the term "anyone" includes any State, any instrumentality of a State, and any officer or employee of a State or instrumentality of a State acting in his or her official capacity. Any State, and any such instrumentality, officer, or employee, shall be subject to the provisions of this title in the same manner and to the same extent as any nongovernmental entity.

(b) The legal or beneficial owner of an exclusive right under a copyright is entitled, subject to the requirements of section 411, to institute an action for any infringement of that particular right committed while he or she is the owner of it. The court may require such owner to serve written notice of the action with a copy of the complaint upon any person shown, by the records of the Copyright Office or otherwise, to have or claim an interest in the copyright, and shall require that such notice be served upon any person whose interest is likely to be affected by a decision in the case. The court may require the joinder, and shall permit the intervention, of any person having or claiming an interest in the copyright.

(c) For any secondary transmission by a cable system that embodies a performance or a display of a work which is actionable as an act of infringement under subsection (c) of section 111, a television broadcast station holding a copyright or other license to transmit or perform the same version of that work shall, for purposes of subsection (b) of this section, be treated as a legal or beneficial owner if such secondary transmission occurs within the local service area of that television station.

(d) For any secondary transmission by a cable system that is actionable as an act of infringement pursuant to section 111 (c) (3), the following shall also have standing to sue: (i) the primary transmitter whose transmission has been altered by the cable system; and (ii) any broadcast station within whose local service area the secondary transmission occurs.

(e) With respect to any secondary transmission that is made by a satellite carrier of a primary transmission embodying the performance or display of a work and is actionable as an act of infringement under section 119(a)(5), a network station holding a copyright or other license to transmit or perform the same version of that work shall, for purposes of subsection (b) of this section, be treated as a legal or beneficial owner if such secondary transmission occurs within the local service area of that station.

§ 502. Remedies for infringement: Injunctions

(a) Any court having jurisdiction of a civil action arising under this title may, subject to the provisions of section 1498 of title 28, grant temporary and final injunctions on such terms as it may deem reasonable to prevent or restrain infringement of a copyright.

(b) Any such injunction may be served anywhere in the United States on the person enjoined; it shall be operative throughout the United States and shall be enforceable, by proceedings in contempt or other-wise, by any United States court having jurisdiction of that person. The clerk of the court granting the injunction shall, when requested by any other court in which enforcement of the injunction is sought, transmit promptly to the other court a certified copy of all the papers in the case on file in such clerk's office.

§ 503. Remedies for infringement: Impounding and disposition of infringing articles

(a) At any time while an action under this title is pending, the court may order the impounding, on such terms as it may deem reasonable, of all copies or phonorecords claimed to have been made or used in violation of the copyright owner's exclusive rights, and of all plates, molds, matrices, masters, tapes, film negatives, or other articles by means of which such copies or phonorecords may be reproduced.

(b) As part of a final judgment or decree, the court may order the destruction or other reasonable disposition of all copies or phonorec-ords found to have been made or used in violation of the copyright owner's exclusive rights, and of all plates, molds, matrices, masters, tapes, film negatives, or other articles by means of which such copies or phonorecords may be reproduced.

§ 504. Remedies for infringement: Damages and profits

(a) In General. Except as otherwise provided by this title, an infringer of copyright is liable for either—
    (1) the copyright owner's actual damages and any additional prof-its of the infringer, as provided by subsection (b); or
    (2) statutory damages, as provided by subsection (c).

(b) Actual Damages and Profits. The copyright owner is entitled to recover the actual damages suffered by him or her as a result of the infringement, and any profits of the infringer that are attributable to the infringement and are not taken into account in computing the actual damages. In establishing the infringer's profits, the copyright owner is required to present proof only of the infringer's gross revenue, and the infringer is required to prove his or her deductible expenses and the elements of profit attributable to factors other than the copyrighted work.

(c) Statutory Damages.

(1) Except as provided by clause (2) of this subsection, the copyright owner may elect, at any time before final judgment is rendered, to recover, instead of actual damages and profits, an award of statutory damages for all infringements involved in the action, with respect to any one work, for which any one infringer is liable individually, or for which any two or more infringers are liable jointly and severally, in a sum of not less than $500 or more than $20,000 as the court considers just. For the purposes of this subsection, all the parts of a compilation or derivative work constitute one work.

(2) In a case where the copyright owner sustains the burden of proving, and the court finds, that infringement was committed willfully, the court in its discretion may increase the award of statutory damages to a sum of not more than $100,000. In a case where the infringer sustains the burden of proving, and the court finds, that such infringer was not aware and had no reason to believe that his or her acts constituted an infringement of copyright, the court in its discretion may reduce the award of statutory damages to a sum of not less than $200. The court shall remit statutory damages in any case where an infringer believed and had reasonable grounds for believing that his or her use of the copyrighted work was a fair use under section 107, if the infringer was: (i) an employee or agent of a nonprofit educational institution, library, or archives acting within the scope of his or her employment who, or such institution, library, or archives itself, which infringed by reproducing the work in copies or phonorecords; or (ii) a public broadcasting entity which or a person who, as a regular part of the nonprofit activities of a public broadcasting entity (as defined in subsection (g) of section 118) infringed by performing a published nondramatic literary work or by reproducing a transmission program embodying a performance of such a work.

§ 505. Remedies for infringement: Costs and attorney's fees

In any civil action under this title, the court in its discretion may allow the recovery of full costs by or against any party other than the United States or an officer thereof. Except as otherwise provided by this title, the court may also award a reasonable attorney's fee to the prevailing party as part of the costs.

§ 506. Criminal offenses

(a) Criminal Infringement. Any person who infringes a copyright willfully and for purposes of commercial advantage or private financial gain shall be punished as provided in section 2319 of title 18.

(b) Forfeiture and Destruction. When any person is convicted of any violation of subsection (a), the court in its judgment of conviction shall, in addition to the penalty therein prescribed, order the forfeiture and destruction or other disposition of all infringing copies or phonorecords and all implements, devices, or equipment used in the manufacture of such infringing copies or phonorecords.

(c) Fraudulent Copyright Notice. Any person who, with fraudulent intent, places on any article a notice of copyright or words of the same purport that such person knows to be false, or who, with fraudulent intent, publicly distributes or imports for public distribution any article bearing such notice or words that such person knows to be false, shall be fined not more than $2,500.

(d) Fraudulent Removal of Copyright Notice. Any person who, with fraudulent intent, removes or alters any notice of copyright appearing on a copy of a copyrighted work shall be fined not more than $2,500.

(e) False Representation. Any person who knowingly makes a false representation of a material fact in the application for copyright registration provided for by section 409, or in any written statement filed in connection with the application, shall be fined not more than $2,500.

(f) Rights of Attribution and Integrity. Nothing in this section applies to infringement of the rights conferred by section 106A(a).

§ 507. Limitations on actions

(a) Criminal Proceedings. No criminal proceeding shall be maintained under the provisions of this title unless it is commenced within three years after the cause of action arose.

(b) Civil Actions. No civil action shall be maintained under the provisions of this title unless it is commenced within three years after the claim accrued.

The Uniform Trade Secrets Act

In contrast to the patent, trademark, and copyright laws, the trade secrets laws curently exist primarily at the state level. Though there is no reason Congress could not pass a federal trade secrets law if it chose to, thus far it has left the regulation of trade secrets to the states. Possibly the main reason Congress has not passed a federal trade secrets law is that nearly all states have adopted laws modeled after the Uniform Trade Secrets Act. The Uniform Trade Secrets Act is not a law itself, but rather a draft statute proposed by an organization tasked with preparing a trade secrets law that could be adopted by every state. Because nearly every state legislature has passed some form of the Uniform Trade Secrets Act, the result is a trade secrets law that is nearly uniform from state to state. This appendix includes the Uniform Trade Secrets Act in its entirety. Note, however, that although most states have adopted some form of the Uniform Trade Secrets Act, few states have adopted in its exact original form.

§ 1. Definitions

As used in this Act, unless the context requires otherwise:

(1) "Improper means" includes theft, bribery, misrepresentation, breach or inducement of a breach of duty to maintain secrecy, or espionage through electronic or other means.

(2) "Misappropriation " means:

(i) acquisition of a trade secret of another by a person who knows or has reason to know that the trade secret was acquired by improper means; or

(ii) disclosure or use of a trade secret of another without express or implied consent by a person who

(A) used improper means to acquire knowledge of the trade secret; or

(B) at the time of disclosure or use knew or had reason to know that his knowledge of the trade secret was

(I) derived from or through a person who has utilized improper means to acquire it;

(II) acquired under circumstances giving rise to a duty to maintain its secrecy or limit its use; or

(III) derived from or through a person who owed a duty to the person seeking relief to maintain its secrecy or limit its use; or

(C) before a material change of his position, knew or had reason to know that it was a trade secret and that knowledge of it had been acquired by accident or mistake.

(3) "Person" means a natural person, corporation, business trust, estate, trust, partnership, association, joint venture, government, governmental subdivision or agency, or any other legal or commercial entity.

(4) "Trade secret" means information, including a formula, pattern, compilation, program device, method, technique, or process, that:

(i) derives independent economic value, actual or potential, from not being generally known to, and not being readily ascertainable by proper means, other persons who can obtain economic value from its disclosure or use, and

(ii) is the subject of efforts that are reasonable under the circumstances to maintain its secrecy.

§ 2. Injunctive Relief

(a) Actual or threatened misappropriation may be enjoined. Upon application to the court, an injunction shall be terminated when the trade secret has ceased to exist, but the injunction may be continued for an additional reasonable period of time in order to eliminate commercial advantage that otherwise would be derived from the misappropriation.

(b) If the court determines that it would be unreasonable to prohibit future use due to an overriding public interest, an injunction may condition future use upon payment of a reasonable royalty for no longer than the period of time the use could have been prohibited.

(c) In appropriate circumstances, affirmative acts to protect a trade secret may be compelled by court order.

§ 3. Damages

(a) In addition to or in lieu of injunctive relief, a complainant may recover damages for the actual loss caused by misappropriation. A complainant also may recover for the unjust enrichment caused by misappropriation that is not taken into acount in computing damages for actual loss.

(b) If willful and malicious misappropriation exists, the court may award exemplary damages in the amount not exceeding twice any award made under subsection (a).

§ 4. Attorney's Fees

If (i) a claim of misappropriation is made in bad faith, (ii) a motion to terminate an injunction is made or resisted in bad faith, or (iii) willful and malicious misappropriation exists, the court may award reasonable attorney's fees to the prevailing party.

§ 5. Preservation of Secrecy

In an action under this Act, a court shall preserve the secrecy of an alleged trade secret by reasonable means, which may include granting protective orders in connection with discovery proceedings, holding in-camera hearings, sealing the records of the action, and ordering any person involved in the litigation not to disclose an alleged trade secret without prior court approval.

§ 6. Statute of Limitations

An action for misappropriation must be brought within 3 years after the misappropriation is discovered or by the exercise of reasonable diligence should have been discovered. For the purposes of this section, a continuing misappropriation constitutes a single claim.

§ 7. Effect on Other Law

(a) This Act displaces conflicting tort, restitutionary, and other law of this State providing civil remedies for misappropriation of a trade secret.

(b) This Act does not affect:

    (1) contractual remedies, whether or not based upon misappropriation of a trade secret;

(2) other civil remedies that are not based upon misappropriation of a trade secret; or

(3) criminal remedies, whether or not based upon misappropriation of a trade secret.

§ 8. Uniformity of Application and Construction

This act shall be applied and construed to effectuate its general purpose to make uniform the law with respect to the subject of this Act among states enacting it.

§ 9. Short Title

This Act may be cited as the Uniform Trade Secrets Act.

§ 10. Severability

If any provision of this Act or its application to any person or circumstances is held invalid, the invalidity does not affect other provisions or applications of the Act which can be given effect without the invalid provision or application, and to this end the provisions of this Act are severable.

§ 11. Time of Taking Effect

This Act takes effect on _____, and does not apply to misappropriation occurring prior to the effective date.

§ 12. Repeal

The following Acts and parts of Acts are repealed*****:.

Economic Espionage Act of 1996

The Economic Espionage Act of 1996 was passed by Congress in recognition of the increasing damage caused by trade secret misappropriation. Note that the law carries criminal penalties for trade secret misappropriation and economic espionage.

Title I -

Protection of Trade Secrets

Sec. 101. Protection of Trade Secrets

(a) In General.—Title 18, United States Code, is amended by inserting after chapter 89 the following:

Sec.

1831. Economic espionage.

1832. Theft of trade secrets.

1833. Exceptions to prohibitions.

1834. Criminal forfeiture.

1835. Orders to preserve confidentiality.

1836. Civil proceedings to enjoin violations.

1837. Conduct outside the United States.

1838. Construction with other laws.

1839. Definitions.

Chapter 90—

Protection of Trade Secrets

Section 1831 Economic espionage

(a) In General —Whoever, intending or knowing that the offense will benefit any foreign government, foreign instrumentality, or foreign agent, knowingly -

(1) steals, or without authorization appropriates, takes, carries away, or conceals, or by fraud, artifice, or deception obtains a trade secret;

(2) without authorization copies, duplicates, sketches, draws, photographs, downloads, uploads, alters, destroys, photocopies, replicates, transmits, delivers, sends, mails, communicates, or conveys a trade secret,

(3) receives, buys, or possesses a trade secret, knowing the same to have been stolen or appropriated, obtained, or converted without authorization,

(4) attempts to commit any offense described in any of paragraphs (1) through (3), or

(5) conspires with one or more other persons to commit any offense described in any of paragraphs (1) through (3), and one or more of such persons do any act to effect the object of the conspiracy, shall, except as provided in subsection (b), be fined not more than $500,000 or imprisoned not more than 15 years, or both.

(B) Organizations—Any organization that commits any offense described in subsection (a) shall be fined not more than $10,000,000.

Section 1832. Theft of trade secrets

(a) Whoever, with intent to convert a trade secret, that is related to or included in a product that is produced for or placed in interstate or foreign commerce, to the economic benefit of anyone other than the owner thereof, and intending or knowing that the offense will injure any owner of that trade secret, knowingly—

(1) steals, or without authorization appropriates, takes, carries away, or conceals, or by fraud, artifice, or deception obtains such information;

(2) without authorization copies, duplicates, sketches,. draws, photographs, downloads, uploads, alters, destroys, photocopies, replicates, transmits, delivers, sends, mails, communicates, or conveys such information;

(3) receives, buys, or possesses such information, knowing the same to have been stolen or appropriated, obtained, or converted without authorization;

(4) attempts to commit any offense described in paragraphs (1) through (3); or

(5) conspires with one or more other persons to commit any offense described in paragraphs (1) through (3), and one or more of such persons do any act to effect the object of the conspiracy, shall, except as provided in subsection (b), be fined under this title or imprisoned not more than 10 years, or both.

(b) Any organization that commits any offense described in subsection (a) shall be fined not more than $5,000,000.

Section 1833. Exceptions to prohibitions

This chapter does not prohibit—

(1) any otherwise lawful activity conducted by a governmental entity of the United States, a State, or a political subdivision of a State; or

(2) the reporting of a suspected violation of law to any governmental entity of the United States, a State, or a political subdivision of a State, if such entity has lawful authority with respect to that violation.

Section 1834. Criminal forfeiture

(a) The court, in imposing sentence on a person for a violation of this chapter, shall order, in addition to any other sentence imposed, that the person forfeit to the United States -

(1) any property constituting or derived from, any proceeds the person obtained, directly or indirectly, as the result of such violation; and

(2) any of the person's or organization's property used, or intended to be used, in any manner or part, to commit or facilitate the commission of such violation, if the court in its discretion so determines, taking into consideration the nature, scope, and proportionality of the use of the property in the offense.

(b) Property subject to forfeiture under this section, any seizure and disposition thereof, and any administrative or judicial proceeding in relation thereto, shall be governed by section 413 of the Comprehensive Drug Abuse Prevention and Control Act of 1970 (21 U.S.C. 853), except for subsections (d) and (e) of such section, which shall not apply to forfeitures under this section.

Section 1835. Orders to preserve confidentiality

In any prosecution or other proceeding under this chapter, the court shall enter such orders and take such other action as may be necessary and appropriate to preserve the confidentiality of trade secrets, consistent with the requirements of the Federal Rules of Criminal and Civil

Procedure, the Federal Rules of Evidence, and all other applicable laws. An interlocutory appeal by the United States shall lie from a decision or order of a district court authorizing or directing the disclosure of any trade secret.

Section 1836. Civil proceedings to enjoin violations

(a) The Attorney General may, in a civil action, obtain appropriate injunctive relief against any violation of this section.

(b) The district courts of the United States shall have exclusive original jurisdiction of civil actions under this subsection.

Section 1837. Applicability to conduct outside the United States

This chapter also applies to conduct occurring outside the United States if

(1) the offender is a natural person who is a citizen or permanent resident alien of the United States, or an organization organized under the laws of the United States or a State or political subdivision thereof, or

(2) an act in furtherance of the offense was committed in the Untied States.

Section 1838. Construction with other laws

This chapter shall not be construed to preempt or displace any other remedies, whether civil or criminal, provided by Untied States Federal, State, commonwealth, possession, or territory law for the misappropriation of a trade secret, or to affect the otherwise lawful disclosure of information by any Government employees under section 552 of title 5 (commonly know as the Freedom of Information Act).

Section 1839. Definitions

As used in this chapter

(1) the term *foreign instrumentality* means any agency, bureau, ministry, component, institution, association, or any legal, commercial, or business organization, corporation, firm, or entity that is substantially owned, controlled, sponsored, commanded, managed, or dominated by a foreign government:

(2) the term *foreign agent* means any officer, employee, proxy, servant, delegate, or representative of a foreign government:

(3) the term *trade secret* means all forms and types of financial, business, scientific, technical, economic, or engineering information, including patterns, plans, compilations, program devices, formulas,

designs, prototypes, methods, techniques, processes, procedures, programs, or codes, whether tangible or intangible, and whether or how stored, compiled, or memorialized physically, electronically, graphically, photographically, or in writing if

(A) the owner thereof has taken reasonable measures to keep such information secret; and

(B) the information derives independent economic value, actual or potential, from not being general known to, and not being readily ascertainable through proper means by the public, and

(4) the term *owner*, with respect to a trade secret, means the person or entity in whom or in which rightful legal or equitable title to or license in, the trade secret is reposed.

(b) Clerical Amendment. The table of chapters at the beginning part I of title 18, United States Code, is amended by inserting after the item relating to chapter 89 the following: "90. Protection of trade secrets 1831"

(c) Reports.—Not later than 2 years and 4 years after the date of the enactment of this Congress of this Act, the Attorney General shall report to Congress on the amounts received and distributed from fines for offenses under this chapter deposited in the Crime Victims Fund established by section 1402 of the Victims of Crime Act of 1984 (42 U.S. C. 10601).

Sec. 102 Wire and Electronic Communications Interception and Interception of Oral Communications

Section 2516(l)(c) of title 18, United States Code, is amended by inserting "chapter 90 (relating to protection of trade secrets)," after "chapter 37 (relating to espionage),"

Suggested Reading

Bryant, Joy L. *Protecting Your Ideas.* Academic Press, 1997.

Chisum, Donald S., and Michael A. Jacobs. *Understanding Intellectual Property Law.* Matthew Bender, 1995.

Clapes, Anthony. *Softwars: The Legal Battles for Control of the Global Software Industry.* Quorum Books, 1993.

Dorr, Robert C., and Christopher H. Munch. *Protecting Trade Dress.* John Wiley & Sons, 1992.

Fishman, Stephen. *Copyright Your Software.* Nolo Press, 1994.

———. *Software Development: A Legal Guide.* Nolo Press, 1996.

Godwin, Mike. *Cyber Rights: Defending Free Speech in the Digital Age.* Times Books, 1998.

Keet, Ernest E. *Preventing Piracy.* Addison-Wesley, 1984.

McGrath, Kate, and Stephen Elias. *Trademarks: Legal Care for Your Business & Product Name.* 3d ed. Nolo Press, 1997.

Pressman, David. *Patent It Yourself.* 6th ed. Nolo Press, 1997.

Rosenbaum, David G. *Patents, Trademarks, and Copyrights: Practical Strategies for Protecting Your Ideas.* Career Press, 1994.

Warshofsky, Fred. *The Patent Wars.* John Wiley & Sons, 1994.

Index

About the Author

LAWRENCE D. GRAHAM practices patent, copyright trademark, and other intellectual property law at the Seattle law firm of Christensen, O'Connor, Johnson, and Kindness, PLLC. He is also an adjunct professor at the Seattle University School of Law and a member of the editorial board for *IEEE Software* journal.